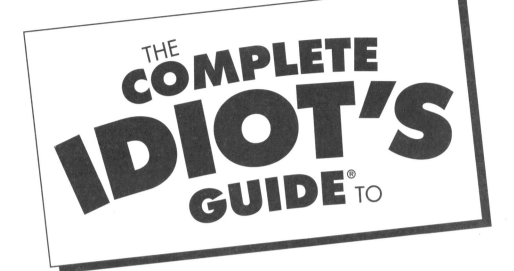

Bike Maintenance and Repair

by Terry Meany

ALPHA

A member of Penguin Group (USA) Inc.

Copyright © 2001 by Terry Meany

All rights reserved. No part of this book shall be reproduced, stored in a retrieval system, or transmitted by any means, electronic, mechanical, photocopying, recording, or otherwise, without written permission from the publisher. No patent liability is assumed with respect to the use of the information contained herein. Although every precaution has been taken in the preparation of this book, the publisher and author assume no responsibility for errors or omissions. Neither is any liability assumed for damages resulting from the use of information contained herein. For information, address Alpha Books, 800 East 96th Street, Indianapolis, IN 46240.

THE COMPLETE IDIOT'S GUIDE TO and Design are registered trademarks of Penguin Group (USA) Inc.

International Standard Book Number: 0-02-864139-6
Library of Congress Catalog Card Number: 2001088751

05   04   03   8   7   6   5   4   3

Interpretation of the printing code: The rightmost number of the first series of numbers is the year of the book's printing; the rightmost number of the second series of numbers is the number of the book's printing. For example, a printing code of 01-1 shows that the first printing occurred in 2001.

Printed in the United States of America

Note: This publication contains the opinions and ideas of its author. It is intended to provide helpful and informative material on the subject matter covered. It is sold with the understanding that the author and publisher are not engaged in rendering professional services in the book. If the reader requires personal assistance or advice, a competent professional should be consulted.

The author and publisher specifically disclaim any responsibility for any liability, loss, or risk, personal or otherwise, which is incurred as a consequence, directly or indirectly, of the use and application of any of the contents of this book.

Publisher
Marie Butler-Knight

Product Manager
Phil Kitchel

Managing Editor
Jennifer Chisholm

Acquisitions Editor
Mike Sanders

Development Editor
Tom Stevens

Production Editor
Billy Fields

Copy Editor
Rachel Lopez

Illustrator
Jody P. Schaeffer

Cover Designers
Mike Freeland
Kevin Spear

Book Designers
Scott Cook and Amy Adams of DesignLab

Indexer
Tonya Heard

Layout/Proofreading
Svetlana Dominguez
Stacey Richwine-DeRome

Contents at a Glance

Contents

Appendixes

Foreword

It was 1959, I was seven years old. School was over for the day, and my best friend Ray and I were playing in the basement of his parents' house in Boonton, New Jersey. The basement was a large magical place for us. It was filled with the echoes of his grandfather's cycle-racing career, which ended just after the turn of the twentieth century. I remember the high-wheeled bike and the pneumatic safety bicycle with the name *Humber* on the front. We would play with these fantastic machines. Spinning the pedals, turning the heavy steel cranks, watching the wheels spin faster and faster. I'm sure such moments in time were what sparked my interest in bicycles.

Riding, repairing, restoring, and collecting bicycles has been a part of my life since then. Like most mechanics/shop owners/enthusiasts who are now 40- or 50-something, we learned about repairing our bicycles by tearing our Schwinn "Americans," "Tornadoes," and "Corvettes" apart in our garages and driveways. Occasionally we would have to run to local bike shop with a coffee can (usually A&P Eight O'Clock blend) filled with sturmey archer three-speed parts because we forgot to pay attention to where the pawl springs and planet gears went. Few repair manuals existed at the time. Coaster brakes were simple to fix, but those three-speed hubs could reduce your dad to tears.

In the late 60s, a few how-to bicycle repair manuals became available. Some of these were hand-illustrated, some had actual photographs to help us, beginners, along the bicycle-repair path. These books gave us the guts to at least attempt to adjust brakes and gears on our own. These paperbacks helped demystify our wonderful machines.

In the last few years, I have discovered just how important being able to fix bicycles and related things has become for most of us in the professional bike business. Mechanics develop relationships with their customers through their machines, realizing what an important part in people's lives these kinetic sculptures play. The bike shop traditionally was a place where you could get a key made or a lawnmower repaired or even have knives sharpened. Cycle shops were and still are the only "fix-it" shops left in our modern world. The world famous "Pop" Brennan cycle shop of Irvington, New Jersey, had a sign over the counter that read, "We fix everything but a broken heart." The Brennans weren't kidding. The Wright brothers, as we all know, were bicycle men first and aeronautical engineers later.

I've always believed that with a little help you can figure out just about anything. Having had the honor to know some of the greatest bicycle mechanics of the twentieth century has proven this to me. Bill Brennan, Oscar Juner, Oscar Wastyn Jr., Spence Wolf were not only great mechanics but real magicians, the original MacGuyvers. They really wrote the book for the rest of us.

Terry Meany's new book, *The Complete Idiot's Guide to Bike Maintenance and Repair,* will help many people take that first step to repairing and maintaining their own bikes. He covers all the basics and goes even deeper in some of his sections explaining wheels and derailleurs in plain simple language. The book is laid out in easy-to-read chapters that walk the reader through all the systems of the modern bicycle and its many incarnations. I'll be pleased to have this book on the shelves of my shops.

Yours in cycling,

Jeff Groman

Classic Cycles of Kingston, WA, and Bainbridge Island, WA

Jeff Groman's professional bicycle career started in Northern New Jersey. He worked with Marty Epstein at the now famous "Marty's Reliable Cycle" in Morristown, NJ. In 1985, Jeff opened "Sacks Feed and Cycle," which was the first farm garden and bicycle shop in the United States. The Classic Cycle shops in Kingston, WA, and Bainbridge Island, WA, are also part museums. With an amazing collection of U.S. cycle-racing memorabilia, Jeff is also a voting member of the United States Bicycle Hall of Fame. The shops house an extensive cycle history archive with some of the most famous pieces of American cycle-racing hardware on display.

Introduction

I wonder if there's some cultural correlation between the huge sales of SUVs and pick-up trucks and those of mountain bikes. Both of them are built for rough roads, but most SUVs never leave the pavement. Hardcore off-road cyclists would go off the World Trade Center if they could find a bike with a suspension system that could handle hitting the pavement. One-speed cruisers have made a comeback, and road bikes are still used for competitive riding and touring. We are surrounded by more bicycle choices than ever before—and we're making good use of them.

Compared to an automobile, the main mode of transportation for many people, a bicycle is a simple machine. All the components are visible to the rider and most are user friendly when it comes to repairs and adjustments. Just try to figure out what's wrong with your sport coupe when it won't start. For the price of the tow, you could have your bike overhauled by a mechanic—or do it yourself for the price of this book.

We tend to take our machines for granted, whether it's a clothes dryer or the garage door opener. We expect them to work and get frustrated when they don't. There's always the simple matter of reading the owner's manuals, which we often conveniently ignore until something goes wrong; that's where *The Complete Idiot's Guide to Bike Maintenance and Repair* comes in. It doesn't take a genius to keep your bike running and you riding, but it does take a few tools, some spare parts, and some know-how. Reading the following chapters will give you enough knowledge to fix the big maintenance items in the comfort of your garage and handle any on-the-road emergencies.

Some bike components—such as hydraulic disc brakes—have become more complicated; but don't let this scare you off. Although some repairs are best left to an experienced mechanic, you don't need to go running to your bike shop every time you hear a strange grinding sound or your tire goes flat. Save those trips for the really complicated repairs that require special tools and experience. Meanwhile, you'll be able to take care of the regular maintenance yourself—and stay on the road with confidence.

The Complete Idiot's Guide to Bike Maintenance and Repair is divided into sections that will introduce you to your bicycle and its components (a fancy word for parts) as well as repairs and fixes. We'll start with the simple and work through to the more complicated. With each section, you'll become more knowledgeable and analytical about bike maintenance.

Part 1: "Bike Basics," shows you why your bike works the way it does and throw in some history as well. Where once only a few choices existed for the consumer, today we have a bike for every rider and every purpose and we'll look at them in Chapter 3, "Bike Details." Bike maintenance requires tools and spare parts and we'll cover those so you can yak up the benefits of a good cone wrench the next time you're down at your local bike shop.

We'll ease into repair in **Part 2, "Repairs Lite,"** covering the one repair everyone has to do eventually (fixing a flat tire), brake adjustments, and some rules to live by. No one likes rules that much, but you need to know enough to stay out of trouble and get the job done. Clean-up follows many repairs and is just part of general upkeep and we will discuss that as well.

If you ride a bike long enough, you'll need to do more major repairs so you can ride it even longer. Bearings need to be cleaned and lubricated, cables will get replaced, and wheels will have to be straightened out from time to time. As you get into **Part 3, "Bigger Repairs,"** you will have had more hands-on experience and be ready to tackle these. You'll also add a few more tools to your workspace so you can do this work.

Part 4: "Specialty Areas," discusses some repairs you should be aware of, but will most likely leave to a bike shop. You'll also find out a thing or two about saddles (bike seats) and how to both fit and adjust them to your own measurements and riding style. We will also do an introduction to mountain bikes, by far the most popular bike on the road today.

To help you through this book, you'll find the following useful sidebars throughout:

Freewheelin' Facts

A little bit of history and related anecdotes about bicycles.

Bike Bites

Hint, tips, and quick advice to simplify your repairs.

The Spoken Word

In addition to the Appendix A Glossary, here you'll find **bolded** terms with definitions for *italicized* terms in the text.

Derailed

Tells you the problems you can run into during your repair work and how to avoid them. It's easier to read about them than experience them!

Acknowledgments

The idea of a lone author holing up in an attic somewhere producing a masterpiece is at best a partial truth. Friends, editors, and production departments all help in bringing about the finished product. I would like to thank Jeff Eichstedt at Finn Hill Bikes, who as this book's tech editor has offered ongoing advice and comments on the manuscript. I also would like to thank Nick Sanders at Sturmey-Archer, Dan Garceau at Park Tool USA, and Kurt Fykerud at Trek Bicycle Corporation for all the artwork they generously provided. To Francesco Zenere and Joseba Arizaga at Campagnolo a huge *grazie* for sending artwork from the company's Italian headquarters. Finally, my thanks to my agent Andree Abecassis for once again ferreting out an interesting project.

Special Thanks to the Technical Reviewer

The Complete Idiot's Guide to Bike Maintenance and Repair was reviewed by an expert who double-checked the accuracy of what you'll learn here to help ensure that this book gives you everything you need to know about bike maintenance and repair. Special thanks are extended to Jeff Eich-stedt.

Trademarks

All terms mentioned in this book that are known to be or are suspected of being trademarks or service marks have been appropriately capitalized. Alpha Books and Penguin Group (USA) Inc. cannot attest to the accuracy of this information. Use of a term in this book should not be regarded as affecting the validity of any trademark or service mark.

Part 1
Bike Basics

It can be hard to believe in these days of SUV fever and an imported car in every garage (at least here on the West coast) that the hottest pairs of wheels in town once belonged to bicycles. America in particular went bike-crazy during the last decade of the nineteenth century, and the country was full of manufacturers until the bike boom became the bike bust at the end of the 1890s. Today's bicycles are essentially based on the design of the safety bicycle that came out of that era.

A bicycle is one of the most efficient manual means for transporting human beings. Two wheels lined up with one another coupled with a means of steering the front wheel seems simple—and it is—but it took nearly a century of experimentation to produce this model. Modern bicycle production has brought about an unprecedented use of new materials and designs, creating vastly improved bikes and accessories.

You don't need to know all the physics involved with designing and riding a bicycle, but it helps to know some essential facts. With a little knowledge, you can more intelligently choose the type of bike you want to ride and understand the importance of regular maintenance (wheels, for instance, spin a lot faster when their bearings are well-greased and adjusted). Your bike—and you—will also be safer once you understand its workings and how to keep them tuned up and running smoothly.

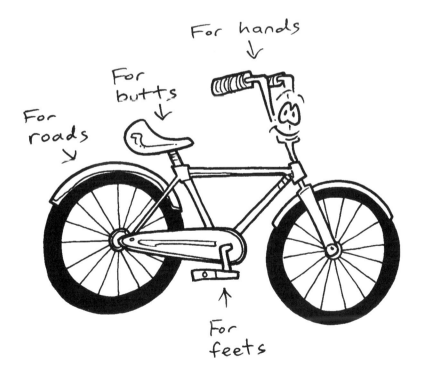

Chapter 1

Pedal Power

In This Chapter

➤ Simple and elegant transportation

➤ Frame finesse

➤ Leveraging leg power

➤ You have to stop sometime

➤ Wheel wise

Bicycles provide us with a recreational outlet, serve as personal transportation, and are a means to move goods around. Regardless of how you use a bicycle, this chapter will make you a more informed rider and consumer.

On first appearance, a bicycle is a pretty basic-looking machine. A rider's feet push down on a pair of pedals that turn some chain rings, which in turn move a chain. The chain moves the rear sprockets in a forward motion. The sprockets are attached to a wheel that moves at the same time. Some type of braking system allows the rider to bring the bike to a stop, and a saddle or seat provides a place to sit. It's simple, but deceptively so.

A contemporary bicycle is a conglomeration of materials, physics, chemistry, and art. Every manufacturer brings his own ideas on bike design and performance to the marketplace. In the end, even as the technology evolves, you still have to pedal to move the bike. The trick is to understand how each component and its design contribute to a bicycle's operation. Some designs and components work better than others.

An Anatomy Lesson

Buildings, bodies, and bicycles are based on some kind of skeletal system to which all kinds of parts are attached. Bicycle parts don't vary in function from one bike to another—all brakes are supposed to help you stop, after all—but they do vary in design, quality, and efficiency. How these parts combine with the bicycle frame will affect your comfort and handling when you ride.

All standard bicycles are constructed with the following parts:

➤ A frame

➤ Wheels

➤ Handlebars and stem

➤ Brakes

➤ A saddle or seat

➤ Gearing components

Frames and components go hand in hand. The finest components in the world can't make up for all the drawbacks of a clunky, heavy frame that looks as if it's made out of sewer pipe. Because a bicycle frame can last a lifetime, it's important to choose one that's appropriate to your personal dimensions and riding style.

A bike showing the chief components.

(Photo courtesy of Trek Bicycles)

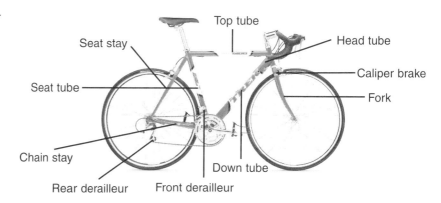

Frames

A bike frame is all about geometry, materials, measurements, and construction methods. Frames come in a variety of flavors, including …

➤ Mass-produced.

➤ High-end frames produced to nonspecific measurements.

➤ Custom frames built to a customer's specifications.

Freewheelin' Facts

When we think of a bike frame, we normally think of metal construction. However, during the late nineteenth century some bike manufacturers experimented with wood frames held together with brass lugs. These must have been beautiful bicycles and more forgiving on rough roads than heavy steel frames; of course, durability was an issue, as were pesky, wood-loving insects.

Walk into any bike store, and you'll see plenty of mass-produced frames. Better-quality models will suit most riders, but they're like mass-produced shoes: They'll work, but they'll never be perfectly suited to you. Many independent shops also carry high-end frames that are built according to common body measurements. These frames are built from better materials than those that are mass-produced and have wonderful paint finishes.

If you have plenty of money and aren't in a big hurry, you can custom order a frame built specifically to your body measurements and whims. This is the ideal frame, especially if you fall far from the norm for your body size (say, a short trunk and really long arms).

Most bike frames are the classic diamond design, which consists of a front and a rear triangle. A conventional frame consists of the following:

➤ Top tube

➤ Head tube

➤ Down tube

➤ Seat tube

➤ Chain stays

➤ Seat stays

Metal frame tubes and stays are connected to each other by some form of *brazing*, welding, or a combination of the two, using either lugs or lugless construction (see the following figure).

Traditional steel frame construction is done with external lugs, and some of the classic frames are quite beautiful and artistic, giving the frame builder a chance to show off a bit. Bikes with oversized tubes have a lugless construction that is referred to as *fillet brazing*. Instead of soldering the tubes to a lug, the manufacturer builds up the area between the tubes and outside of the joint with plenty of solder. Cannondale, a popular American bicycle manufacturer, builds lugless aluminum frames that are welded, but they clean away all the excess weld, leaving a smooth, seamless joint.

The Spoken Word

Brazing refers to joining two pieces of metal together using solder, which bonds to both pieces and holds them tight. Solder is an alloy with a low melting temperature. Brazing differs from welding; the latter is the fusing of two pieces of metal together by heating them directly.

This lugless Trek bike frame combines strength, aluminum tubes, and beautiful finish work.

(Photo courtesy of Trek Bicycles)

A Materials World

Metal is the traditional material for bike frames; steel, or a steel alloy, is the most common metal used. Manufacturers use different grades of steel and alloys in their bikes depending on the price level and the type of bike.

Carbon is added to steel as a simple way to increase its strength. Chrome-moly and manganese-molybdenum are the best steel alloys used in frame building. Among the best known manufacturers of these tubes are Reynolds, Columbus, Vitus, True Temper, and Tange.

No Steel Allowed

Many mountain bikes are made with aluminum frames for lightness and rigidity. The more rigid the bike, the less flex it has, so more of your muscle power goes directly toward moving the bike forward. Titanium occasionally is used by custom frame builders and, like aluminum, is highly resistant to corrosion.

Leaving the world of metallurgy, we enter the world of exotic materials, such as Kevlar™ and carbon. Fibers made from these materials typically are mixed with an epoxy resin, called a composite, and then formed into tubes. The end result is a lightweight frame that stands up to moisture and mud. These frames are more expensive than their steel counterparts. The advantage of a *composite frame,* particularly one using carbon, is that through the manufacturing process, a section of the frame can be infinitely adjusted to very exact specifications—add a little here, shave off a bit there, and end up with a true custom frame that would satisfy the most finicky cyclist.

If you're thinking, "Wait a minute, you can't braze a composite frame without deforming it," well … you're right. Composite frames and some aluminum frames are held together with epoxy at the joints. Think of them as being glued together with something about 100 times stronger than Crazy Glue.

Strength in Numbers

There's more to frame tubes than meets the eye; otherwise, we could build bikes out of plumbing pipes. A seamless tube is manufactured from a steel bar that is heated, drawn over a form, and rolled until the desired diameter and tube thickness are achieved. An alloy tube, one made from different metals for superior strength, can be drawn out thinner, thus be lighter, than a plain steel tube.

Bike Bites

Good-quality bikes will have a sticker on the top of the seat tube indicating how the frame was built. "Chrome-moly" indicates an alloy material with greater strength and more desirability. Others will indicate how many of the tubes are butted. Traditionally, the very best road bikes (both touring and racing bikes built for paved road use) were completely double-butted and sometimes triple-butted.

To increase the strength of the frame at the points where the tubes are brazed, *butted tubes* are used. A butted tube has thicker walls on one (or both) of its ends than in its center sections. A double-butted tube is thicker at both ends. Some tubes are even triple- and quad-butted, offering three- and four-wall thickness.

Bike Bites

Good luck if you expect to find two frame makers who agree on the more esoteric notions of frame construction, whether it's a choice of materials or geometry. All these builders have their followers and their biases. Add to that the choice of components and the wheel construction options, and you almost need a spreadsheet to keep track of the different design possibilities.

Distances Matter

A bicycle frame is designed and built with a certain end use in mind. This end use—touring, racing, or hauling around ice-cream treats while ringing annoying bells that bring children running—determines the size and geometry of the frame tubes. Adding an inch here or increasing an angle there will affect the ride and efficiency of the bicycle.

As a rider or potential purchaser of a bicycle, you need to pay attention to the following dimensions and angles:

➤ The seat tube angle

➤ The steering tube angle or head angle

➤ The *fork rake*

➤ The length of the chain stays

➤ The top tube length

➤ Drop or bottom bracket height

The Spoken Word

The **fork rake** refers to the shortest distance between the front wheel axle and an imaginary line traveling through the head tube toward the ground. The straighter the fork, the smaller the rake, stiffer the ride, and quicker the steering. The head angle measures the distance from this same line to a horizontal line traveling through the axle. Shallow head angles usually accompany large rakes.

Suddenly, this sounds complicated; it's really not. The differences in measurements from one brand to another might be enough to sway your purchasing decision—that's why it helps to know about this stuff. Basically, all you have to keep in mind is that the steeper the angles, the more rigid and less forgiving the frame will be when you ride the bike. This is terrific if you're aiming for the 2006 Tour de France, but not so if you just want to tour in France.

If you're traveling long distances, the distances between the axles and bottom bracket are important. A longer distance is more forgiving when it comes to bumps and potholes. Longer chain stays also give plenty of room to hang *panniers* (those touring bags that hang off the bike) so you don't hit them with the back of your foot when pedaling.

Got a Tape Measurer?

The length of the frame tubes affects your ride. A top tube that's too long for your arms to comfortably reach the handlebars means you'll always be bent over at an uncomfortable angle. One that's too short will require that you install a longer seat post to move you back and a longer handlebar stem to move the handlebars forward; neither of these is a satisfactory solution.

As a rule, you don't need to be concerned about the angle of the seat tube; manufacturers design their frames so a rider is seated in the proper position for pedaling. The seat or saddle can always be adjusted by moving it backward or forward a bit.

The *drop,* or bottom bracket height, determines whether you end up scraping the road or trail with your pedals every time you go into a steep turn. Racers require higher bottom brackets so they can pedal around corners (to a racer, the idea of coasting and not pedaling is evil unless coasting past the finish line). A lower bottom bracket helps provide better stability to a heavily loaded bicycle.

Freewheelin' Facts

Despite the usual advice about buying a bike with a long wheelbase and more forgiving angles for touring purposes, I rode from Boulder, Colorado, to Seattle on a Mercian Superlight (an English road-racing frame with steep angles and short wheelbase). The ride was stiffer than I would have liked at first, but I got used to it and came to appreciate the Mercian's speed and handling. It took a bit more effort to keep it stable given the load I was carrying, but it certainly was doable. If you find a bike you really like and you're willing to adapt some, you can do a tour on just about anything.

All these measurements, aside from determining the comfort and efficiency of your bike, also affect whether the bike is a suitable size for you. A bike that's too tall, too short, or too long in the top tube will be uncomfortable and even unsafe to ride. A good bike shop can assist you in getting properly measured. When in doubt, go to a second shop and see if you get the same results. Even though fitting a person to a bike should be a finite science, there can be infinite interpretations of your measurements.

Changing the Rules a Little

Mountain bikes stretch the rules a bit when it comes to frame materials and measurements. A mountain bike will have a smaller frame than most other bikes, but the longer seat post will position the rider correctly above the pedals and crankset. The seat tube is shorter to accommodate shorter chain stays for maneuverability, especially if you're jumping over logs and climbing hills. This rough riding also calls for oversize tubes that still must be engineered to keep the overall weight of the frame down (see the following figure).

Tough riding calls for a tough mountain bike.

(Photo courtesy of Trek Bicycles)

The Sum of Its Parts

A frame might be the main building block of a bicycle, but it's pretty useless without all those sundry parts that make it run. And there are a lot of them—everything from a pedal bearing to the handlebars. They all work in unison (or should), and you have plenty of latitude to mix and match to get just the kind of bike you want. I know one bike mechanic who took a very expensive, custom road racing frame and made it into a three-speed with upright handlebars and a bell to boot.

Over the years, bicycle parts have become increasingly sophisticated and expensive. They still perform the same functions as parts made decades ago, but with greater efficiency and smoothness. However, the basics haven't changed: Brakes still have to stop spinning wheels and a crankset has to move a chain.

You Push, It Moves

Bicycles make good use of your energy. When compared to walking, cycling is quite an efficient way of moving your body around, at least on level surfaces. Frame geometry will affect the comfort of your ride and the responsiveness of your bike, but even the lightest frame can take a lot of work to get up a hill if your gearing leaves something to be desired.

Any brake set will stop your bike; some will just stop it better than others. Newer disc brakes have tremendous stopping power and are slowly replacing other types of brakes on mountain bikes. Traditional road bikes might well see disc brakes as an option some day as well.

Wheels come in a great variety of hub, spoke, and rim combinations, depending on their usage. A tandem bicycle wheel, with its extra weight demands, will be built different from a wheel on a track bike. All the parts just mentioned contribute to your bike-riding experience.

Gearing Up ... and Down

Gearing, or the selection among a number of gear combinations, allows the rider to choose a comfortable rate of pedaling given the ever-changing conditions during a ride. The idea is to find a rate of pedaling that won't tire out the rider regardless of the speed of the bike. This is particularly true during steep climbs when you might not be going very fast; a good range of gears can at least make the climb tolerable. The opposite is true as well: On a level road, you want gears high enough that a moderate rate of pedaling will keep you from tiring out your legs.

The Spoken Word

A **gear ratio** is the result of dividing the number of teeth in a chain ring by the number of teeth in a chosen sprocket. A 52-tooth chain ring combined with a 20-tooth rear sprocket produces a gear ratio of 2.6 to 1.

On derailleur-equipped bicycles, gearing is a combination of the front chain rings and the rear sprockets. Each has a different number of teeth and, when combined, produce the *gear ratio.* Lower gears make it easier for you to climb steep hills or deal with windy conditions; higher gears allow you to go screaming fast down the other side of that same steep hill.

When the gear ratio is multiplied by the diameter of the wheel, the product of these two figures is the gear as measured in inches. If we take the 2.6 (see the following sidebar) and multiply it by 27 (for a 27-inch wheel), we'll have a 70.2-inch gear. This is the equivalent of the distance the bike would move with a 70.2-inch wheel directly attached to the crankset. The greater the inch measurement of the gear, the farther you'll go with every turn of the cranks.

An easier measurement to use shows the distance traveled with each revolution of the crankset. Engineer and author Rob Van der Plas in his book titled *Bike Technology* (Bicycle Books, Inc., 1991), illustrates this with the following formula:

$$D = \pi \times D \text{ (wheel)} \times T \text{ (front)} \div T \text{ (rear)}$$

Freewheelin' Facts

Gears as measured in inches go back to the old high wheeler days. A gear with a 100-inch measurement, for instance, is the same thing as directly pedaling a 100-inch wheel. The idea is that a large wheel covers more ground when it's pedaled than a smaller wheel. Of course, trying to budge a wheel this size would be very difficult, thus the advantage of modern gears.

In case this isn't perfectly clear, here's the translation:

> The distance traveled in meters is equal to pi times the diameter of the wheel (also in meters) times the gear ratio. Because the metric system will never take hold in America in our lifetime, you can use this formula to annoy your bike mechanic if the need ever arises.

Highs and Lows

A crankset can have one, two, or three chain rings. More often, and especially on mountain bikes, a bike will have a triple chain ring and seven to nine *cassette sprockets* or rear gears on the rear wheel. This gives the rider a wide range of gearing possibilities, even if some of the gear ratios end up being the same.

Regardless of the number of gears you have available, a few rules apply to all chain ring/rear sprocket gearing systems:

➤ The lowest gear is a combination of the smallest chain ring and the largest sprocket.

➤ The highest gear is a combination of the largest chain ring and the smallest sprocket.

➤ You want to avoid combining the largest chain ring with the largest sprocket and the smallest chain ring with the smallest sprocket because crossing the chain over in this extreme wears both it and the gear teeth down prematurely.

You can custom-select your chain rings and rear sprockets or cogs, but there is little reason to do so unless you're a competitive racer. Modern index shifters are designed to work smoothly with limited jumps from one gear to the next. Mucking with the gearing can affect the shifting. Older-style friction shifters, which stayed in adjustment by the tightening of a screw or bolt, depend on the rider to locate the chain rings and sprockets, are more flexible in this respect; but when ten-speeds were the standard, it made more sense to customize the gearing. With 21 to 27 speeds standard on today's bikes, a rider has more than enough gear options.

Derailed

Choosing extreme gears (largest chain ring to the largest sprocket and the smallest chain ring to the smallest sprocket) not only stresses the chain and wears down the gear teeth; it's unlikely that your rear derailleur can be adjusted to properly handle these combinations. These really aren't usable gears and should be avoided.

Stopping Power

I'll get into brakes later (see Chapter 6, "Gimme a Brake!"), but depending on the age of your bike, you'll have one of the following brake systems:

➤ Side-pull or center-pull caliper brakes

➤ Drum brakes

➤ Disc brakes

➤ Coaster brakes

➤ Cantilever brakes (including U-brakes and V-brakes)

➤ Rollercam brakes

The traditional braking system on ten-speed bikes uses either side-pull or center-pull brakes. These brakes work when a cable pulls on them and forces the arms or calipers to push a pair of brake shoes against the rim of the wheel. The range of quality spans the cheapest steel side-pulls on mass-produced three-speeds to the finest Campagnolo and Dura-Ace side-pulls. The old-style drum and disc brakes are quite heavy and not easy to service as they are internal hub mechanisms. New disc brakes are operated by hydraulic systems and are simply awesome in their stopping power and reliability. These are externally mounted and easier to service than earlier disc models.

Cantilever brakes, whose individual arms (or cantilevers) are bolted directly to the bike frame, are most often seen on mountain bikes. These are highly effective in part because each brake arm is mounted on its own pivot bushing that is brazed directly to the bike frame and provides a sturdy anchor for the arms.

Wheels

If you think about it, a bicycle wheel is a fascinating bit of physics. You have a sturdy rim, a pile of not especially sturdy-looking spokes, and a hub. Screw them all together, and you get a wheel capable of supporting you, your bike, and your gear for a zillion revolutions under all kinds of riding conditions. A bicycle wheel carries its load through tension rather than compression, as in most other wheels. Because it depends on tension, it's important that spokes are kept properly adjusted and taut.

Wheels are sized according to the bicycle frame. Mountain bikes typically have wheels that accommodate tires that are 26 inches in diameter. Road bikes, both touring and racing, have either 700C (700 millimeters) or 27-inch tires. However, sizes are not interchangeable! If your bike is built for 27-inch tires and you try to install 700C tires, the brake pads might not reach the wheel rim (more on wheels in Chapter 3, "Bike Details").

Different types of riding demand different wheel construction. Everyone wants a strong and sturdy wheel; a racer wants lightweight wheel, whereas an off-road rider wants a wheel that will withstand riding over logs and gullies. Wheel construction includes …

➤ Rim selection.

➤ Spoke selection and spoke patterns.

➤ Hub selection.

Bike Bites

Wheels are often referred to by the tire size, but in reality, they are narrower in diameter. It's easier to simply say "27-inch wheel" because bike mechanics and sales people will know what you're talking about. Also, there is some variance in the wheel diameters even when they accommodate the same size tire.

Quality new bikes come with *extruded aluminum rims*, which sometimes are referred to as *alloy rims*. They feature a box-style construction and are quite strong despite their relatively light weight when compared with steel rims. Steel rims usually are found on cheaper bikes or on bikes with hub gears such as three-speeds. The rim's spoke holes are drilled in an offset pattern, that is, slightly to the right and left of a line running down the center of the rim.

Just about every wheel is built with *tangential spoking* patterns, in which one spoke crosses one or more other spokes before connecting to the rim. The alternative, *radial spoking,* in which spokes do not cross, sometimes is used for track racing. The more spokes a single spoke has to cross, the longer the spokes used in the wheel construction. This makes for a somewhat more forgiving ride as the spokes help absorb some of the road shock. Spokes are hooked around a hole in the hub and then attached to the rim with screwed-on nipples.

Hubs, the Centers of Attention

Hubs and rims have to match up in terms of their holes; for example, a 36-hole hub goes with a 36-hole rim. The more holes, the more spokes to cushion your ride. Hubs come in several flavors: high *flange,* low flange, and those with internal brakes or gears.

Some will argue that one size flange offers benefits over another, but high flange hubs seem to have won the popularity contest.

Speaking of Spokes

The best spokes are made from stainless steel because of its strength and rust resistance. Double-butted spokes, which have extra strength at each end, just like double-butted frame tubes, are used in all quality wheels. Spokes come in different lengths to accommodate the different sizes of rims and hubs, as well as different spoking patterns.

Spokes attach to the wheel rim with nipples that typically are nickel-plated brass. This combination is fairly rust resistant, which is a good thing considering the amount of water they can be exposed to.

Choosing the Tires

Tires come in different diameters, widths, and types. Fortunately, there are only two styles to choose from—*sew-ups* (also called tubulars) and *clinchers* (also called wired-on tires). The vast majority of tires are clinchers. A clincher tire is simply one that has a separate inner tube. A tubular tire has a tube sewn inside its casing. Tubulars are very light, very fast, and used almost exclusively in racing and time trials.

Mountain bikes come equipped with fat, wide, knobby tires that perform well in off-road use, especially in mud and rough terrain. The tires generally have lower pressure than narrow, road-bike tires; however, this is appropriate for riding over softer, uneven ground versus smooth, hard, paved roads.

Bicycle tires must meet a variety of loads, demands, and riding conditions the world over, from ice-cream vendors to time-trial racing. You can buy several types for the same set of wheels and swap them around as the seasons or the type of terrain you ride over changes. The same is true for other bike components as well, making bicycling a versatile pastime. With a few tools and some extra parts, one bike can serve you well for all types of riding.

The Spoken Word

A **flange** is simply a projected rim on a wheel hub that provides a connecting point to the rim. High flange hubs, because they offer more material (more hub), are viewed as being stronger than low flange hubs.

Bike Bites

For all you aerodynamic addicts out there, elliptical spokes are available. Go to your local bike shop and take a look at the Wheelsmith Aero spokes if you're really interested. These are really geared toward racers who are trying to shave a few seconds off their time.

The Least You Need to Know

➤ Bicycles are more complicated than the casual rider would think.

➤ Bike types are designed and equipped for different types of riding; as a consumer, you have an endless combination of frame and components to choose from for your bicycle.

➤ It's critical to your riding comfort and safety that your bike frame is the correct size for your body.

➤ There is a bike for every terrain and road surface; from one-speed children's models to twenty-seven–speed mountain bikes.

Two-Wheeled History

In This Chapter

➤ Walking machines

➤ The first big wheels

➤ A bike designed for everyone

➤ America goes bike-crazy

➤ Modern bicycles

I don't think the wheel ever was actually invented; but as our ancestors discovered the benefits of round discs, everything changed—especially transportation. No more pulling all the household goods on sleds or riding early versions of the subway on rotating tree trunks. A simple wheel allowed people to move themselves and their stuff with previously unknown ease.

It was inevitable that our independent streaks would call for some kind of private, solo transportation that would run on the user's own power instead of using something with four legs and a huge appetite. Early versions of bicycles were uncomfortable, heavy, and not at all consumer friendly, but they were a start. Every version added to the collective knowledge of bicycle design, culminating in the bikes that we have today. It's a good thing, too, because none of us would be willing to ride the one-speed machines of the nineteenth century.

Early Bikes

In the last few centuries, personal transportation, especially along city streets, was due for a change; it came in the form of a bicycle. Some writers date the first doodlings of bicycle design to the fifteenth century. According to *Richards' Ultimate Bicycle Book* (Dorling Kindersley, Inc., New York, 1992), Leonardo da Vinci sketched out an early prototype bicycle with a chain drive and pedals as early as 1490. Others say this never happened and the first bicycle prototypes came more than two centuries later.

Freewheelin' Facts

Although they're getting harder to find, older bikes from the 1950s and 1960s still find their way to secondhand and thrift stores. Some bike shops sell only used bikes and specialize in older models. These bicycles are fun to collect and good for practicing repairs.

In the late 1700s, a Frenchman named de Sivrac came up with the Celerifere, a two-wheeled machine with a beam connecting the wheels. The rider had the fun job of pushing his or her feet along the ground to get moving. In 1817, the German Baron Karl von Drais took this "hobbyhorse" one step further and made a front wheel that could be steered; it had no pedals and was constructed entirely of wood. The baron took out a patent and called his invention a velocipede (for "fast foot"). As you can guess, this wasn't exactly a bestseller and was usable only on smooth paths. The upper classes of Europe—ever ready to jump on the latest fad—only briefly took to this less-than-accommodating mode of transportation. Fortunately, German engineering has taken huge leaps since the hobbyhorse.

Learning Curves

Early machinists and inventors were among the first garage-based entrepreneurs, although in those days they called them barns or blacksmith shops. Anyone with a forge, an anvil, and an idea could put some kind of a bicycle together. Things moved slowly even after *cranks* and *pedals* were brought into the equation (credited in 1840 to both Scottish blacksmith Kirkpatrick Macmillan and another Scotsman, Gavin Dalzell; bike history can be a little sketchy at times). The pedals and cranks were connected directly to the rear wheel, which meant one gear. This also meant that touring the Scottish highlands—let alone the Alps—was out of the question. Macmillan did manage to ride a 140-mile trip to Glasgow and back and at one point hit his stride with a speed of 8 mph.

The Spoken Word

Cranks refer to the metal arms that are attached to the front chain rings and are attached to a spindle or axle that passes through the bottom bracket of a bicycle frame. The **pedals** basically are footrests that allow the rider to move the crank arms.

A Mover and a Shaker

The next notable move in bicycle design came in the 1860s with another two-wheel velocipede known less-than-affectionately as the boneshaker. Unlike earlier bikes, this one had the pedals attached to the front wheel, similar to a child's tricycle. Pierre Lallement, a French mechanic, is credited for this innovation, as well as building the first velocipede in America in 1865. Constructed from wood and later from metal tubing, the boneshaker was available in both a two-wheel and a three-wheel, or tricycle, version. The front wheel typically was larger than the rear wheel. The wheels themselves sometimes were built from metal rather than wood and added to the general discomfort of the riding experience. It was not uncommon for one of these velocipedes to weigh 60 pounds.

A Penny for Your Farthing

Bike design became even stranger with the development of the high-wheeler, sometimes called a "penny farthing," which had a huge front wheel (up to five feet across) and a much smaller rear wheel; these appeared in the 1870s. Manufacturers discovered that the larger the front wheel, to which the cranks and pedals were attached, the farther the rider could travel with one revolution of the cranks. One welcome change was the smoothness of the ride, which greatly improved with solid rubber tires and long wheel spokes.

The riders of these bikes, typically young men with more money than sense, sat high off the ground on a precarious center of gravity. Stopping was accomplished when a rider stopped pedaling, used a spoon brake that pressed a metal shoe against a solid rubber tire, or fell off the high-wheeler—more than a few riders took a rough tumble. As the front wheel shrank, the new versions became known as high-wheel safety bicycles, whereas the older models were referred to as "ordinary" bicycles or, more simply, "ordinaries."

Bike Bites

Some of the earliest manufacturers of bicycles were sewing machine companies, such as Singer, because they had the machinery and the craftsmen to do precision metalworking. Colonel Albert Pope, a nineteenth-century industrialist, figured out how to mass-produce bicycles and eliminated the need for more expensive machinists. He built his own die-making equipment and even manufactured the ball bearings needed for the final assemblies. His Columbia brand of bicycles was quite popular and less costly than the more traditional hand-built machines.

Riding Like a Girl

As one can well imagine, high-wheelers and late nineteenth-century women—encumbered by long dresses and strange, restrictive undergarments—weren't exactly a match made in heaven. Adult-size tricycles allowed women and less daring men to enjoy cycling. However, these were still one-speed, fixed-gear steel bikes. They might have been lighter than their earlier wooden counterparts, but they still required a fair amount of effort to keep them moving.

Safety Arrives

The safety bicycle of the 1880s and 1890s didn't exactly bring bike design into the jet age (more like the biplane age), but they were early versions of what bikes would look like in years to come. The diamond frame set a new standard, and the wheels shrank

Freewheelin' Facts

One bike model (called the "sociable") fitted parts of two bike frames together so a couple could sit side by side while they pedaled. The alpha male of the couple typically did the steering.

dramatically with the introduction of gears and the chain drive. The idea was simple: Gear sprockets and a chain allowed the rider to multiply his or her leg power to the rear wheel instead of using cranks and pedals directly attached to a front wheel. This was a lot easier than pumping away on a high-wheeler—and much safer to ride. For the first time, large numbers of women could take up cycling and hit the road with the boys.

Finally, Some Gears

Using a chain to connect the gears on a rear wheel with the gears attached to the cranks and pedals seems pretty self-evident now, but this wasn't always so. Although most turn-of-the-century bikes had a single, fixed gear, a manufacturer could vary the gearing for different bikes. Racing bikes could be geared to the preferences of the rider, for example.

Bike Bites

Early bike racing took place on the road and in *velodromes*, which were enclosed, banked tracks that accommodated the movement of the bicycles. Modern track bikes are very similar to these earlier models in that they have a single, fixed gear and no braking system.

A Social Revolution on Wheels

It's interesting to see what brings about changes to the social order. Technological innovations throughout history, from the horse saddle to the personal computer, have allowed human beings to become more independent and self-reliant. The bicycle was one of these inventions.

Bicycles allowed people to travel more easily. Younger people could take off and get away from the old neighborhoods and see what was on the other end of town. Workers had more options for employment because they could commute farther than they could comfortably walk. Women took to wearing less restrictive *bloomers* and hit the road with an unprecedented sense of personal freedom. According to some writers, the popularity of bicycling and its required physical movement helped to do away with the bustle and corset, two highly restrictive items of women's clothing at the turn of the twentieth century.

The Spoken Word

Bloomers were a style of women's dress promoted by Amelia Bloomer, a New York woman, around 1850. This fashion included a short skirt, loose trousers buttoned around the ankle, and a broad-rimmed hat. Bloomers of the 1890s were a loose type of pants gathered at the knee and worn by women for cycling and swimming.

Bikes Were Big Business

According to authors Jay Pridmore and Jim Hurd in their book *The American Bicycle* (Motorbooks, 1995), bikes and their manufacturing were a big deal by the late nineteenth century. Bicycling exploded in the 1890s with the bike boom and at least one third of all new patent applications in the United States at that time were bicycle related. The bicycle manufacturing and factory systems were forerunners to later automobile assembly lines. The Wright brothers, who were America's most famous bike mechanics, even took their expertise and applied it to flying, resulting indirectly in the incomprehensible ticketing systems and mysterious airline food that we have today.

Bicycle sales peaked in 1897 in the United States. At that time, the authors estimate that close to 3,000 firms were involved in the manufacturing of bikes and bike parts. They collectively sold an estimated 2,000,000 bicycles that year.

However, with the introduction of motorized bikes and automobiles (why cycle when a gasoline motor will do the job for you?) and a glut of manufacturers, bike sales were bound to take a hit. As the twentieth century rolled on and cars took over the roads that had been developed for bicycles, adults in America began to view bikes as more of a child's toy rather than serious transportation. In Europe, bicycling flourished between World War I and World War II, although it, too, declined in the late 1940s as car production increased.

Bike Bites

Susan B. Anthony, known for her work in the women's suffrage movement and for a one-dollar coin that barely made it out of the U.S. Mint's storehouses, made a very perceptive comment on cycling in the late nineteenth century. She said, "Let me tell you what I think of bicycling. I think it has done more to emancipate women than anything else in the world. I stand and rejoice every time I see a woman ride by on a wheel. It gives women a feeling of freedom and self-reliance." She would have loved motorcycles.

After Revolution Comes Evolution

Bicycle manufacturing was one of the high-tech industries of the late nineteenth and early twentieth centuries. Designers and manufacturers were regularly coming up with new components and styles to stay competitive and improve the bike's performance. Some manufacturers even experimented with solid wood frames (wheels often were made with wood rims and steel spokes) to soften the ride!

One of the biggest improvements was the introduction of a pneumatic tire; that is, a tire with an air-filled inner tube. John Dunlop, an Irish veterinary surgeon, invented the pneumatic tire when he apparently wanted to come up with a more comfortable tricycle ride for his young son who was in poor health. Pneumatic tires replaced the less forgiving solid rubber tires that were standard at that time.

Modern Times

As automobiles took over the world, some manufacturers attempted to revitalize the bike industry by introducing children's bicycles after World War I. These bikes were very heavy and very flashy, in part because they were made to look somewhat like motorcycles with big frames, large fenders, and cool paint jobs. These designs predominated in America until the 1950s. The first lightweight European bikes (mostly English Raleighs) were imported to the United States after World War II.

Bike Bites

As Americans took to bicycling into the late nineteenth century, bicycle racing became a very popular sport. Some races were endured for 24 hours or longer. One bike, the Tribune Blue Streak, weighed in at just under 20 pounds with 28-inch wheels. This is a very respectable weight given the technology of the time.

Bike Bites

Multi-gear bikes actually were invented many years ago. An early type of derailleur was available around the turn of the twentieth century about the same time the first internal gear/hub system was developed by England's Sturmey–Archer company. Their bestselling three-speed hub, the AW 3, was developed in 1936. The French company Heuret manufactured the first workable derailleurs in the 1940s. Modern derailleurs are light years beyond any of these earlier components.

English Racers

The 1950s brought an influx of three-speed bikes, mainly from England. These were far sleeker than the older-style balloon tire bikes and offered multiple gearing for different road conditions and riding styles. These three-speeds were highly reliable bicycles and can still be found today at garage sales and thrift stores. Sturmey-Archer, the English manufacturer of multi-speed hubs, also offered a four-speed mechanism. The company, which recently fell into receivership, manufactured three-, five-, and seven-speed gear systems.

Leaner and Meaner

Finally, in the 1960s, lightweight bikes with derailleur systems became available in the United States as European imports took off. Schwinn gave its blessing to this movement with its 8-speed, and later 10-speed, Varsity series. As European and Japanese bikes made inroads here, Schwinn and other American manufacturers responded with lighter, faster bikes with more responsive handling and frames.

Several factors contributed to the resurging popularity of bicycling, including ...

➤ Obviously improved bicycle design.

➤ A new emphasis on physical fitness.

➤ Rising energy prices.

➤ Increased acceptance of bike commuting.

➤ A rediscovery of the fun in cycling and a renewed interest in serious racing.

Rediscovering the Clunker

The old balloon tire bikes from decades past became affectionately known as clunkers, and for good reason: They were heavy! As with many trends that start on the West coast, Californians found that these bikes were perfect for racing down mountain trails in areas such as Marin County. These cruisers were used as models for the first mountain bikes.

Freewheelin' Facts

Modern mountain bikes are expensive and built for abuse. If you want to do only some moderate trail riding, consider picking up an old clunker at a garage sale. You can retrofit it with some modern components or just tune it up and use it on flat trails. You can buy a lot of clunkers for the price of one new bike. Outfit one with a three-speed hub if you want the option of more than one gear.

Like so much else that starts out as simple, cheap fun, these old clunkers were gradually replaced with state-of-the-art mountain bikes that now can cost thousands of dollars. So much for taking an old Schwinn, packing the bearings with a ton of grease, and racing it down a hiking path until it was semi-destroyed.

It's a New Day

The last few decades have brought out all kinds of fascinating bicycles and off-the-wall designs. Some of these have included …

➤ Muscle bikes.

➤ Recumbent bikes.

➤ Frames made from carbon fiber, aluminum, and titanium.

➤ Moto-Cross (BMX) models.

➤ Aerodynamic frames.

➤ An increase of available gears (up to 27 speeds).

Freewheelin' Facts

The National Bicycle History Archive of America (NBHAA) is an archive of historical materials that relate to bicycles. The archive contains over 30,000 articles, photos, and catalogs pertaining to bicycles. E-mail them at OldBicycle@aol.com or call 714-647-1949. Their mailing address is NBHAA, PO Box 28242, Santa Ana, CA 92799. Contact them for assistance in identifying a bicycle or component.

Some bicycles now cost as much as a used car. Components range from heavy and inexpensive to ultra-light and ultra-costly. Virtually any riding style or riding purpose can be accommodated at a good bike shop, and the future will bring even more exotic materials and construction.

The Least You Need to Know

➤ Early bicycles, known as velocipedes, were heavy, unwieldy, and uncomfortable.

➤ America went through an unprecedented bicycle boom in the 1890s, only to be followed by declining sales as automobiles and motorcycles gained in popularity.

➤ Multi-speed bikes didn't really catch on in the United States until the 1950s with the heavy importation of three-speed bikes.

➤ Modern derailleur bicycles gained popularity in the 1960s and have markedly improved with modern design and components.

Chapter 3

Bike Details

In This Chapter

➤ A bicycle for every ride

➤ Tandems and recumbents

➤ When bikes go on diets

➤ Small parts make big differences

One-speed bicycles were the norm in America for decades. These bikes were heavy and dependable; and one way or another, they got their riders up hills that we tackle today only with multi-speed bikes. Technological advances have brought us an array of bicycle designs, from titanium components to full-suspension frames, and there's no end in sight to future improvements. Of course, there's no end to the cost of these bikes, either.

Some ardent cyclists have a number of bicycles, each one set up for a different type of riding: commuting, off-road, touring, and so on. Those who are slightly less possessed (or have less storage room) usually find one bike is sufficient. The key is determining normal riding activity and purchasing an appropriate machine. This means, for instance, that you don't use a traditional English touring bike for weekend rides on old, abandoned logging roads.

This chapter introduces you to the myriad of bicycles available at your local bike shop and listed in the want ads. Some can be used for more than one type of riding with little compromise. If you're not sure what you like, try all of them—eventually something will strike your fancy.

What's Your Type?

There's a bicycle for every body type and riding style. You can ride solo or ride with your partner on a tandem (a bicycle built for two). No matter where you intend to ride, even across the North Pole, you can find a bike that will get you there.

The Spoken Word

Drop handlebars provides multiple hand positions for the rider and are found on touring and racing bikes. The center of the bar is usually its highest point while the ends of the bar are the lowest. These are the opposite of upright bars typically found on children's bikes and three-speed bikes.

Bike Bites

Uncertain about buying a particular type of bike? Rent one for a weekend from a bike shop that offers rentals and put it through the paces. Use it on a typical ride. You'll find out quickly enough if, say, a mountain bike is suitable for your purposes.

All the hipness of the 1950s with better components on this Trek Cruiser Classic.

(Photo courtesy of Trek Bicycles)

Many factors will affect your choice of bicycles, including …

➤ The intended use.

➤ Budget.

➤ Preference in riding style.

➤ Frequency of use.

➤ Road conditions.

What's your riding style? Are you a racing traditionalist who likes leaning over a pair of *drop handlebars,* or do you prefer being more upright? Are you a speed demon or more even-paced and steady? If you ride every day or depend on your bicycle for most of your transportation needs, it will be worth it to spend a little more money and get yourself a comfortable, responsive bike rather than settling for something less.

Some people ride all year around, even through winter snow and ice. If your main intention is to commute to and from work, you might choose a mountain bike to cope with potholes and uncertain weather conditions. Or, you might only have a short distance to ride on flat roads; in this case, consider a second-hand three-speed that you can safely leave locked outside without worrying about it being stolen. Occasional weekend rides on flat roads in warm weather can be done on just about anything. The right bike will see you through it all.

Cruisers

Modern-day cruisers resemble the early Schwinns from the 1920s through the 1950s with their heavy frames, upright handlebars, and sometimes even shock absorbers. These aren't racing bikes; traditionally, they come with only one gear and a coaster brake, or built-in rear hub brake, on 26-inch wheels (this size includes the tire). Fat tires are standard for these classic bikes that seem custom-built for beachfront riding. There's a good reason that they found early resurgence in surf-crazy California. No longer limited to one gear, you can buy a new cruiser with three-, five-, or seven-speed internal rear hubs with either hand brakes or a coaster brake (see the following figure).

Derailed

The off-road bike craze started out with old cruisers, some of which were modified with additional gears and hand brakes. Cruisers work for some off-road use, but they are not as strong or as durable as modern mountain bikes built specifically for this type of riding. A used cruiser and strenuous trail riding aren't a great combination.

Remember, these bikes are heavy. They're terrific for occasional riding on flat roads, but any childhood notions of easy riding will quickly disappear when you try to sprint up your first major hill. Cruisers are great for college campuses or beach towns such as Lahaina, Maui, but I wouldn't try them in hilly San Francisco unless you're trying to prove something.

Mountain Bikes

By far, the mountain bike is the bestselling current bike model and has been for years. What a mountain bike lacks in elegance (they're not exactly the prettiest bikes ever built) it makes up for in utility. Their popularity is easy to understand considering that they ...

➤ Are extremely durable.

➤ Can be used off road.

➤ Are more practical than many traditional road bikes.

Derailed

Just because it's a tough mountain bike doesn't mean you can go jumping off a 10-foot ledge onto a cobblestone street and expect to go riding off undamaged (or uninjured, for that matter). Riders who are excessively tough on their bikes end up replacing wheels, cranks, pedals ... you name it. Enjoy your bike, but understand its limitations.

Some mountain bikes are built for speed, both cross-country and downhill; others are built for rough terrain. Typically, mountain bikes have the following:

➤ 26-inch wide wheels (includes the tire)

➤ Up to 27 gears

➤ Rugged components and frames

➤ Wide, knobby tires

➤ Upright handlebars

Mountain bikes are divided into several categories. Utility is the guiding principle to mountain bike design; the major differences among them are the strength and dimensions of the frame and components.

Rigid Models

A rigid mountain bike is the least forgiving and least expensive bike of this type; it has no added suspension. Some riders prefer the stiffer frame for climbing hills because it has less give than a frame with suspension, and therefore is more efficient for transferring energy from pedals to wheels. Forget about comfort—a rigid bike will give you a blow-by-blow description of every rock and hole encounter.

Hardtail

A mountain bike with only front suspension (some type of spring or shock absorber in the fork) is a hardtail bike. This bike is faster climbing than a full-suspension bike, (that is, a bike with front and rear suspension), but it's not as comfortable. A hardtail is most often used in racing, partially because of its lighter weight. Higher-end models allow the rider to adjust the suspension's stiffness to the road or trail conditions.

Full Suspension

This dual suspension bike has shock absorbers on both wheels and is quite comfortable to ride, especially when riding off road and downhill. These bikes are more expensive than hardtail models. Manufacturers use different designs for placement of the springs and pivots (the attachment points for the rear springs).

Comfort and Cyclocross Bikes

Comfort bikes make no pretense about being fast or cornering on a dime, but they are comfortable (see the following figure). The rider sits upright on a soft saddle and lightweight steel frame. Comfort bikes usually have 21 or 24 gears, are similar in design to a hybrid bike (a cross between a mountain bike and a touring bike), and often come with partial suspension. These bikes are built for pavement or flat, dirt roads.

The Trek Navigator 500 comfort bike offers an easy ride for short trips or a longer cruise.

(Photo courtesy of Trek Bicycles)

Another cycling style is *cyclocross*, which started in Europe as a way for road racers to continue riding in the off-season months. It's a sport in which riders race around an off-road course over various obstacles, including mud pits and hills. At some points on the course, the riders must dismount and carry their bikes around or up an obstacle and then continue riding. A cyclocross bike has the following features:

➤ Wide tires (but not as wide or knobby as mountain bikes)

➤ Drop handlebars

➤ Cantilever brakes

➤ Extra rugged frame

➤ Multiple speeds

A cyclocross bicycle is faster than a mountain bike, but not as rugged. It's one thing to go around a track and get around obstacles and quite another to go bouncing over rocks and logs on a trail. Still, for overall winter commuting, a cyclocross bike can make sense for some riders.

Hit the Road

A modern-day, relatively lightweight road bike is built for racing or touring. These bikes resemble the old drop-bar 10-speed bikes that were imported by the truckload in the 1960s. They are built to require a bent-over riding position that decreases wind resistance and are intended for paved roads, not dirt trails. A true road bike will have a longer *wheelbase* for greater comfort.

A road bike comes with either 700C wheels or, less often, 27-inch wheels. These measurements refer to the diameter of the tire, but the term is often used to define the wheel when combined with the tire. A 27-inch wheel is slightly smaller than a 700C (or 700 millimeters), but the latter is narrower and offers less rolling resistance.

An older road bike will have 10 speeds, whereas newer ones will have up to 27 speeds. Some touring models will have a classic wide leather saddle for added comfort. All will have a variety of small fittings—called braze-ons—and eyelets for attaching water bottles, bike racks, and tire pumps. Racing models typically have fewer braze-ons because they are not intended to carry racks or more than one water bottle.

The Spoken Word

The **wheelbase** of a bicycle is the distance between the front and rear wheel axles. A short base gives a stiffer ride and comes in handy for cornering during a race. A longer wheelbase cushions the rider from road shock by distributing the load over a larger area.

Freewheelin' Facts

For years, the bicycle industry has faced issues of size standards for everything from threads to tires. It seemed every country used its own measuring system until standardization finally prevailed. The International Organization for Standardization, or IOS, has developed a universal tire sizing system based on the width of the tire and the rim diameter as measured in millimeters.

Hybrid

What happens when you cross a mountain bike with a road bike? You get a hybrid, a good choice for commuting and recreational riding on pavement and some minor off-road riding on smooth trails. Hybrid bikes feature 700C, or sometimes 27-inch, wheels and usually at least 21 gears. These generally are short-distance road bikes (you won't be doing a coast-to-coast ride on them), with upright seating and handlebars and a wide saddle. A hybrid offers versatility. It will never be terrific for any one type of riding, but will allow you to experience a variety of biking (see the following figure).

Trek 7700 Hybrid lets you hit the road and do some light trail riding, too.

(Photo courtesy of Trek Bicycles)

Recumbents

You might see a *recumbent* bike with its rider sitting back with outstretched legs and wonder why it doesn't tip over with its small (20- or 24-inch) wheels. They can look a bit strange, but these bikes offer the advantage of decreased wind resistance, no weight on the rider's wrists, a large seat instead of a narrow saddle, and an ability to see straight ahead without bending the neck. Don't expect recumbents to ever become a mainstream bike, they're just too weird and slow going uphill.

One issue with recumbents is visibility because both bicycle and rider are lower to the ground than other bicycles. Some reports suggest that drivers are more alert to these bikes because they are so unusual, although this might be less true in heavy traffic. Personally, I wouldn't want to test this theory in downtown Manhattan.

The Spoken Word

Recumbent refers to the seated or reclining position that the rider of a recumbent bike assumes. Some enthusiasts also call these bikes "bents."

However, recumbent bikes have many advocates, including the International Human Powered Vehicle Association (IHPVA:http://ihpva.org; HPVA Membership, PO Box 1307, San Luis Obispo, CA 93406-1307). In events sanctioned by the IHPVA, all the land-speed records are held by recumbent or semi-recumbent designs. Recumbent enthusiasts tout the bike's design as superior to a standard diamond-framed bike, claiming it is far more comfortable and efficient. As a bonus, if you fall while riding a recumbent bike, you rarely get hurt because a rider is already close to the ground and the frame itself protects the rider (see the following figure). For current information on recumbent bikes, contact the Recumbent Cyclist News at www.recumbentcyclistnews.com or RCN, PO Box 2048, Port Townsend, WA 98368.

Sit back and relax on a Trek Recumbent.

(Photo courtesy of Trek Bicycles)

Tandems

The classic bicycle built for two, a *tandem* (from the Latin for "at length") can be great fun for the right two people and torture for the wrong two. It helps if the riders are roughly equivalent in riding skill or enthusiasm—or at least are willing to meet somewhere in the middle. If one of the two insists on riding as though he (it's almost always a he) were trying to outrun a flock of vampires at sunset, most likely he will find himself riding alone.

Tandems come with two sets of handlebars, *saddles,* pedals, and cranksets. They range from one-speed rentals at coastal resorts to twenty-seven–speed mountain bike tandems. A tandem can be custom-ordered and built to fit both riders. Special tandem considerations include wheel strength, frame geometry, and the *drivetrain.*

Tandem riders of equal ability can travel faster together than either can do individually. This calls for extra weight on the wheels, and for this reason, some tandem builders use wheels with more spokes than the standard 36-hole hub-and-rim combinations. Each builder also has ideas on the proper frame geometry for stiffness and rigidity. Frame builders are an opinionated lot, which makes purchasing a custom-made tandem bike a lively experience.

The Spoken Word

The **drivetrain** is all those components that connect your leg power to the wheels, including the chain, pedals, and gears. A tandem has two sets of pedals and cranks (the arms where the pedals attach) and two chains. There are also two sets of handlebars and two saddles, of course.

Kids Only

Juvenile bikes include everything from tricycles to dirt bikes. As a rule, these have small wheels (12- to 24-inch), one speed, and a coaster brake. Older kids and younger adults often use these bikes—including BMX or dirt bikes, trick or freestyle bikes, and jumpers—for competitive purposes.

BMX stands for Bicycle Motocross and usually comes with a rear hand brake. It is used for both racing (on the more expensive models) and general-purpose riding. BMX bikes are simple, durable, and well-suited for kids, although adults race them, too (you're considered an old guy once you reach age 19).

Trick bikes are designed for freeform stunts that often defy gravity and, in the minds of nonriders, general intelligence (but that's usually generational jealousy in my humble opinion). These bikes are strong and specially designed for fun tricks, such as standing on the pedals and spinning the handlebars around and around. Jumpers are built to survive ramp jumping and are reinforced and strengthened at all stress points—a salient point for larger, heavier riders (see the following figure).

The Spoken Word

A **saddle** refers to a bicycle seat and goes back to the days of the early hobbyhorse, which borrowed some terminology from real horses; the term "saddle" has stayed with us to this day. Many riders still swear by the comfort of a well-broken-in leather saddle.

Kids and kid-like adults can get plenty of dirt-track riding fun on a Trek T.1.1 BMX.

(Photo courtesy of Trek Bicycles)

Weighing In

One of the first things we do when considering the purchase of a bike is to pick it up. We want to know how heavy it is, even though the weight of a bicycle is only one factor that affects its performance. One bike can be lighter than another, but uncomfortable to ride. Still, we don't want to be pushing around any more weight than we have to when we're out riding.

Several factors affect the effort required for a rider to move a bike along. These include …

➤ The weight of the bike.

➤ The stiffness of the frame.

➤ The size of the wheels and the wheelbase itself.

➤ The quality of the bearings.

➤ The sitting position of the rider.

➤ Tire pressure.

➤ Gear ratios.

The Spoken Word

Rolling resistance is simply the friction between the road and the tire as it compresses against the road surface. The higher the air pressure in the tire, the less it compresses and the lower the rolling resistance.

I must add that the weight of the rider also counts—the more weight you have to move, the slower you will move it, all things being equal. A lighter bicycle that also has a stiffer frame and components will be the best combination of all because together these elements will more efficiently transfer your energy from pedaling into moving the bike. A shorter wheelbase also transfers this energy more efficiently, especially during a climb.

Weight distribution counts, too. A superlight frame with heavy steel wheels will be slower than the same frame with light, efficient alloy wheels. As a rule, narrow, high-pressure tires offer less *rolling resistance* than wider, lower-pressure tires, depending on the road conditions and tire design.

Watching Those Ounces

For most riders, it isn't necessary to shave off every extra gram of weight from a bicycle. Weight differences at this level matter only to racers who have been known to drill holes in components to decrease their weight. The key for most riders is to get the lightest bike they can afford. It's going to weigh just as much the first mile you ride it as the thousandth mile—the less weight you have to push around, the better.

All this comes at a cost to your budget, of course. Extremely light-weight bikes are made from top-of-the-line tubing and components with top-of-the-line price tags. For instance, there's a noticeable difference between 29 pounds and 26 pounds; but not enough between 26 pounds and 24 pounds to justify a lot of extra dollars to the average rider. And put your drill away! You can weaken components by drilling holes in them.

Wheel Weight

With few exceptions, you'll find alloy wheels only on new, multi-speed, derailleur bikes sold at independent bike shops. You'll find heavier steel wheels on cheaper bikes from department stores. The latter are worth avoiding, especially for a serious adult rider. Older 10-speeds and bikes with internal hub gears often have steel wheels and hubs. All of this extra weight adds up to more rolling resistance, which means less distance covered for the leg power you exert.

Freewheelin' Facts

A decent-quality mountain bike with alloy components probably will weigh about 26 pounds. It can cost hundreds of dollars to lighten the bike by a single pound. Lighter components also are expensive, as is a lighter frame. For most riders, this extra expense is hardly worth it.

Smart Parts

As you move up the ladder of bicycle quality, small things start adding up. For instance, quick-release wheels are a great convenience when it comes to repairing flats. Instead of removing a nut from each side of the axle, the rider or mechanic simply flips the quick-release lever to loosen the wheel.

Every component of a bike changes as the price and quality increase. A standard nut and bolt is replaced with a recessed hex fitting, which will be either an Allen nut or an Allen bolt. Derailleurs are smoother. Bottom brackets spin with less resistance. Other changes include the shift levers (gear shifters), *sealed bearings,* and braze-ons.

Sealed bearings are contained in cartridges that protect them from dirt and moisture. Older bikes rarely had sealed bearings, but they are a mainstay on new bikes.

Nifty Shifters

Gear shifters or shift levers come in a range of models. The old-style friction shifters, which typically were installed on the down tube, are a thing of the past. Modern index shifters will move the chain up or down the rear cogs or sprockets ("gears") or the front chain rings automatically with a "click." The shifter is designed to move just enough to shift into the selected gear. There's no guesswork on the part of the rider to change gears, although purists might think that index shifters reduce the rider's skill level ("In my day, we found our own gears; and we built our own tires, too"). Index shifters also have relocated from the down tube to the brake levers or handlebars, allowing the rider to maintain a hands-on position at all times. This is important for racers, but perhaps less so for recreational riders.

The Spoken Word

A **sealed bearing** unit also is called a "cartridge bearing." The unit contains ring-shaped bearings set in grease unlike loose ball bearings, which are sphere-shaped. One advantage of loose ball bearings, however, is that anyone can service them.

Getting Your Bearings

Most quality new bikes come with some sealed bearings. Older bikes have individual ball bearings that are not protected by any kind of cartridge. They work just fine, but are subject to infiltration by dirt and water, especially during wet weather riding. Consumers can service some sealed bearings; others must be taken to a bike shop.

Crazy for Braze-Ons

Braze-ons—those convenient, small, permanent attachments to the frame that accommodate racks, water bottles, shifters, and brakes—are generously added to some bikes; others are a bit stingier. In lieu of braze-ons, various clamps and attachments can be bolted to the frame to accomplish these tasks, but braze-ons are much neater and cleaner.

Some older, inexpensive 10-speeds will have all kinds of bolt-on clamps, sometimes made of plastic. Higher-quality bikes, though, will have plenty of braze-ons, making some of your bike repairs a bit more convenient.

The Least You Need to Know

➤ There is a bicycle model for absolutely every type of riding and rider.

➤ Some bikes can be used successfully for multiple riding purposes, such as a mountain bike as commuter transportation.

➤ You'll pay more for a lighter bicycle, but you'll also get a faster and more efficient bike.

➤ Modern bikes have wholesale improvements over older models, especially in the components.

Chapter 4

Tools and Parts

In This Chapter

➤ Minimal repair tools

➤ What they all do

➤ Spares to carry with you

➤ Setting up a home shop

The world of bicycling calls for some very specialized tools. They're not necessarily expensive—a chain tool costs only a few dollars—but you need them to do repairs properly. You won't find most of these at a hardware store, and trying to substitute needle-nose pliers for a cone wrench just isn't going to work. A basic set of tools will get you started without breaking your budget. As you get into more intricate bike repairs or fulfill your dream of opening a bike shop in your garage, you can look into more expensive and more specific tools. Bike tools are available at your local bike shop or through various catalogs. Begin with the basics and work from there.

Every cyclist should have a modicum of spare or extra parts around for emergencies. The most obvious are inner tubes and tube repair kits—everyone gets a flat tire once in a while. I'll discuss the spares that will get you home when you're off the beaten path and there isn't a bike shop in site.

Got Tools?

Bicycle tools can be divided into two simple categories: those that you can carry with you when you ride and those that stay in your workshop. You probably already have some tools at home that can be used for bike repair. Some of these include ...

➤ Hammers.

➤ An adjustable (crescent) wrench.

➤ Different types of pliers.

➤ Various screwdrivers.

These tools are fine for some purposes, but they cannot replace the more specialized tools you'll need to adjust, disassemble, and reassemble your bike. If you use the wrong tool, you could end up chewing up a component.

Freewheelin' Facts

A great alternative to individual hand tools is one of the multi-tools made by various manufacturers. For example, the Park Micro Toolbox Multi-Tool, which sells for around $30, contains 21 separate tools including a chain tool, spoke wrenches, hex wrenches, tire levers, screwdrivers, and a tire patch kit (see the following figure). Multi-tools fit inside a bike bag or backpack in one convenient kit.

The Park Multi-Tool is the Swiss Army knife of bike tools.

(Courtesy of Park Tool)

Start Small

A bicycle periodically needs its moving parts adjusted. After so many miles of pedaling, stressing brake and derailleur cables, and rotating wheels, parts begin to loosen. To tighten them, you'll need screwdrivers, wrenches, and pliers. These are simple enough and relatively inexpensive. You'll also need some rags, solvent, and lubricants to keep moving parts moving and clean.

Additionally, you'll want a frame-mounted tire pump. Patch kits and tire levers (see the following section) won't do you much good if you can't pump up the tire when you're done repairing or replacing the inner tube. It's a good idea to have a regular air pump (a foot pump or floor pump with a big, T-shaped plunger) in your workshop since they work a lot faster than a frame-mounted pump.

Spare a Part, Buddy?

Simple, dumb repairs on the road will stop a fun afternoon ride every time. They will also hold up a cross-country tour or a hell-on-wheels careening down an abandoned logging road. Be prepared, and you'll be able to finish your ride. Here are the basic spare parts that you should carry with you when you ride:

> ➤ One tire patch kit
> ➤ One inner tube
> ➤ Tire levers
> ➤ Tire gauge
> ➤ Tire pump
> ➤ Roll of electrical tape

Freewheelin' Facts

It's a good idea to throw a few individually wrapped, disposable hand-cleaning wipes into your bike bag, too. Roadside repairs can be messy, especially if you have to move the chain. A quick cleaning will get the worst of the grease off your hands.

You never know when you're going to need a roll of tape. A tire might have a hole in it and not be able to hold an inner tube securely. Wrapping a lot of tape around it might not be very elegant, but it can get you home. If you're riding long distances, such as a day long trip, you also should carry the following:

> ➤ A spare brake cable
> ➤ An extra derailleur cable
> ➤ Two or three spare spokes
> ➤ Screwdrivers (slotted and Phillips heads)
> ➤ Extra chain links

Every time you squeeze a brake lever or pull back on a gear shifter, you put tremendous pressure on their respective cables. These cables can snap and require replacement. This is not a difficult repair to do on the road (see Chapter 6, "Gimme a Brake!") it sure beats losing half of your gearing or the use of one of your brakes.

A broken spoke isn't the end of the world; but you can ride some distance on a wobbly wheel. It's not an ideal situation: A broken spoke puts stress on the wheel, so you're better off if you replace it as soon as possible.

The Well-Packed Pack

You can't pack for every contingency. Well, you could, but *panniers* would weigh a ton. You want to carry enough tools and spare parts to ensure that you can handle most repairs and emergencies that can occur during a bike ride, regardless of the duration. In addition to the items just listed, consider taking the following on a long ride, especially if you're not going to be near a bicycle shop:

➤ Cable cutters

➤ Spoke wrench

➤ Chain tool

➤ Crank extractor

➤ Freewheel remover

➤ Cone wrenches

➤ Channel locks

Many of these tools can be found in a convenient multi-tool. It helps to have a freewheel remover and crank extractor—you might find yourself at a small-town bike shop that doesn't have the specific tools to match your components (some shops are run out of someone's garage). Channel locks take up a bit of room, but can be used in emergencies to tighten up headsets, bottom brackets, and straighten out blips in a wheel rim. To avoid scratching any surfaces, wrap the jaws of the channel locks with a bit of tape first.

The Spoken Word

Panniers are the pairs of bags carried on either a front or rear rack on a bicycle. It comes from the Old French word meaning "breadbasket."

What Do They Do?

I've thrown out a lot of tool names; now I'll identify them. There are a lot of wrenches used in bike maintenance, so I'll start with those. If you want your tools to last, use them for the purpose for which they were designed. On the other hand, if you're really stuck, you can always improvise. A rock can always be used to straighten out a bent crankarm if you're really desperate. No spoke wrench around when you must replace a spoke? Carefully use a pair of pliers instead or even a large adjustable wrench. They'll both work, albeit more slowly.

The Wrenches

Bicycles can be very demanding, especially when it comes to tightening and adjusting their components. Some require very specific types of wrenches. You can't just hack your way around with a big pair of pliers and hope to get the adjustment right. Use the wrong tool, and you can strip the head of a screw or bolt.

Derailed

Cone wrenches or hub spanners are very narrow and made to fit the narrow space between the cone on a wheel axle and the locknut that secures it. Don't damage the heads of these wrenches by using them to ream down on other components.

The following wrenches will tighten up your cones, nuts, cups, spindles, and various other bicycle components:

➤ **A six-inch adjustable wrench**   Also called a crescent wrench, this wrench is used on any variety of locknuts depending on your bike. You also can use a set of individual spanner wrenches, which are sold in sets. Note that many bikes will require metric wrenches.

➤ **Headset/pedal spanner**   This has two ends: One is used to remove pedals from the crankarms; the other is used to remove the headset locknut and head cup.

➤ **Cone wrench or hub spanner**   This loosens the cones that are part of the wheel hub/axle assembly. You'll need two wrenches. Be sure they fit your cones, as dimensions vary. Cone wrenches also can be used to remove the pedals from the crankarms.

➤ **Allen wrenches or hex wrenches**   These usually are L-shaped and used to adjust recessed Allen bolts such as the one that often secures the seat post or the chain rings to a crankarm.

➤ **Y-tool**   Consists of three open-end socket wrenches that are super-convenient for tightening up most bolts and nuts on your bike. You'll probably need two of them to tighten the variety of sizes.

➤ **Spoke wrench**   Tightens the nipples that secure wheel spokes to a wheel rim.

Derailed

It's easy for a tool to slip when you're tightening a nut or bolt. Be sure to use a tool that's an appropriate size for the component you're working on. You can strip the head of a screw or bolt, for instance, if your screwdriver head is too small and slips while you're turning it.

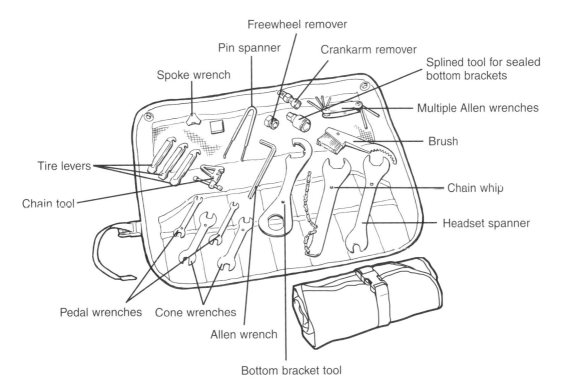

The basic tools you'll need to keep your bike healthy.

(Courtesy of Park Tool)

Tire Tools

The most important tire tools are your hands. Sure, you need them for everything else, too, but strong fingers can prevent an inner tube from being pinched by an aggressively directed tire iron. The main tools needed for tire and tube repair are the following:

Derailed

Be careful using the automated air pumps at gas stations. You can blow out an inner tube in no time if you're not careful. Just let a little bit of air in at a time until you've reached the proper pressure.

➤ A frame or floor pump; preferably both. You'll need a frame pump when you're out riding, of course; but a floor pump makes quick work of inflating a tire when you're at home. Be sure to get a pump that fits the valve on your inner tube, which will be either a Schrader valve (the type used on an automobile tire) or a presta valve (a skinny valve used on some bikes).

➤ A set of three inexpensive tire levers will remove any reluctant tire from its rim when you have a flat.

➤ Always carry a tire repair kit consisting of a small piece of sandpaper for roughing up the inner tube repair area; patches; glue; and several small sections of an old bike tire, about 1" × 4", for patching punctured tires.

➤ In case your tube is really trashed or you don't want to mess with repairing it, carry an extra inner tube. Be sure to buy the same size and valve type as the existing tube.

Freewheelin' Facts

If you're faced with a choice of several different tool manufacturers when you go to your local bike shop and are not sure which are suitable, explain your purposes to the shop owner. Some tools are high-end and not necessary for occasional use. Others are less expensive, but won't offer a lot of durability and long-term use. The shop owner can explain your options so you can make an intelligent choice.

Wheel Tools

Wheel building and *truing* are true art forms. Some mechanics specialize in wheels and attract a core of loyal customers, especially racers, for their services and skills. You might not be Michelangelo when it comes to your wheels but you can keep them reasonably straight and properly tensioned, and keep the hubs rotating smoothly. As mentioned earlier in the chapter, you'll need a set of cone wrenches for the hub and a spoke wrench for the spokes. If you get into wheel building, you'll need a couple of other tools such as a truing stand and a dishing tool. The stand supports the wheel while you tighten and adjust the spokes, and the dishing tool lets you know if the rim is off-center.

When replacing spokes, you have to remove the rim strip, a thin rubber strip that stretches around the inside of the rim and acts as a protective barrier between the heads of the nipples and the inner tube. Sometimes a rim strip can tear when it's removed. If you don't have a replacement available, wrap a couple of layers of electrical tape or one layer of handlebar tape around the nipples and replace the strip later. You don't want the inner tube rubbing against the nipples because it can puncture.

Screwdrivers

If you have a Swiss Army knife with both a slotted and a Phillips screwdriver, you have enough screwdrivers to get by on the road. At home, a screwdriver with changeable heads often will do the trick. For some purposes, a long screwdriver with a thin shaft can be very convenient.

Cutters and Pliers

Avoid using a pair of pliers to tighten a nut or bolt on a bicycle when a wrench is available to do the job. A wrench is less likely to slip or mar the surface of whatever it's tightening because it's designed to lock onto a nut or bolt of a specific size. A pair of pliers, on the other hand, has jaws that really are designed for gripping irregular or round surfaces. For instance, you can use pliers to pull brake and derailleur cables through their housing and hold them tightly while they are attached to their respective components. For this job, needle-nose pliers will work just fine.

Cable ends should be cut clean, and this means using a separate cable cutter. Some tools, such as a lineman's pliers, also can cut cable and wire, but they tend to get dull faster than a pair of cutters made specifically for bike cables. The same is true with diagonal cutters, which aren't always made to the same quality standards as bike tools.

Specialized Tools

Campagnolo, a highly respected manufacturer of bicycle components, also distributes a beautiful tool set for servicing these and other components. It would be a great treat to own one of these sets, but overkill for anyone but the most serious home or professional mechanic. Still, if you want to completely overhaul your bicycle and keep it in top form, you'll need some additional tools to the ones just mentioned.

You won't use these tools very often, although this will depend on your riding style. For instance, here in the Northwest a regular trail rider rolls through a lot of mud and puddles. (Don't let those sunny photographs of Seattle in the travel magazines fool you; it rains here, and rains often.) This rider will need to clean and lubricate the bearings and the exposed components more often than someone riding in a warm, dry climate. Each rider needs a few specialized tools.

The Spoken Word

Truing a wheel refers to tightening and tensioning the spokes to the point that the wheel spins straight without any wobble or variation in the spin. **Lateral truing** means the wheel doesn't vary from side to side as it rotates. **Vertical truing** means the wheel does not move up or down while rotating. Ideally, it should spin the same as a solid, flat disc with an axle in its exact center.

Derailed

However tempting it might be, don't use screwdrivers to change a flat tire. They are almost guaranteed to puncture the inner tube during either the removal or the reinstallation. Use your hands or tire irons instead.

Freewheelin' Facts

A good cable cutter will cut the cable clean and leave all the wire strands intact in a tight coil. A cheap cutter tends to chew up the end of the cable and leave the strands loose. Loose strands just look sloppy and can cut you if you accidentally run your hand up against them. A quality cutter also will far outlast a cheap one, making it a good investment.

Yanking Your Chain

Multi-speed bikes with derailleurs have chains that are removed by driving out one of the rivets that hold a pair of links together. A chain tool is inexpensive, but does a unique job by removing and reinstalling these rivets (see the following figure). One size chain tool does not fit all chains, so be sure the tool you buy is the correct one for your chain. Some chain tools come with an extra pin or tip in case you lose the one attached to the screw drive. The pins can loosen or bend on occasion, so be sure to save this extra one.

There is no substitute for a chain tool, so don't leave home without one.

(Courtesy of Park Tool)

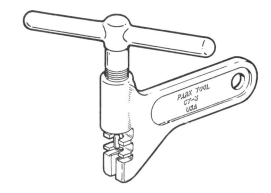

When Cranks Can't Be Nice

The crankset is attached to a spindle or axle that passes through the bottom bracket of your bike's frame. Each crankarm is attached to this spindle with a crank bolt, and this calls for—as you might have guessed—a special tool. You'll need a crank extractor designed for your crankset. In the biking world, different manufacturers often require different tools to service their parts.

A crank extractor often is used in conjunction with a large crescent wrench. Some extractors come attached to a long handle that provides enough leverage to do the jobs.

Bottoming Out

The bottom bracket sits, appropriately enough, at the bottom of the bike frame. It's here that the spindle attaches to the crankarms and spins against two sets of ball bearings. Ball bearings can wear down, and the bottom bracket itself can become contaminated with dirt and water. A complete bike overhaul includes disassembling the bottom bracket and replacing or repacking these bearings. As you can imagine, different types of bottom brackets require different tools (see Chapter 12, "Bottoming Out").

Cassette and Freewheel Tools

The rear sprockets on your bike come in one of three forms: a single, fixed sprocket; a freewheel; or a cassette. You'll find a fixed sprocket on one-speed bikes and any multi-gear bikes with internal hub gearing (three-speeds, for example). Freewheels and cassettes, which you find on all road, racing, and mountain bikes, each contain anywhere from five to nine individual sprockets ("gears").

Freewheels require a remover that is either splined or two-pronged depending on the freewheel design. Cassettes are removed in two steps:

1. First, the cogs or sprockets come off, using chain whips if it's an older model or removing the lockring on newer versions.

2. The cassette body is removed with a large Allen wrench.

Cassettes have surpassed freewheels in usage, and the latter will eventually become obsolete.

Your Own Bike Shop

Basic bicycle repairs can be done in a studio apartment if that's all the space you have available. All you need is a drop cloth or sheet of plastic to put under the bike to catch any greasy parts or dripping oil, and you're all set. It's not the most convenient arrangement, but it's doable. More doable is a basement or garage space with all your tools, work lights, and a bike stand.

A separate space for your bicycle repairs gives you plenty of room to spread out the different parts and components and to leave your work unfinished for a while if it's getting too frustrating to deal with. You don't need to tie up a lot of space (an 8' × 4' area will suffice). The important thing is getting the bike off the ground with its wheels and cranks spinning free so you can make your adjustments.

Bike Stands

Bike stands come in various styles and designs, including freestanding, tripod, and workbench (see the following figure). A freestanding bike stand holds the bicycle in a clamp roughly at shoulder level to the mechanic. Some allow you to rotate the bike to different positions. A tripod stand has hooks that hold the rear of the bike off the ground, allowing you to adjust all the gears and the rear brake and remove the rear wheel. They are less expensive than a freestanding stand, but not as versatile. A workbench stand is supported by a vise-grip style workbench such as a Black & Decker Workmate.

Freewheelin' Facts

For road use, buy a crank extractor that comes with a slide-through handle. The handles are only about five inches long, provide enough leverage to remove the crank bolt, and still fit conveniently in your bike pack. The handle eliminates the need for a crescent wrench (and who wants to carry one of those on a long trip?).

Derailed

If you're not sure what kind of system you have (freewheel or cassette), ask at your bike shop. You don't want to get on the road only to discover that you have the wrong tool. Most cassette models will have the word "cassette" or "freehub" on them.

If you want to go really bargain-basement, you can hang a couple of ropes from the ceiling and loop them around your bike. They won't keep it very steady while you do your repairs, but they will keep it off the ground and you can hang your bike at any level that's comfortable for you to do your work.

Your bicycle repair work will be much easier to do with some kind of work stand.

(Courtesy of Park Tool)

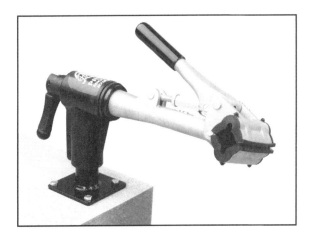

Truing Stand

A truing stand is used when building a wheel or adjusting the spokes. It holds the wheel by the hub axle and allows you to spin the wheel between stand's guides. Truing stands are either freestanding or fit inside a workbench vise. The latter model is more than adequate for home use.

The truth is, you should use a truing stand for really accurate wheel adjustments.

(Courtesy of Park Tool)

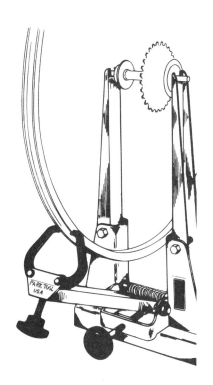

Lending a Third Hand

A third-hand tool is a clever device for holding the brake arms and pads tight against a wheel rim while you adjust the brake cable. This tool is both inexpensive and indispensable for many brake adjustments (see the following figure).

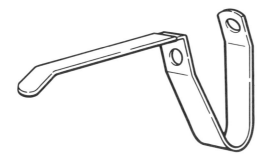

A third-hand tool leaves your hands free to adjust the brakes.

(Courtesy of Park Tool)

Solvents, Cleaners, and Lubes

Bikes have a lot of moving parts and they require lubrication. Unfortunately, lubricants attract dirt that has to be cleaned away and, well, then you need more lubrication. It's kind of a vicious cycle (pardon the pun), but you can't avoid it unless you ride your bike indoors all the time.

Bearings that lack adequate lubrication will wear down unevenly and offer a less than satisfactory ride. Other moving parts—the chain, cables, brakes, and derailleurs—also need lubrication from time to time. Every mechanic has a favorite approach to lubrication; here are a few guidelines (you can find more in Chapter 5, "You Need Some Stinkin' Rules"):

➤ Use a lithium-based grease made for bearings and buy it in a tube rather than an open can. Your bike shop will have an appropriate product (Phil Wood Waterproof Grease is an excellent choice).

➤ 30-weight motor oil is okay for lubing a chain, but the spray cans of synthetic lubricants sold at your bike shop are better and will last longer.

➤ All kinds of solvents, including gasoline and paint thinner, will clean your chain and bearings. Use them outside and away from any open flame. Gasoline is quite volatile, so avoid using it whenever possible. As an alternative, try one of the citrus-based cleaners made for degreasing.

➤ Any automobile paste wax will work for protecting the paint on the frame. Wax/polish combinations will clean off blemishes and marks at the same time.

There are so many lubricants to choose from, and they vary from one bike shop to another. A good quality automotive grease also will work for many lube jobs, but they are formulated to withstand high temperatures and will not necessarily resist water. High-quality bike grease, sold at bike shops, will always be the most appropriate choice.

Derailed

Keep your solvents and cleaners in clearly marked cans, preferably their original containers. Store them high, away from any heat source, and out of the reach of children. This sounds self-evident, but you'd be surprised how sloppy a work area can get when you're repairing bicycles.

Keep a supply of clean rags and a roll of paper towels nearby when you do your bike repairs. The paper towels can wipe the worst of the old grease and gunk off the components and then can be tossed away. Greasy rags should be kept in an airtight metal container and, unless you're really attached to them, thrown out when they get too dirty to use any longer. There's little point in laundering them if you have a regular supply of old T-shirts and towels ready to take their place.

Think of it this way: If it moves on a bicycle, it probably needs to be lubricated. Everything needs to be cleaned, especially the bearings that you cannot see. You'd be surprised how much gunk can accumulate inside a neglected wheel hub. As an incentive, consider how much smoother your bike will work when the lube is fresh and that gunk is cleaned out.

The Least You Need to Know

➤ You'll want to have enough tools to do the basic, everyday bike repairs; most tools will fit inside a handlebar bag.

➤ Bike repair requires some specialized tools that cannot be duplicated with common, hardware store tools.

➤ Be sure the tools you're purchasing are appropriate for the specific brand name of components on your bike.

➤ Your local bike shop will be your best source for lubricants specifically made for bicycles.

Part 2

Repairs Lite

Think about the way you learned to cook: Your first creation as a child might have been a peanut-butter sandwich. Later, you moved up in the culinary world to baking cookies, making mashed potatoes, and eventually preparing entire meals. You learned some rules about baking times, seasoning, and using kitchen utensils. The same agenda applies to bicycle repair. Bikes have their own rules about adjustments, tightening, and lubrication; if you know the rules, your repairs will be successful. Ignore them, and you might end up visiting Mr. or Ms. Professional Bike Mechanic to redo the job.

Some of your most important repair tools are your eyes and ears. A chain will let you know when it's rubbing against the front derailleur cage and needs an adjustment. Many repairs can be avoided by simply performing regular maintenance checks and adjustments. A quick check before a ride will let you know if you need to tighten a cable or oil a chain before it becomes a problem on the road.

The chapters in this part cover the smaller but critical issues such as brake adjustment and the most common repair, the flat tire. Everyone gets a flat if they ride long enough, so it's probably the single most useful repair that you'll learn how to do. The last thing you want is to be stuck on the road or trail because of something as easily repairable as a flat tire. Other repairs don't require a lot of disassembly and are really just adjustments to your components. And although it's not really a repair, we'll cover general cleaning as well.

Chapter 5

You Need Some Stinkin' Rules

In This Chapter

➤ Getting acquainted with bike repairs

➤ Preventing large problems

➤ Knowing when to leave it

➤ Solvents and lubricants

➤ Regular inspections and maintenance

We all have individual talents in different areas; some people know their way around a kitchen, but not a dance floor. Bike repair isn't as cerebral as computer science nor as difficult as coming up with the perfect homemade piecrust. However, it does have a few guidelines that, when followed, make your job easier.

Some professional mechanics go to school to learn their trade; others learn on the job. The latter usually start working on their own bikes, find they have a knack for it, and get hired on in a shop where they learn more from a master mechanic. You can learn basic repairs on your own and do them competently. No, you won't do them as fast as an experienced mechanic, and you might have to redo some repairs if the first attempt doesn't quite do the job, but you'll figure it out. This chapter gives you some orientation to guide you along.

A Lot of Small Things

The immediate bike components that hit you are the big ones such as the wheels, the handlebars and stem, and the frame. Next, you'll probably notice the crankset, derailleurs, brakes, and saddle. Break down these components further, and you'll see that there are smaller and smaller parts that keep everything together. It is these parts that often need servicing of some kind. They include bearings, cables, and fasteners.

Fasteners—screws, bolts, and nuts—are critical. You can overtighten them or not tighten them enough and end up with problems either way. Cables allow you to activate the brakes and move the derailleurs. Bearings, however, allow the bike to move smoothly. And because they always have something moving around them, they need regular servicing.

Get Your Bearings Straight

Most anything that moves in a circle on your bike has some form of bearings. They come in different sizes, and you can't mix and match them. Every component that uses bearings requires a set number of them: trying to stuff an extra one in or do with one less won't work, so pay attention to the count when you do your work.

You'll find bearings in …

➤ The headset.

➤ The wheels.

➤ The bottom bracket.

➤ The pedals.

➤ Freewheels and cassettes.

All these bearings, except in freewheels and cassettes, should be periodically serviced, depending on their usage. Bearings like grease. When you think of bearings, think grease—copious amounts of grease—enough to thoroughly coat the bearings without being ridiculous about it. You'll find four types of bearings:

➤ Loose ball

➤ Bearings held in a retainer

➤ Sealed

➤ Sealed cartridge

Bike Bites

When replacing bearings, take some of the old bearings with you to the bike shop. This way you'll be certain that you're getting the correct size and type.

Loose ball bearings are just that: individual steel balls held in place by their placement in a component. Bearings in a retainer are secured inside a closed metal ring, which makes the bearings easier to manage. A bearing unit or cartridge that is enclosed with a removable or non-removable plastic dust cap is considered a sealed bearing. A bike owner with a sharp knife and a careful hand can service those with a removable cap. Others are serviceable only at a bike shop. If you're not sure, ask your mechanic before you start messing with things.

Your bicycle doesn't care if it's gotten its bearings straight, but it wants them well lubricated.

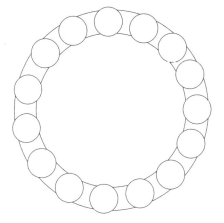

This Isn't a Muscle Contest

Bicycle components must be secure, but they also must be able to move freely. Small fasteners, such as the various nuts and bolts that secure your brakes, can break if you apply too much force to them. A number of installations, including the headset, bottom bracket, and hubs, require a locknut or lockring to be tightened against a cup or cone. If you overtighten the wrong piece, the bike isn't going to move.

Trying to muscle a rusted nut or bolt off isn't the greatest idea, either. Wrenches can slip, and you might end up with chipped paint on the frame or a skinned finger or two depending on what component you're working on. Keep in mind a few rules:

➤ Always use the proper size wrench.

➤ Soak rusted bolts, nuts, and screws with penetrating oil and let them sit overnight if necessary.

➤ When tightening a fastener, stop after you've reached reasonable resistance.

"Reasonable resistance" is a little hard to define; you'll know it when you encounter it. If the tool slips and you've stripped the head off of a bolt or screw, it's safe to say you've gone too far.

Follow the Clock

Almost every threaded component in bicycledom tightens when it's turned clockwise. Clockwise is defined as following the hands of a clock when the mechanic is standing directly in front of the section of the component. That said, there is one exception to this rule: The left-side pedal will tighten by turning the spindle to the left when attaching it to the crankarm. Why the exception? Because the pedals rotate in a forward direction, and the pedal eventually will loosen if it is not tightened in the same direction.

You Have a Screw Loose

Most components stay pretty well secured through normal riding, but remember that a bicycle is always absorbing vibrations from the road and stresses from use. This is why screws, nuts, and bolts come loose; thus, they must be maintained regularly. Size doesn't matter here, as even larger nuts and lockrings, such as those in the headset (where the handlebars turn) and bottom bracket respectively, can loosen up. Ignoring loose screw, bolts, and nuts can cause bigger problems later and can be a safety issue. The last thing you want to discover while commuting home on a rainy night is a loose brake shoe.

Keeping Small Problems Small

Most of us have heard, and have regularly ignored, all those parental voices in our lives telling us to take care of _____ (fill in the blank here) before it becomes a real problem.

Bike Bites

Note that some threads (those spiral-like ridges on the side of a screw or bolt and inside a nut) are lightly lubricated before fastening. This makes future removal easier without jeopardizing the tightness of the fastened component.

Derailed

There is one other exception to the clockwise tightening rule: In English threading, on the bottom brackets, the fixed cup (the one on the chain ring side) tightens to the left. Of course, the English are the same people who, according to most of civilization, drive on the wrong (left) side of the road. So much for adapting to world standards.

It's great advice even if it fell on deaf ears as we scrambled to get high school English papers written the night before they were due. Nonetheless, here comes my parental voice.

A bicycle is full of moving parts and components. Each one contributes to the bike's function and the enjoyment and efficiency of your riding. If you ignore the lubrication needs of a chain, it can rust and require replacement. It's a lot easier to lube it once in a while than to go to the trouble and expense of replacing it. Ignore a rear derailleur that's not working properly, and it might end up going into your spokes and causing major damage. Routine maintenance sounds boring, but there's nothing exciting about doing major repairs that could have been avoided.

Observe First, Repair Second

You can't very well repair your bike without knowing what the problem is; however, the cause can be a bit elusive. When you read the chapter on derailleurs, for instance, you'll find out about the adjusting screws that control how far the derailleur cage can travel. If it travels too far in either direction, the chain can fall off of the chain rings. You can fix this by adjusting the correct screw. But what if the chain is falling off because your bottom bracket is loose and the chain rings are moving in and out? You'll want to look at all the possible causes before electing one course of action.

You might find that your brakes aren't working as effectively as they should. It could be anything from a stretched-out cable to a dirty rim. Even if the cause seems obvious, take a minute to check a little further. You might need some additional maintenance.

You Hear Something?

Bikes can be kind of vocal. Gears grind, brake pads shriek, and dry bearings and chains grate when they need attention. Your hearing can be just as good a diagnostic tool as your sight. Pay attention to new noises; they could be normal wear and tear or something more serious.

Know Your Limitations

Some bike repairs are best left to a shop because of the tools and skill required. Unless you've got a fleet of bikes to maintain, you'll rarely run into these repairs, and there's little point in becoming adept at them. The jobs you might want to take to a mechanic include …

➤ Straightening out and aligning a frame.

➤ Tapping out bottom bracket threads.

➤ Repairing hydraulic disc brakes.

➤ Overhauling internal hub gears.

➤ Certain shock and suspension adjustments on mountain bikes.

Building wheels could be included in this list, but that's actually a pretty intriguing exercise; you might try building an extra set sometime if you're interested. If nothing else, you can get it to the point where it's assembled and roughly straight before taking it to an experienced mechanic for the final truing.

Nap Time

Sometimes the best solution to a mechanical problem is to simply walk away from it for a while. Adults are subject to the same emotions as kids when they are tired, hungry, or cold: They get cranky and start making mistakes. I watched one mechanic undo a wheel he was building twice because he kept getting the lacing pattern wrong. He was experienced and had built dozens of wheels, but was tired and kept messing up. Repairing a bike isn't like fixing the only toilet in the house: The toilet really can't be left in pieces and not working, but your bicycle usually can.

When You Slip, Paint Chips

It's easy to chip the paint on the bike frame if a small hand tool slips. You can avoid this by using tools that are in good shape and working carefully. Screwdrivers and Allen wrenches should have well-defined tips or heads, not ones that are rounded or deformed. Cutting tools should be sharp (dull tools can be more dangerous than sharp ones). Tools slip for various reasons, including the following:

➤ Too much pressure is applied.

➤ The tool is worn (especially screwdriver heads) and doesn't properly grasp the component.

➤ The wrong size tool is used.

Solvent Solutions

Until an organic, vegetable-based lubricant is developed for moving machine parts, we will still be dependant on petroleum-based products. This means you'll need strong solvents to clean bearings, chains, and all other greased and oiled parts. You can use milder solvents to clean other components. And some mechanics and riders are quite satisfied with citrus-based solvents in place of petroleum-based for even the dirtiest jobs, such as lubricating chains.

The most readily available solvent is plain paint thinner, some of which is available in a low-odor formula (artists use this). You can buy it at any paint or hardware store. Other solvents, such as lacquer thinner, should be avoided because of their volatility and odor. Gasoline is another one to avoid, especially in closed rooms. Of course, avoid any kind of open flames or cigarettes around open containers of solvents.

Popular spray solvents such as WD-40 are convenient for quickly cleaning chain and derailleurs and can act as a mild lubricant for these parts (emphasize, *mild*). The solvent in WD-40 flashes off pretty quickly and actually has a bearable smell to it, unless you're very sensitive to solvents.

The mildest solvent of all is soap and warm water. This is the best solution for cleaning dirty frames, tires, wheels, and other metal parts that are not lubricated. For tougher stains, try a spray cleaner such as Formula 409 to cut through grease on these surfaces.

Bike Bites

Be sure your work area is well lighted and clean. It's a lot easier to work in this kind of environment than one that's dim and messy. You'd be surprised how fast small parts can get lost on a messy workbench.

Bike Bites

Pour your used solvent in a separately marked container and let it sit undisturbed for a week or more. The solid gunk will sink to the bottom leaving clear solvent on top. Carefully pour the clear liquid into another marked container for future cleaning use.

Bike Bites

You can clean and shine your bicycle frame with the same materials that are used on automobiles. Car waxes and cleaners work just fine on the nonlubricated parts of a bike. There is more detailing to work around, but small toothbrushes or rags wrapped around wood dowels will do the trick.

Love That Lube

Lubrication does more than to simply make your bike riding easier. It also prevents damage to moving parts, stops rust, and makes it easier to disassemble bicycle components. (Just try removing a seat post that wasn't lightly greased first.) There are all kinds of greases, oils, and specialty lubricants available for bicycles, but basically all you need are white lithium grease, oil, and spray lubricant.

Every bicycle shop sells appropriate grease for bike maintenance. Any of these will do the job. They are sold in small tubes, anywhere from 3 ounces on up. You also can go to an automotive parts store and get a tube (you'll need a caulk gun) or tub of white lithium grease, which will give you plenty of grease for future overhauls.

Freewheelin' Facts

Phil Wood is a San Jose, CA–based manufacturer of bicycle components. One of their oldest products is Phil Wood Waterproof Grease, which has been manufactured since the 1970s. If you're uncertain about which grease to use on your bicycle, this product will always do the job.

Bike riders and mechanics can be a temperamental lot when it comes to their bikes and how they're maintained. You'll hear a number of opinions on lubricants, but you won't go wrong with grease sold by a bike shop. You *will* go wrong if you use overly thick grease used for other types of bearings because it will be too sluggish. The point is not so much to keep looking for the holy grail of lubricants, as it is to keep your bike clean and properly lubricated.

Oil

Most any medium-weight oil will work on your chain and rear cassettes or freewheel. It's more convenient to buy your oil in a small can, but if you prefer to use motor oil (30-weight will do), you can pour a small amount into a plastic squeeze bottle for dispensing. The one oil you don't want to use is one of the vegetable-based, three-in-one types, because they will gum up the works (they're fine for other household purposes).

Spray Stuff

Lubricants in spray dispensers are the perfect answer to our desire for gadgets and convenience. Why use a slow-dripping oilcan when we can push a button and spray it out so much faster? There are plenty of products to choose from and again, you'll hear a lot of opinions. For instance, WD-40 isn't great as a long-term lubricant for bicycle parts because of weather exposure and wear and tear. Spray silicone is better and has water-repellant properties. Teflon sprays are better yet. Some mechanics prefer specific brand names, such as those made by DriSlide. Again, stop in and see what your bike shop is using and selling.

Bike Bites

Various brands of chain lube provide a convenient way to keep your chain in good shape. This terrific product is a foaming agent that penetrates the chain links with the push of a button and spreads faster than oil.

Before You Ride, Inspect

Taking a minute or two to check your bike out before hopping on for a ride is a good investment of your time. The last thing you want to do is ride off on a soft tire that's got a slow leak or a wobbly wheel with a loose quick-release. Here are some things you should look for:

➤ The tires should be pumped to the recommended pressure (look on the side of the tire for the psi—pounds per square inch—rating).

➤ Give the wheels a spin and look for wobbles; they should be centered evenly between the brake pads.

➤ Give the brake levers a couple of hard squeezes to ensure that the brakes are working properly and there isn't any excess slack in the cables.

➤ Move the wheels back and forth to be sure they're tight to the frame.

➤ Check that you have a frame pump and small tools (tire patch kit, tire wrenches, mini-tool or equivalent, spare tube).

➤ Check that the brake shoes are firmly attached to the brake arms.

➤ Inspect your chain and spray it with chain lube if it looks dry.

The Spoken Word

To **taco** a wheel is to really trash and bend (a la taco) the rim during a ride. Sometimes the wheel can be straightened out enough to ride home, but it will have to be rebuilt if the damage is extensive.

A few minutes of your time will ensure that your bike is ready to roll. By my observations, mountain bikers are particularly good about giving their bikes a once-over before hitting the trails. Given the type of riding they do, this is especially critical for them. Aggressive off-road riding can break bottom bracket spindles, bend cranksets, or *taco* a wheel.

Your Cycle's Maintenance Cycle

You can break your maintenance schedule down according to the type of riding you do and how often you ride. If you ride only on dry weekends during the summer and then only on clean, dry roads, you won't have much to do. On the other hand, if you ride all year round, rain or shine, and go off road at least a couple of days a week, you're looking at more frequent maintenance.

One set of guidelines doesn't fit all, but the goal is the same: a safe, efficient bike. Think in terms of monthly and yearly maintenance and tasks that should be done after hard or lengthy rides.

Monthly Jobs

The type of riding you do will determine your maintenance schedule. My tech editor, for instance, rides often and rides hard. He's been known to trash components that would last a recreational rider forever after just a month of challenging trail riding and jumbing. Of course, when you have your own shop, you can afford to be an extreme rider.

More moderate riders should do the following once per month:

➤ Spray the chain with WD-40, wipe it with a rag, and apply lubricant.

➤ Lubricate the brake levers and brake pivots.

➤ Check tightness of cables and adjustment of derailleurs and brakes.

➤ Check all fasteners for tightness.

➤ Check that the wheels are true (straight without wobbles) and adjust spokes as necessary.

➤ Wipe down the bike, including chain rings, with mild cleaner and clean rags.

➤ Check brake pads for wear (be sure to wipe down wheel rims).

If you're a more aggressive rider, especially off road, also do the following:

➤ Check that the stem is tight in the head tube (do so by holding the front wheel between your legs and trying to turn the handlebars in both directions).

➤ Clean the rear sprockets with solvent, an old toothbrush, and a clean rag.

➤ Clean and lube suspension forks (check air pressure in air-sprung style forks).

➤ Tighten rear suspension bolts if necessary.

➤ Check the condition of the chain.

➤ Look for any cracks in the frame or components.

➤ Check for wear and tear on chain, chain rings, and rear sprockets.

➤ If you have a leather saddle, treat it with an appropriate cleaner and preservative.

A bike that's ridden off-road, especially in wet weather, is more likely to get dirt and grit washed up near the various components that contain bearings. It's important to clean the bike after really dirty rides. You can use a hose, but all you need is a light spray. You don't want to have a lot of direct water pressure on any of these components because it can force water and dirt into the bearings.

Every six months, check all the components that have bearings (hubs, bottom bracket, headset, pedals) for adjustment. If they're sticking or not moving smoothly, they should be disassembled, checked, and probably overhauled.

Happy New Year!

Once a year, if you've ridden your bike regularly, give it a complete overhaul. Disassemble, clean, and lubricate everything with bearings and replace any that are worn. If you've done a lot of riding, replace your brake and derailleur cables. Replace any worn or questionable parts. Remove the chain; soak it in solvent; and then soak it in oil or chain lube, wiping off the excess before reinstalling it. Remove your freewheel or cassette, clean it thoroughly, and oil the bearings.

While the wheels and chain are off, polish and wax the frame with an automotive cleaner/wax. Now you're really ready for your next ride.

Let's face it, maintenance isn't much fun, but an out-of-order bike is less fun. Unless you're going to buy your way out and drop your bike off at a shop (in which case, you wouldn't be reading this book), you'll need to attend to your bike. Just think of the time spent doing repairs and upkeep as an investment in your enjoyment and safety—and more miles on your bike!

The Least You Need to Know

➤ Breaking down your bike into a series of systems and components makes the maintenance more manageable for novice mechanics.

➤ When you think bearing, think grease.

➤ Not every adjustment on a bike requires brute strength; finesse is called for, too.

➤ The proper solvents and lubricants make the job easier and safer.

➤ Regular maintenance and safety checks will keep you from bigger problems in the future.

Chapter 6

Gimme a Brake!

In This Chapter

➤ Different brakes, same stopping

➤ Loose cables and brakes are unstable

➤ When pads and rims meet

➤ Without brake levers, nothing's going to happen

➤ Hydraulic disk brakes: awesomeness defined

Riding a bike and steering it in the direction in which you want to go is great fun—but that fun can end in a heartbeat if you can't stop. Bicycles come with an array of braking systems, some of which have been around for years. Take a look at your brakes: Are they mounted on or attached to the bike frame or are they built into one or both of the wheel hubs? I cover them all in this chapter.

Stopping Is Everything

Braking isn't complicated: Mechanical force is applied to one or both of the wheels to stop their movement. This is simple enough if your brakes are in good working order. In most situations on dry pavement, it's best to use the front brake for most of your stopping. This is just as true with automobiles.

A one-speed bike usually has a coaster brake in the rear. This would seem to refute the idea of a front brake offering superior stopping power, but remember that most one-speed bikes aren't out to break any overland speed records. On these slower bikes, a rear brake is fine.

Breakdown, or How They Work

Every bicycle brake stops the motion of one or both wheels, but the methods are different. Some press against the wheel rims, others work inside one or both wheel hubs, and new hydraulic disc brakes squeeze pads against discs attached to each hub. Each type of brake has its own series of working parts including ...

Bike Bites

High-wheelers, the old penny–farthing bikes of the 1900s, had spoon brakes to stop them. These were metal shoes shaped like a flat spoon that were pressed against a hard rubber tire when the rider pushed on a lever. Spoon brake production dropped big time with the introduction of tires with inner tubes, which could not accommodate this brake design.

Freewheelin' Facts

If you absolutely cannot stop quickly enough—but must—try not to panic (easy for me to say!). Carefully place one of your feet near the front wheel and gradually press your foot against the side of the tire. Be sure to keep an eye on the road and watch your steering. If you're wearing gloves, you can reach down with your hand and gradually press against the tire.

The high-quality Campagnolo side-pull brake is found on high-end racing bikes.

(Courtesy of Campagnolo)

➤ A mechanism to start the braking action.

➤ A means of connecting this mechanism to the brake itself.

➤ The brake body.

Brake action is started when the rider either squeezes a brake lever by hand (a rim, disc, or drum brake) or pushes backward on the pedals (in the case of a foot brake or coaster brake). Cables connected to the brake levers pull up and activate the arms of a brake or a drum or disk mechanism. With foot brakes, the chain forces the rear sprocket to move in reverse and activate the hub brake.

Caliper brakes are the simplest to work on whereas disc, drum, and coaster brakes are more complicated and less user-friendly when it comes to servicing. Nevertheless, if you want to be safe—and being able to stop is pretty important in terms of safety—you'll need to maintain and troubleshoot your brakes.

Hand Brakes

The higher speeds of multi-gear bikes combined with the demand for weight savings have made hand brakes the most commonly used system on bicycles today. These brakes range from the cheapest steel side-pulls to high-tech hydraulic disc brakes. (High-end Shimano and Campagnolo side-pull brakes often are installed on expensive racing and road bikes.)

Hand brakes include a lot of different models:

➤ Side-pulls

➤ Center-pulls

➤ Cantilever

➤ Disc brakes

➤ V-brakes

➤ Rollercam

➤ U-brakes

Regardless of the design, all hand brakes need to be adjusted so the brake pads are an optimum distance from the wheel rim. The cable also must be sufficiently taut, so the rider doesn't have to use the grip of death to pull back on the brake lever. Cables should be in good condition, and the levers and brake bodies lubricated for easy operation.

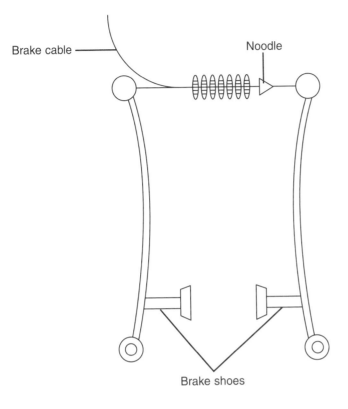

Brake cable

Noodle

Brake shoes

The V-brake looks simple, but is a very effective stopper on mountain bikes.

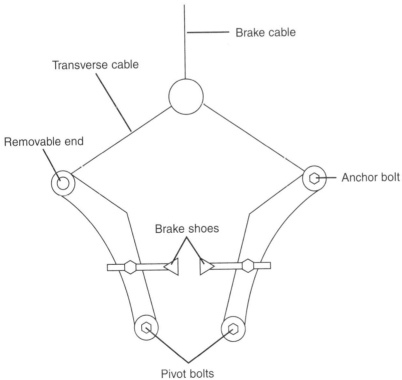

Brake cable

Transverse cable

Removable end

Anchor bolt

Brake shoes

Pivot bolts

Cantilever brakes are attached directly to the bike frame and offer more direct stopping power than older-style center-pull brakes.

Hand brakes have evolved over the years from caliper brakes to modern disc brakes, which would seemingly stop a direct descent down the side of the Empire State Building (don't try this at home). Although they all stop the wheels after being activated by the pull of a lever, their designs vary as described in the following:

➤ A **cantilever brake** has two separate cantilevers, or arms. Each arm is bolted to and pivots on a threaded boss that is brazed to the frame, two on the fork and two on the rear seat stays. A short cable (the transverse cable) connects the two arms. A small yoke or connector on the end of the main brake cable pulls up on the transverse cable, forcing the brake pads against the rim of the wheel. The other end of the cable is attached to a brake lever.

➤ A **V-brake** is a cross between a cantilever and a side-pull brake. The brake cable forms a direct link to the brake arms, eliminating the transverse cable.

➤ Modern **disc brakes** have a disc that screws to the wheel hub and a caliper that attaches to the fork or the rear seat stay. These brakes are essentially impervious to weather and have terrific stopping power.

➤ A **side-pull caliper brake** has two arms that move in opposing directions when the cable, which runs down one side of the brake, is pulled. While the cable is pulling one arm, the cable housing is pushing the other. A single-pivot model pivots both arms on a central point, whereas a dual-pivot model has a separate pivot for each arm.

➤ A **center-pull caliper brake** uses a transverse cable and yoke to move the two caliper arms. The cable, as the name implies, runs down toward the center of the brake.

Is one brake better than another? I think the answer lies in the designs that survive and the ones that disappear. Center-pull brakes did the job for years, but cantilevers and disc brakes are a huge improvement. They also are more expensive and complicated to repair and install. Technology is always accompanied by compromises (just look at computers).

Foot Brakes

Your first bicycle as a child probably was a one-speed with a coaster brake. These are easy to operate and allow the rider to put a lot of pressure on the brake by using legs and feet against pedals instead of hands around brake levers. This is an effective strategy for these relatively slow bikes (going down a steep hill is another matter).

Caliper Brakes

Caliper brakes get their name from the design of the brake arms, which resemble calipers, a type of measuring instrument. They have been used for decades in various styles; everything from steel side-pulls to the center-pull models that showed up in the 1960s; and finally to the high-end Shimano and Campagnolo side-pulls mentioned earlier. In case you're wondering, there is a big difference in quality between cheap brakes and the latter, more expensive brakes.

Caliper brakes function when a brake lever with one end of a brake cable attached to it is pulled in toward the handlebars. This tightens the cable and allows it to pull up on the other end, which is attached to the brake body. This action pulls the brake arms together and forces the brake pads against the rim, slowing down and eventually stopping (you hope) the movement of the wheel.

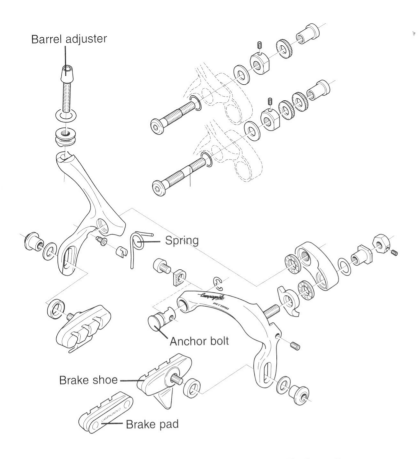

Barrel adjuster

Spring

Anchor bolt

Brake shoe

Brake pad

A side-pull brake is elegant in its simplicity, but still involves a number of small parts.

(Courtesy of Campagnolo)

Caliper brakes are fairly easy to maintain. Their maintenance includes …

➤ Cable adjustment and lubrication.

➤ Lever repairs.

➤ Adjusting the brake shoes.

➤ Adjusting the brake body.

Other components can break down or run at less than top efficiency, but your brakes are critical. You can overhaul your bike to perfection; but if you can't stop, you're going to have big problems. Check your brakes by giving the levers a squeeze. Do they have to travel a bit too far for comfort before the pads lock? Are the pads worn a bit? In either case, you must adjust the cable.

Bike Bites

Before you do any brake adjustments, give your wheels a spin and be certain that they are true and not wobbling. Any wobble can hit a brake pad, in which case you will end up with an imperfect brake adjustment.

Cable Conundrums

Brake cables are connected to the brake lever at one end and the brake body at the other. The tension is set so the brake pads or shoes typically will lock against the wheel rim when the levers are pulled about halfway toward the handlebars. Brake cables typically need adjustment when they stretch from use, or the pads have worn down and thus take longer to reach the rim. There are two ways to adjust a cable: You can either use the barrel adjuster or loosen the respective anchor bolt and pull the cable tighter. The first method is the easier of the two.

The Barrel Adjuster

Hand brakes typically come with a barrel adjuster located close to the brake body. Others have an adjusting sleeve that is located on the lever. When turned counterclockwise, the adjuster increases the cable tension. You can pull off this trick until you run out of adjuster threads, but it's fine for minor tightening. To use a barrel adjuster:

1. Hold the locknut that is located under the barrel (see the second figure below).

2. Turn the barrel counterclockwise until the brake pads are closer to the rim, but still have adequate clearance for the wheel to spin; give the lever a squeeze and check for adjustment.

3. Turn the locknut clockwise toward the adjuster; this will hold the adjuster in its new position.

This side-pull brake has an adjusting sleeve on the brake body, as well as on the brake lever.

(Courtesy of Campagnolo)

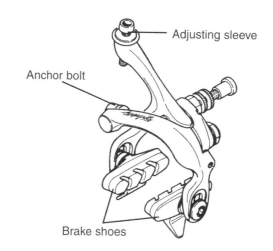

A barrel adjuster located on the brake lever makes quick cable adjustments a snap.

(Courtesy of Campagnolo)

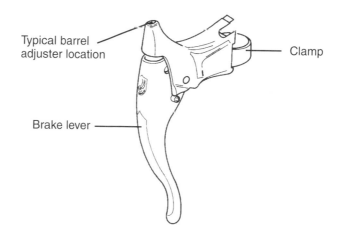

If tightening the barrel adjuster or adjusting the sleeve doesn't do the job (you still have too much play in the cable), back the locknut away from the adjuster and screw the adjuster in a clockwise direction until it can go no farther. In this position, the adjuster is unused and is available for future minor adjustments to the cable. You now will have to do a bigger adjustment to the cable.

Adjusting a Brake Cable

For most hand brakes (hydraulic disc brakes are an exception), adjusting the cable is a similar process for all of them. The job includes ...

➤ Loosening the anchor bolt.

➤ Pulling the slack cable through the bolt.

➤ Tightening the bolt and checking the adjustment.

Hand brakes often come with some kind of a cable release mechanism on the brake body or the brake lever. Old-style center-pull brakes and cantilevers have a transverse cable with one removable end. New V-brakes have a small cable called a "noodle" that does the same thing. With side-pull brakes, there typically is a release mechanism that flips up and leaves the cable slack. You still have to loosen the anchor bolt to tighten or remove the brake cable, but it's much easier to do this after using the respective cable releases.

Cable adjustment and replacement also is a lot easier if you have a *third-hand tool.* This handy tool clamps the brake pads against the wheel rim, effectively leaving the brake cable slack. This allows you to more accurately adjust the cable tension. Without a third-hand tool or some other means of pressing the brake pads against the rim, your adjustment of the cable will require some estimating, which means you might have to redo the job if your estimate is off.

Freewheelin' Facts

If you don't have a third-hand tool or another pair of hands, you can always improvise. Use a small wood clamp, or even wrap the brake arms with twine if you have to.

Side-Pull Brakes

Brake cables will stretch out with use. This is normal, even on new bikes or after the installation of new cables. Minor alterations using a barrel adjuster will normally take care of any adjustment needed for minor stretching, but after repeated use, the barrel adjuster isn't going to cut it. You'll have to loosen the cable and pull it until it's more taut. To adjust a side-pull brake cable, do the following:

1. Loosen the cable using the quick-release lever or other mechanism on the brake body or brake lever.

2. Clamp the brake shoes to the rim using a third-hand tool (see the following figure).

3. Loosen the anchor bolt by holding the head of the bolt with a wrench; with a second wrench, turn the nut *counterclockwise* until the cable can easily slide through the hole in the bolt.

4. Flip the brake release back to its locked position.

5. Pull the end of the brake cable down using a pair of needle-nose pliers so it's a little short of snug.

6. Tighten the nut on the anchor bolt.

7. Remove the third-hand tool and give the brake lever two or three hard squeezes; this will stretch the cable slightly and test your adjustment (if it slips out, you want to find out now instead of when you're careening down the biggest hill in town and have to really pull on the levers).

8. If the cable is too tight or too loose, do the adjustment again.

The Spoken Word

When turning something **counterclockwise,** you're turning it in the opposite direction that a clock's hands travel if you were standing in front of it. When you tighten the nut on an anchor bolt, you'll most likely be standing in front of the bolt, so think backward when you're tightening with a wrench.

A third-hand tool is used to secure the brake shoes against the wheel rim.

(Courtesy of Park Tool)

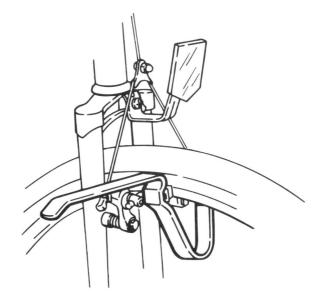

Adjusting brake cables is a bit of an art form. After doing (and maybe undoing) it a few times, you'll have a better idea of how much force to use when you pull the cable through with the pliers. If you're on the road without a third-hand tool, just pull the cable through a bit more tightly (without pulling too hard).

Center-Pull Caliper Brakes

Center-pull brakes adjust a bit differently from side-pulls. You have to loosen the cable at the yoke that pulls up on the transverse cable, which in turns pulls up on the brake arms. The same mechanism is used in many cantilever brakes as well. It's not as slick as a side-pull adjustment, but it's easy to do. Here are the steps:

Derailed

Anchor bolts must be tight; otherwise, they can work just fine until you really pull on the levers and the cable slips out. Always test the brakes after installing or adjusting a cable by pulling hard on the levers several times.

1. Clamp the brake pads against the rim using a third-hand tool.
2. Loosen the anchor bolt on the yoke so the cable slides freely.
3. Check that any barrel adjusters are turned securely clockwise.
4. Pull the cable through the anchor bolt with a pair of needle-nose pliers while pushing up on the yoke with the pliers.
5. Tighten the anchor bolt with a wrench until the cable is held securely.
6. Remove the third-hand tool and test the brakes by squeezing the lever a few times.

After tightening the cable, spin the wheel to be sure it moves freely in the newly positioned brake pads.

Cantilever Brake Cable

To adjust a cantilever brake cable, hold the brake pads against the wheel rim with a third-hand tool. Loosen both the main anchor bolt on the brake arm and any secondary anchor bolt on the yoke. Pull the cable securely and tighten all anchor bolts. Test for adjustment and check that the pads are hitting the wheel rim at the same time.

Rollercam and U-Brakes

Rollercam and U-brakes are no longer manufactured, but you adjust both of them in a fashion similar to cantilever brakes. Rollercams are a particular nuisance to adjust and are best taken to a shop. Depending on the value of your bike and the condition of your brakes, you might consider replacing them with V-brakes.

On Being Centered

Bicycles like symmetry. Handlebars should be centered on the stem, wheels should be centered when they're installed, and brake arms should be centered next to a wheel rim. If a brake is off center, one pad will hit the rim before the other, which leads to premature wear and tear on the pad and uneven stopping.

The easiest brakes to center and adjust are side-pull and center-pull calipers. The adjustments vary somewhat depending on the age and the model of the brake. Both side- and center-pulls are mounted on a single pivot bolt. To center these brakes:

1. Loosen the nut that secures the anchor bolt to the frame (it will be either an acorn nut or an Allen nut).

2. Squeeze the brake pads against the wheel rim (this should move the brake body some).

3. Tighten the nut and check that the brake is centered (see the following figure).

Still not centered? Take a cone wrench to the seating pad and slowly twist the brake body until it's centered.

Along with centering, the brake body should be kept clean and occasionally lubricated. If it's a real mess, the cable can be removed first, and then the body can be removed as well for cleaning and lubricating.

Bike Bites

Old caliper brakes can be resistant to centering so here's a tip: Take a large screwdriver and hammer and tap the top of the spring opposite the pad that's too close to the rim. A light tap or two will move the brake body over. If you go too far, tap the other spring to move the body back again.

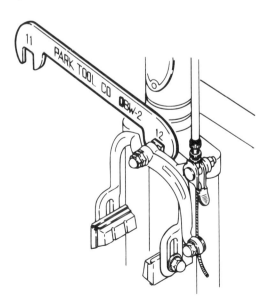

A slight turn of a wrench will quickly fix an off-center brake.

(Courtesy of Park Tool)

Cantilever Adjustments

When your brakes are not in use (when they're resting), each shoe should be the same distance from the rim, indicating that the brake is properly centered. If your cantilever brakes appear to be off-center and your cables are properly adjusted:

1. Check that the wheel is installed correctly and that it's true.
2. Release the transverse cable and check that each cantilever moves freely.
3. If the cantilevers are sticking, unscrew and remove them from the frame, clean any rust or grit off the boss with steel wool or sandpaper, wipe it clean, and apply a light coat of grease before reinstalling the cantilevers.

Sometimes this is all it takes to adjust cantilevers. If everything is moving freely and the brake pads still aren't centered, you might have to adjust the tension in one or both of the cantilever springs. The springs adjust in one of two ways:

➤ Remove the cantilever and turn it so the spring moves up and into the next hole on the mounting boss (there usually are three of them with the top hole, which provide the most tension; the middle hole is the most frequently used).

➤ On newer and better brakes, you can adjust the spring tension by turning a small Phillips or Allen screw at the base of the arm; by adjusting the tension you will center the cantilevers.

Dia Compe uses a different system. Instead of inserting the spring into the hole in the boss, it comes with a spring block that fits into the boss and holds the spring. You can adjust this by loosening the bolt that secures the cantilever to the brazed-on, threaded boss and rotating the block with a cone wrench until the cantilevers are centered. While still holding the block with the cone wrench, tighten the bolt that secures the cantilever to the boss.

Bike Bites

Note that some bike frames have cable stops that allow sections of brake cables to run outside of the cable housing. At the point where the cable intersects with a stop, the housing stops and the cable is exposed until it reaches the next stop or a brake yoke. Cable housing is always used from the brake lever to the first stop or brake—whichever comes first.

Cables and Their Installation

You can have the most mechanically advantaged, awesome-looking brakes made, but their performance will suffer if their cables aren't installed properly. You want to avoid excessive looping and friction, as well as too much play in the cables.

The brake cable, which consists of fine steel wires twisted together, is given shape and form inside of flexible cable housing. The core of the housing consists of wound wire with a colored plastic exterior. You need both components to connect the brake lever to the brake body.

A Home for Your Cable

The big enemy of brake cables is friction. Modern cable housing usually comes with a plastic liner, such as Teflon, that separates the brake cable from the woven wire inside the housing, thus reducing friction. One key to a smoothly operating cable is properly installed and cut cable housing. Here are a few tips to keep your cables from getting hung up:

➤ Use a high-quality diagonal cutter or a cutter made specifically for cutting bicycle cables when cutting your housing (see the following figure).

➤ When you cut your housing, be sure to leave a clean end (no crushed ends or burrs).

➤ To assure a clean, square end, file down the cut housing with a fine metal file.

➤ Install a *ferrule* at the end of the housing whenever a housing stop or adjusting barrel will accommodate one. Ferrules aren't critical, but they do help with the housing's function.

There is some disagreement about applying grease or other lubricant to a cable before running it in cable housing. Some manufacturers recommend not using grease, claiming it slows the movement of the cable. Certainly, a small amount of lubricant is useful wherever a cable runs through a sharp turn in the housing. You're always safe using a small amount of oil instead of grease.

The Spoken Word

A **ferrule** is a small metal cap that fits over a cable housing end. It provides support for the cable where it fits into a cable stop on the frame or a cable hanger.

Bike Bites

Dirt, gunk, and ground-off brake material can end up on your wheel rims and affect your braking. Check the condition of your rims from time to time, especially after a hard ride. Clean them with a rag or fine steel wool and alcohol.

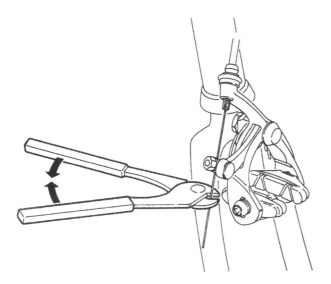

Remember to cut off any excess cable from the brakes.

(Courtesy of Campagnolo)

The shortest route isn't the best route for your brake cables. You have to have enough of an arc so the cable doesn't kink. A cable that's too long can get in the rider's way and create friction. When installing the brake cables, follow these guidelines:

➤ Be sure the handlebars can turn all the way to the left and to the right without being restricted by the cable.

➤ When the rear brake cable leaves the top tube, it should gradually bend downward, not up and down.

➤ Bends should be gradual—not sharp—and still keep cable lengths short.

As a rule, the rear brake is controlled by the right lever and the front brake by the left lever. This is part tradition and part pragmatism in that the rear brake takes a bit more strength to operate, so it's assigned to the right hand.

Installing Cables

Brake cables occasionally break. Old brake cables become ... well, old and should be replaced just for safety's sake. The end that fits into the brake lever will need either a barrel fitting or a ball fitting. Universal brake cables, the most common replacement type of cable, come with both fittings; simply cut off the one that you don't need. Even if your cables seem to be in good shape, it's a good idea to replace them once a year or so when you do a major overhaul.

Road Bike Cable Replacement

Most road bikes have drop-style handlebars, and that's what this installation addresses; but it also can apply to some upright bars depending on the type of brake levers. When you buy your brake cable, be sure you have the right type for your levers (either a barrel end or a ball end). Here's what you do:

1. Remove the old cable by loosening the anchor bolt and give the lever a squeeze; this will loosen the cable so you can pull it out of the housing.

2. Remove the cable from the housing and prod and wiggle the ball end (drop bar levers) or barrel end (usually upright bar levers) from the brake lever.

3. Cut off the excess cable fitting on the new cable.

4. Put a small amount of grease or oil on your fingers and lightly lubricate the cable.

5. Carefully insert the cable through the body of the brake lever and into the housing, making sure that any barrel adjusters are turned all the way clockwise; leave a little extra cable on the lever end so it can be connected to the lever.

6. When the cable has passed through the housing and out the brake end, install the other end of the cable at the lever (see the following figure).

7. Check to make sure that all ferrules, barrel adjusters, and quick-releases are in correct positions.

8. Connect the cable to the brake, following the same procedures used in adjusting a brake cable.

9. When the cable has been tested, cut off any excess past the anchor bolt, leaving about $1^{1}/_{2}$" of cable exposed.

10. To keep the end of the cable from unraveling and fraying, install a small plastic or metal cap (available at bike shops) over it.

If your housing has seen better days, replace it, following the route of the original housing. Be sure to cut the ends off clean and square.

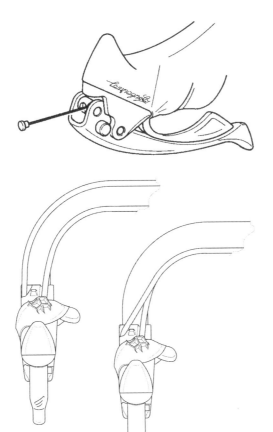

One example of installing a brake cable on a road bike.

(Courtesy of Campagnolo)

Sample cable routing with combination levers that have both brake cables and derailleur shifter cables.

(Courtesy of Campagnolo)

Mountain Bike Brake Cables

Mountain bike brake levers, like other upright handlebar levers, are different from road bike brake levers. Instead of curving in toward the bars, they extend outward for, well, better leverage when pulling on the cables. The adjustments aren't radically different, though. Use the same procedures described in the previous section and add the following:

1. Turn the adjusting barrel and any lockring until the slots are lined up.

2. Squeeze the lever all the way out and push the barrel end of the cable out.

3. Install the new barrel end into the lever; make sure it's lined up with all the slots in the adjusting barrel, any lockring, and the lever.

4. If you're satisfied with the cable routing, follow it; otherwise, route the cables in a manner that will least interfere with the turning of the handlebars.

5. Give the lever a few hard squeezes to check your work.

Checking and testing your work accomplishes two things: It assures you that the job was done properly and it stretches the cable somewhat so you can fine-tune your adjustment.

Levers

The simplest rule with brake levers is to use the levers that come with the brakes or replace them with the same brand. V-brakes, for instance, typically require their original equipment levers. Brake levers for drop handlebars are not meant for upright handlebars, nor can those for uprights work that well on drop handlebars (although I have seen some people try it).

Some levers integrate all the gear shifters into a single unit. You will find these on both road bikes and mountain bikes. With the advent of disc brakes and V-brakes, manufacturers are returning to separate shifter and brake lever components.

Leveraging Those Levers

Decent quality levers on road bikes will last for years unless you have an accident and bend them. Otherwise, about the only time you'll replace them will be if you replace the brakes themselves. A clamp on the back side of the lever encircles the handlebars and is tightened with a bolt or screw. On drop bars, you have to remove either the handlebar tape or padding, which will prevent you from slipping the lever off after you've loosened the clamp.

To replace the brake levers on drop-style handlebars, do the following:

1. Remove the handlebar tape or padding.
2. Remove the brake cable (plan on replacing it).
3. Squeeze the handle to expose the fastener (bolt or screw) that is securing the lever to the handlebar (you'll need a screwdriver, an Allen wrench, or a socket wrench to loosen it).
4. Loosen the fastener until the lever can be moved and slide it off the handlebars.
5. Remove both levers and clean off the sticky residue from the tape.
6. Position your new levers and tighten the clamps (check that the lever position is comfortable for your riding style).
7. Retape the handlebars.

New brake levers call for new handlebar tape as well.

(Courtesy of Campagnolo)

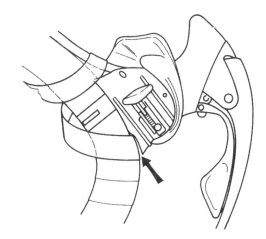

Check your bike shop for different types and colors of handlebar tape and wrapping. Padded tape is available for more shock-absorbing qualities, but it's thicker and might be uncomfortable for you to grip if you have small hands. Another alternative is to use regular handlebar tape and wear biking gloves to absorb some of the shock.

Upright Bars

On upright bars, you'll have to remove any grips before you can remove the brake levers. It's often easiest to just cut these off and replace them; but if yours are in good shape, slip a narrow screwdriver blade between the grip and the handlebar and spray in some silicone, twisting the grip as you go. Remove the grip and wipe off the handlebar. Make sure that the new levers are positioned so that your wrists are comfortable when squeezing them—you don't want your wrists sitting at any weird angles every time you use the brakes.

When Pads Protest

Brakes aren't much good without decent brake pads, and the pads aren't much good if they're worn, out or alignment, or loose. Brake pads should hit the wheel rim and only the rim squarely and evenly and at the same time. Worn pads should always be replaced.

There are two types of brake pads: a one-piece (pad and shoe), which screws to the brake arm and a cartridge pad, which can be replaced while the shoe is retained. The pad (sometimes called a *brake block*) is held inside a shoe; it's the shoe that is adjusted and positioned on the brake arm. Cantilever brakes generally offer adjustable pads, whereas center-pull and side-pull calipers do not.

Caliper brake pads can screech, especially when they're new. You can stop this by toeing in or bending the brake arms so that the front of the pad hits the rim before the rest of the pad. Do this by grasping the brake arm under the pad with an adjustable wrench and then slightly bending the arm (see the following figure).

Cantilever brakes have a series of washers attached to the shoes on the pole section, which attaches to the arm or cantilever. Using these washers, adjust the pad so that it hits toed-in against the center of the rim.

Toeing in brake arm requires a small twist of the wrench.

(Courtesy of Park Tool)

Hydraulic Brakes

The newest disc brakes are hydraulic systems that use formulated oil in their cables to control the braking action. These are low-maintenance braking systems and should be serviced by an experienced shop.

Freewheelin' Facts

Hydraulics refers to fluid mechanics. In the case of hydraulic bicycle brake systems, it's the pressure of the fluid in the brake cable, which is activated by squeezing the brake lever as it acts on the brake. The liquid greatly amplifies the force applied by the lever, offering a measurable mechanical advantage over conventional brake cables.

Coaster and Hub Brakes

Each type of hub brake, including coaster and drum models, is configured differently. Some are even integrated with multi-speed hub gears, which add to their complexity. A coaster brake can have close to 24 separate parts—it's a bit beyond the scope of this book to dice and slice all of them here. These are good projects for a bike shop, but be sure the shop's mechanic is experienced with these types of brakes. Some mechanics, for instance, have never repaired a three-speed hub; you don't want yours to be part of someone's learning curve.

Bike Bites

Allen wrenches are used for a lot of adjustments on bicycles. Unlike most other tools, a worn Allen wrench can be easily renewed. All you have to do is grind off the worn end of the wrench using a bench grinder until you have a flat, square end again.

General Maintenance

Brakes don't need a lot of care and feeding, but you do need to monitor them and keep them in good working order. A bike that stops when you want it to ensures that you stay in good working order, too. All braking systems will work best when the following maintenance is done:

➤ Check that all cables are taut and in good shape; replace corroded or frayed cables.

➤ Be sure that all rim brakes are tightly secured to the bike frame.

➤ Align brake shoes so they hit the rim squarely and uniformly.

➤ Clean and lubricate all moving parts of a brake when called for.

➤ Replace all worn brake pads.

➤ Keep your rims clean for better brake contact.

➤ Test your brakes by giving the levers a hard squeeze. Be hard on them because you want to be sure they work in an emergency situation.

It will start sounding like this book's mantra after a while, but regular maintenance and safety checks are important. When they come to your brakes, they will assure you of stopping power when you need it.

The Least You Need to Know

➤ Caliper brakes, once the mainstay of 10-speed bikes, have taken a distant second place to cantilever-style brakes.

➤ Rim brake cables should be kept taut, reasonably short, and replaced when frayed or corroded.

➤ Brake pads should hit the rim squarely and simultaneously for affective stopping power.

➤ Cable housing and cables should be cut with sharp, appropriate cutters for clean, square ends.

➤ Brake systems are critical and should be examined regularly for defects and needed maintenance.

Chapter 7

When Tires Retire

In This Chapter

➤ All tires are not created equal

➤ The pressure should be on

➤ Inner tube interruptions

➤ A pitch for patches

➤ Tires to tread for

Early bicycles didn't have tires as we know them. The nineteenth century hobbyhorse had wooden wheels with strips of leather attached to their rims. Later, riders struggled along on iron or steel wheels until solid India rubber was added around 1860. The riders of those days weren't necessarily extra tough; they just didn't have any alternatives. Hard rubber was an improvement, but it still made for a bone-rattling ride. When Dunlop patented the pneumatic tire, the comfort level of cycling increased dramatically.

Like just about every other bicycle component, tires come in a variety of styles, sizes, and types. (Life probably was easier when you were three years old and the only option your parents had was the color of the tricycle they picked out for you at Sears, but I doubt you want to go back to that kind of riding.) A tire and inner tube serve several purposes:

➤ They absorb shocks from the riding surface.

➤ They protect the wheel from damage.

➤ They offer less rolling resistance than a metal wheel, therefore allowing for a faster ride.

➤ They can accommodate all kinds of terrain due to the availability of different tire types.

Tires and tubes are easy to ignore until they give us trouble, usually because they are air-deprived. This chapter covers tires, tubes, repairs, and installations; it even has a few tips for avoiding leaks. With some basic repair knowledge, you never need to walk your bike and its flat tire home again.

Tire Types

There are two types of bicycle tires: *clincher,* or *wire-on* tires and *tubular,* or *sew-up* tires. I feel confident saying that every bike you ever buy will have clincher tires unless your name is Lance Armstrong (current two-time winner of the Tour de France). A clincher, or wire-on, tire is coupled with a separate inner tube, kind of a ring-shaped bladder, which holds air and keeps the tire from collapsing. The tire is made of thicker, tougher material and protects the inner tube. This is a nice, symbiotic relationship of sorts until a thorn, a shard of glass, or some overly enthusiastic air pump intrudes. The term "wire-on" refers to the two wire beads that are fitted into the edge of the tire and tucked into the wheel rim.

Tubular tires combine the tube and tire in one unit with the inner tube sewn inside the tire casing (that's why they're also called sew-ups). These are fast, high-pressure tires, most of which have been replaced by high-pressure clinchers.

Bike Bites

Check your tire pressure weekly. Bicycle tires naturally lose some air on their own; the lost air must be replaced. Improper inflation—either too much or too little—can cause damage to tires and wheels. A blowout from too much air pressure can cause an accident, which is the last thing you want during a high-speed descent.

Clinchers

Pneumatic tires are held in place by their fit on and around some type of wheel rim, and by air pressure. A pair of steel wire hoops along the edge of a clincher tire are tucked around a corresponding edge of a wheel rim. The inflated inner tube presses against the tire with enough pressure to maintain firmness. With too much pressure the tire can blow off the rim; with too little it will be more likely to pinch the tube and cause a flat.

Between the two wire beads a cloth fabric, usually nylon cord, is woven in layers to form the body of the tire. The fabric is coated with rubber, the formula of which varies according to each manufacturer's specifications. The rubber has two sections: the thicker *tread* that comes in contact with the riding surface and the narrower *sidewall.*

Freewheelin' Facts

The wonderful world of chemistry has brought Kevlar, the same material used in bullet-proof vests, to bicycle tires. Some high-performance tires are constructed with Kevlar beads, which reduce the weight of the tire and allow it to be folded up for storage. A belt of Kevlar is used in some tires under the tread area to beef it up against punctures. In this case, the Kevlar makes the tire heavier than tires constructed without it.

Tubular Tires

Everything about tubulars is different from clinchers. They require special rims, repairs are a nuisance, and they are glued to the rims as they have no wire beads. They were quite common on high-end, high-performance bikes at one time, but quality 700C clinchers have mostly replaced them. Tubular tires and wheels are lighter than many clincher tire/rim combinations, but tubulars are more expensive. Because they do not have a bead, tubulars are foldable and fit under the saddle. To repair them on the road, the rider carries a spare tire or two and slips one over the rim after peeling off the flat.

Once you're back home, you have to find the leak in the tubular. Carefully undo the stitching so you can get at the tube, repair the tube, and then restitch the tire. You're not done yet. Now clean all the glue from the rim. It helps to install the new tire over the clean rim and let it stretch out before applying two separate coats of glue. (It's not too tough to figure out why so many riders choose clinchers over tubulars.)

In addition to their general nuisance and expense, new tubular tires are considered to be "raw" and are best aged for at least six months on a spare wheel rim, suspended off the floor, to toughen the casing.

Valves

Bicycle tires come with one of three types of valves, one of which you'll probably never see. The two most common types are the Schrader valve and the Presta valve. You'll recognize Schrader valves because they're the same ones that are used on automobile tires. (If you don't recognize them, let this serve as a not-so-subtle reminder to check the pressure in your car tires every week or so.)

A Schrader valve has a small pin inside the valve that allows air in and out of the tube when it's pushed in. The valve itself sits inside a stem—that short, cylinder-shaped thingy that sticks out of the tube. Presta valves have a smaller diameter and a knurled or ridged nut inside the core (the Presta equivalent of a stem). In order to pump up a Schrader valve, push a pump head onto it until the pin is depressed. On a Presta valve, you must loosen the nut and tap it slightly to break the seal. Tighten the nut after pumping up the tire. Presta valves are used on most high-performance clincher tires and on all tubulars.

Unfortunately, air pumps come with only one fitting, so you can't use one pump for both types of valve unless you also have a Presta valve adapter. Also, a rim built for a Presta valve will not work for a Schrader valve unless you ream out the hole to accommodate the larger valve. There is no point in doing this, so stick with Presta valves for these rims.

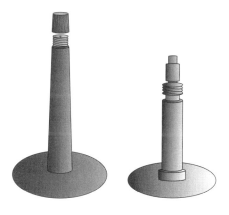

A Presta valve on the right and a Schrader valve on the left.

The third type of valve, a rarity in the United States, is the *Woods,* or *Dunlop* valve. It's one of those strange British things that you expect from the same people who came up with Monty Python's Flying Circus. You will probably never, ever see one.

Tread Heartily

The tread of a tire is the pattern of groove, lugs, and knobs that comes in contact with the riding surface. Different treads offer different traction and handling characteristics. These distinctions generally are more critical in off-road riding and winter riding than riding on smooth roads. In fact, with high-pressure tires, a pronounced tread isn't much benefit because it's really designed for lower-pressure tires. The best-performing high-pressure racing tires actually are smooth and have no tread at all, or very little.

For off-road use, the pattern of *knobs* is its own science. The spacing of knobs and ridges affects the tire's performance on different surfaces. Pronounced knobs, for instance, work well in loose dirt, but not as well on hard pack or mud. The spacing and number of knobs will determine the type of surface on which the tire works best. Generally, more knobs are desirable on harder surfaces and fewer on soft surfaces.

The Spoken Word

A **knob** (or lug) is a thick section of rubber designed to dig into soft riding surfaces. Think of knobs as rubber spikes.

Freewheelin' Facts

The whole idea of tire treads started with automobile tires, which are inflated to relatively low pressure compared to bicycle tires. Low pressure means less contact pressure with the road. On wet roads, this causes hydroplaning or skidding when a film of water forms between the tire and the road. This keeps the tire from making solid contact with the asphalt or concrete—skid city for the driver. Treads act as channels to remove the water and allow the tire to maintain more contact. High-pressure bike tires maintain more road contact; consequently, there is less chance of skidding.

You Can't Resist Resistance

Pick up the front end of your bike and give the wheel a spin. When all the wheel has to do is spin through thin air, the tire has virtually no rolling resistance because it isn't running on any kind of surface. This resistance is affected by the tire's contact area; that is, the area of the tire that makes contact with the road or trail as the wheel rotates. Several factors affect the rolling resistance, including …

➤ Tire pressure.

➤ Condition of the riding surface.

➤ Weight of the rider, bicycle, and equipment.

A tire has to work its way over all kinds of surface conditions. A choppy, bumpy trail forces the tire to deform every time it comes in contact with that surface; a smooth road doesn't demand as much deformation. Deformation causes friction or rolling resistance. The ideal tire would have very high pressure, thus less deformation; but still would be able to adapt to logs, gopher holes, and ruts in the road. However, along with higher pressure comes a less comfortable ride; thus, a wider tire would be desirable, which means more weight to move around. These are tough criteria to meet because they're contradicting properties. A relatively high-pressure mountain bike tire comes close, though.

Tires are designed for specific surfaces and riding conditions. On a dirt trail, the weight the tire supports is distributed over a greater area, so the wheel doesn't sink into the dirt the way a narrower tire would. You can try a narrow, high-pressure road tire on an old logging road, but you'll regret it. On the other hand, a fat, knobby mountain bike tire will be slow going on a smooth asphalt road.

Bike Bites

After you've sifted through all the tire opinions, one bit of wisdom remains true: Watch the tire pressure. An under-inflated tire has more rolling resistance and is prone to flats. An over-inflated tire is more prone to damage from sharp objects and is less comfortable to ride on. Use the psi stamped on the side of the tire as your guideline.

Feeling Low?

The term "flat tire" is a bit misleading. Sure, the tire isn't thick and happy any longer, but it's the tube that's not cooperating. A tire will still work with a thorn in it or other small, sharp objects; but a tube will deflate. There are several types of flats:

➤ Punctures

➤ Slow leaks

➤ Pinch cuts

➤ Big blow-outs

Run over a thorn, shard of glass, or any other opportunistic sharp object, and you'll often end up with a flat. A slow leak is just that: one that gradually deflates the tube over time. It might take overnight or only a few hours. These holes are very small and sometimes difficult to find. You can get by pumping up the tire regularly, but tire punctures should be repaired; otherwise, you risk damaging your tire from riding with it under-inflated.

A *pinch cut* happens when you hit a stone, curb, or hole in the road and the inner tube gets pinched between the rim and whatever you hit. These also are called "snake bites" because they regularly result in two holes in the tube. (Of course, your tire actually might get bitten by a snake, but that's another matter altogether.) Pinch cuts happen more often if your tires have low air pressure.

A blowout results from too much air pressure. Sometimes it won't blow right away, but after you've been riding for a while, heat builds up to exacerbate this pressure. The tube has to be held inside the tire; with too much pressure, it's forced outside of the wire bead.

Bike Bites

On some old center-pull brakes, such as the French-made Mafac series, you can squeeze the brake pads against the rim and pull out the removable end of the transverse cable from the brake arm. This is necessary only if there isn't any kind of a quick release available.

Step 1: Examine the Wheel

Before you remove your wheel, examine it, as well as your brakes. Most quality bikes have quick-release wheels and a means of releasing the brake arms so they will back away from the wheel rim. This makes removing the wheel much easier than removing one of the brake shoes. Many caliper brakes have some type of quick-release mechanism located in one of several locations, including ...

➤ A button on the brake lever.

➤ On the brake arm of a side pull.

➤ On the cable hanger of a center pull.

On cantilever brakes, you have to squeeze the brake pads together and release the removable end of the transverse cable. With V-brakes and other linear pull brakes, the releasable noodle is removed from its bracket in the brake arm. Once the brake arms have been released, you can remove the wheel and get at the tire and inner tube.

Removing the Wheel

With more effort than can possibly be worthwhile, you can repair some flats without re-moving the wheel. I can understand this if the bike has a rear wheel with internal gearing or some kind of hub brakes and you don't want to mess with it, but there's no reason to not remove a wheel from a bike equipped with derailleurs and rim brakes. These are the easiest wheels to remove because the bike is designed to move all obstacles—the brake pads, derailleurs, and chain—out of the way of the wheel.

Once the wheel is removed, you can easily remove the inner tube and repair the hole. Bike wheels are secured to the bike frame by one of the following:

➤ Axle nuts

➤ Quick-release mechanism

➤ Internal bolts

Axle nuts are used on inexpensive multi-speed bikes, bikes with internal-hub gears, and wheels with hub brakes. Some axle nuts are butterfly nuts and don't require any tools to remove them. Others will require a wrench. The easiest wheel to remove is one on a bike with quick-release brakes.

To remove the front wheel:

1. Release the brakes.

2. For a quick-release wheel, flip the cam lever 180 degrees; if the fork has a wheel-retention safety feature (small ridges that prevent the wheel from falling out if the quick release is too loose), hold on to the adjusting nut end of the quick release and turn the cam several times in a counterclockwise direction until hub clears the fork and can drop down.

3. If your wheel has some type of axle nuts, loosen them by hand (butterfly nuts) or with a wrench by turning counterclockwise (they shouldn't be completely removed from the axle); be sure to keep all washers.

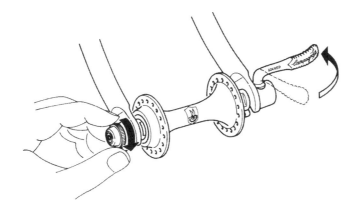

A handy quick-release mechanism makes for fast wheel removal and replacement.

(Courtesy of Campagnolo)

Watch where you put your hands on the tire! You don't want to be cutting yourself on the same piece of glass or metal that's caused the flat in the first place.

If your bike is leaning against a wall or a tree, gently put it down so you don't damage the fork. Removing the front wheel is easy, but the rear wheel is a bit more involved. You can follow essentially the same steps for the rear wheel, except you have to work around that—now pesky—derailleur by doing the following:

1. Spin the cranks around so you can shift the rear derailleur to the smallest or outermost sprocket.

2. Loosen the wheel (either the quick release or nuts).

3. Standing behind the bike, grab the derailleur with your right hand and pull it toward you.

4. Lift the bike a few inches off the ground by grabbing the left chain stay and seat stay with your left hand.

5. Hold the bike in this position with your right hand (it's still holding the derailleur) and pop the wheel out by giving it a whack on top of the tire; if it's loose enough, it will drop out.

6. With the wheel loose, pull the chain back and off the sprockets (yep, you'll get your hands greasy).

7. Lay your bicycle on its left side, never on the derailleur side.

If you're removing the wheel at home, you might as well give the freewheel or cassettes a spray of lubricant while the wheel is off. It's also a good time to wipe off the inside of the chain stays with a damp cloth. And as long as you're at it, wipe down the chain, too.

Bike Bites

The front wheels on the new Cannondale Lefty mountain bikes use a self-extracting bolt inside the hub to secure it to the fork. It's removed with an Allen wrench turned counterclockwise to loosen, although you must remove the disc brake caliper first.

Derailed

Use a wrench to remove axle nuts, not a pair of pliers. Pliers often distort the sides of the nut so it's harder to remove the next time. They also do a mediocre job of tightening during wheel installation.

Removing the rear wheel.

Removing Other Rear Wheels

It's a toss-up over which is the greater nuisance to remove: hubs with internal brakes or hubs with internal gears. Hub brakes, both foot- and hand-operated, have a reaction arm that attaches to the left side of the bike frame near the rear hub. This arm has to be disconnected from its bracket by loosening and removing the nut and bolt that secure it. After the arm has been removed from the bracket, loosely reinstall the nut and bolt so they don't get lost (small bike parts are always getting lost).

Next, remove the axle nuts and push the wheel out of the frame. If your bike has an internal hand brake, disconnect the brake cable from its fittings and remove the wheel.

The Wheel's Off, Now What?

Once the wheel has been removed, you must remove the tire and the inner tube. This is where your handy tire levers do their job. Their flat, smooth ends, when carefully directed, will lift the tire up and over the rim without pinching the inner tube.

To remove the tire and tube:

1. Squeeze all the air out of the tube by depressing the Schrader or Presta valve.

2. Pinch the tire beads all around the tire to loosen them from the rim.

Derailed

Use tire levers to remove a flat tire and tube; don't us a a screwdriver! Every time someone tries this, the tube ends up with another hole or two in it. Save the screwdriver for screws—that's what it was designed for.

3. Insert the round end of one of your three tire levers under one bead of the tire (start opposite the tube valve and make sure not to catch the inner tube) and pry the bead over the edge of the rim, hooking the other end of the tire lever onto a spoke to hold it in place.

4. Insert a second lever two or three spokes down from the first one and pry off the bead here as well, again hooking the lever onto a spoke. (See the following figure.)

Removing a tire with your trusty tire levers.

5. Insert the third iron two or three spokes down from the first if the tire is still kind of stubborn. At this point, the second iron probably will fall out and you can use it to peel the remaining—now loose—tire off the rim by running it between the bead and the rim.

6. After one side of the tire is loose and hanging over the rim, you can reach in and gradually pull the tube out. (See the following figure.)

7. When you get to the valve, carefully push it up against the tire and completely remove the tube from the tire and rim.

With the tube removed, you can more easily remove the tire from the rim using your fingers or, if necessary, a tire lever. Just push the other bead over the edge of the rim with your hands or carefully pry it off with a tire lever.

The first place to look for holes or leaks is around the valve stem. Look for cracks or tears near its base. Inflate the tube and listen for leaks (they'll hiss). Something should show up. If not, pump in some more air (don't get ridiculous about it) and check again. Gently bend the valve, one side to another. If the problem is with the valve, toss it out and replace it—you can't repair this type of leak. If you absolutely cannot find the leak, you can pump up the tube and pass it through a container of water. The leak is where you see bubbles. (The tube will have to be completely dry before you can patch it.)

Once you've found the hole, apply a patch from your repair kit by doing the following:

1. Rough up the area around the puncture with the sandpaper or metal scraper that comes with the kit until the area is dull. Be sure the puncture is in the center of your sanded section. Also make sure the raised molding line that runs the circumference of the tube is sanded flat if it is part of the sanded area.

2. Evenly spread a small amount of glue (you don't want any lumps or drips) over the sanded area using the opening of the glue tube, going a bit beyond the size of the patch you'll be using.

3. Allow the glue to dry completely.

4. Take a patch out of the kit, peel off the foil backing, and press this side of the patch over the glued area as hard as you can.

Bike Bites

If you're on the road and time and weather are considerations, don't even bother patching a tube. Just install a new one (you should have one with you) and stuff the damaged tube in your backpack or bike bag. You can repair it later at home.

Applying a patch.

When patching the tire, two points are worth emphasizing:

➤ It's very important that the area be sanded thoroughly. This doesn't mean you should sand aggressively, but simply that the tube must be dulled completely for the patch to take.

➤ The glue has to dry completely before applying the patch.

After applying the patch, put the tube aside and examine the tire and rim for the cause of the puncture. Carefully run your thumb around the inside of the tire, feeling for sharp objects. Push out anything you find using any available tool and recheck the tire. Also look for wear and tear and holes in the tire itself. If the hole was in the side of the tube that rests against the rim, make sure no spokes are pushing through rim tape and that the rim has no sharp edges. If a spoke is sticking through, cover it with something that will temporarily protect the inner tube (a patch from your repair kit or even a small piece of a business card) and repair it when you get home. A rough spot on the rim can be smoothed out with the sandpaper from your patch repair kit.

Bike Bites

A torn tire, one that allows the inner tube to bulge out, must be replaced. To get home, install a boot or patch that's larger than the cut on the inside of the tire. A boot is a temporary tire patch that is installed between a clincher tire and its inner tube. A piece of scrap tire a few inches long works best, but you can stuff in folded paper, cardboard, or even candy wrappers—anything that's flexible but somewhat firm.

Reinstalling

Satisfied that you've eliminated the cause of the puncture? Good; now you can remount the inner tube and tire. To reinstall your tire and tube, simply reverse your steps. Well, the first time might not seem so simple, but it gets easier with practice (not that I'm hoping you get more flats). Follow these steps to reinstall your tube and tire:

1. Pump a little air into the tube to give it some shape (you absolutely have to do this with a new tube).

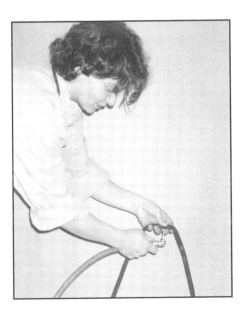

2. Slip one entire bead of the tire over the rim.

3. Find the stem hole and push the second bead against the first bead and far enough over the opposite edge of the rim that the stem hole is exposed freely.

4. Insert the valve stem into the hole, making sure it's snug and straight.

5. Pull the tire over the valve stem and tube.

6. Go around the tire and tuck the tube inside it, making sure to not bunch it up or twist it.

7. Starting on both sides of the valve stem, start working the second bead of the tire back and over the tube so it's secured to the rim, taking care that the tube does not get pinched in the process.

8. The last section of the tire can be difficult to push over the rim—especially if you have a narrow, high-pressure tire. Push it with the palms of your hands or your fingers a bit at a time until it slips over the rim.

9. If you absolutely cannot get the last bit of tire onto the rim, take one tire lever and, making sure the tube is out of the way, pry against the tire bead and force it over the rim.

10. Once the tire is completely installed, move the valve stem up and down a few times to check that it's straight and the tube isn't pinched. Go around the entire tire, squeezing it as you go to ensure that the tube isn't sticking here, either.

11. Inflate the tube a bit and, again, make sure it's securely under the tire.

12. Inflate the tire to the recommended pressure and reinstall the wheel.

Installing the Front Wheel

Front wheels are relatively easy to install, as you have no derailleur or messy chain to deal with. Go ahead and pump them up before you reinstall. Again, reverse your steps by doing the following:

1. Stand the bike upright and slip the axle into the fork making sure any quick-release springs or axle washers are on the outside of the tips.

2. Make sure the rim is centered between the brake shoes (they are still released at this point) and tighten the quick-release lever or axle nuts until the wheel is tight to the fork.

3. Tighten the quick release on caliper brakes and ensure that the wheel is centered; if it isn't, loosen it slightly at the fork and move it over so that it is centered.

4. On cantilever or V-brakes, hold the pads against the rim and reconnect the transverse cable or noodle to the brake; check that the wheel is centered.

Freewheelin' Facts

Some off-road riders mix and match their tires by putting a wider, knobby front tire on for traction and steering control and installing a narrower, smoother rear tire for lower rolling resistance.

Axle nuts should be tight, as should quick-release mechanisms. You'll know if your quick release is tight enough if you meet resistance when you're past the halfway point of tightening it and can completely lock it after moving it 180 degrees.

Reinstalling the Rear Wheel

Reinstalling the rear wheel is messier because of the chain and derailleur, but who ever said changing a tire was a glamorous event? It's tricky to balance the bike, manage the wheel, and pull back the derailleur and chain at the same time when the front wheel is barely cooperating. Here's what you do:

1. Line up the wheel with the dropouts (the slotted ends of the rear stays).
2. Hold the wheel with your left hand and pull back the derailleur cage along with the chain.
3. Maneuver the wheel into the dropouts so the chain drops onto the smallest sprocket (remember, this was its position when the wheel was removed).
4. Pull the wheel all the way back into the dropouts (you might have to jiggle it back and forth a bit) and tighten the quick release or axle nuts, ensuring that the wheel is centered between the brake pads.
5. Adjust the brakes by tightening the quick release or reinstalling the transverse cable or noodle.
6. Give the wheel a spin, again making sure it's centered; give the cranks a spin to be sure the chain isn't rubbing against the derailleur.

You're done. You're on your way again, and you didn't have to walk to the bike shop. A small patch repair kit gives you a lot of power.

Installing Other Rear Wheels

When installing the rear wheel on a one-speed, coaster brake bike, simply pull the wheel back in between the stays while placing the chain over the sprocket. Align the wheel between the chain stays near the bottom bracket. Be sure the reaction arm (it connects and secures the brake to one of the rear stays) lines up with the bracket that secures it to the left chain stay.

Bike Bites

Whenever you've repaired a flat and reinstalled a wheel, take the bike for a short test ride. You want to check your work and eliminate any later surprises.

With the wheel aligned and the axle in the dropouts, hand-tighten the axle nuts, watching that the wheel doesn't move around and become misaligned. When you're sure it's centered, tighten the nuts with a wrench. Attach the reaction arm to its bracket. If you're reinstalling a wheel with a multi-speed hub or hub brake, align the wheel with the stays, tighten the axles nuts; and reattach any brake or control cables.

Flat Prevention

You cannot avoid all flats, but you can take some steps to keep them to a minimum. These steps are divided into two categories: equipment and prevention. Your first line of defense is a good quality tire. If your tires once had deep treads on them and now resemble a pair of slicks, it's a safe bet they should be replaced. Next up are thorn-proof tubes, which really are just heavy-duty versions of regular tubes. They're about three times thicker and in my experience, they really work. You pay a price in terms of additional weight; but when you ride across a stretch of Wyoming that's full of thorns and endure the resultant multiple flat tires as I once did, you won't mind heavier wheels.

Another protective measure is installing Mr. Tuffy (www.MrTuffy.com) protectors, which are plastic wraps that go inside your tire and protect the tube from punctures. This is a more lightweight means of protecting your tubes and even comes in several cool colors—not that you'll ever look at it again once you've lined the tire.

Some cyclists swear by tire sealants such as Slime Sealant (www.slimesealant.com). This comes in a green fluid that is pumped inside the deflated tube, instantly sealing holes up to $1/_4$" in size. It is a nonflammable product that the company claims will last up to two years. A by-product of this strange chemical is the slime tube, an inner tube that comes with the goop already inside and seals punctures up to $1/_{16}$" in diameter as you ride.

Thorn-proof tubes and sealants all add weight to your bike, so unless you live in an area known for its thorns, such as sections of the Southwest, you should consider whether you need to take any extra precautions at all.

Freewheelin' Facts

Winter riders are a breed apart and don't hesitate to ride in snow and on ice. For snow riding, some recommend lowering the tire pressure to 20 psi or so for better traction. Rims such as the SnowCat, which is nearly twice as wide as a normal rim, won't fit all bikes, but it gives lots of traction. Ice riding on frozen lakes or glazed roads calls for studded tires; either manufactured versions such as the Finnish-made Nokian (with tungsten carbide studs) or homemade versions. The homemade versions require you to install stainless steel sheet metal screws through the tire casing from the inside and add a tire liner so the screw heads don't damage the inner tube. For more information, go to www.icebike.com.

Watch Out!

We all talk about prevention, but in most areas of life we're a little rusty in our practice of it. When it comes to your tires, a few simple steps can keep your patch repair kit gathering dust instead of being yanked open for repairs. For longer-lasting tubes, try the following:

➤ Keep your tires properly inflated and check the pressure regularly with a tire gauge.

➤ Check the condition of your tires and replace them when necessary.

➤ Always use a rim strip.

➤ Avoid riding too close to the curb (where much of the glass and road junk seem to accumulate).

Bike Bites

Keep a pressure gauge with your tool kit. A simple pencil gauge has a sliding rod for reading the tire pressure. Be sure to buy one intended for bicycle, not automobile, use as the former reads higher pressure. Other gauges have a dial readout that maintains its reading after removing the gauge from the valve. A reset button sets the needle back to zero.

Tubular Repairs

If you're sophisticated enough to be using sew-ups or tubular tires, you already know how to repair them. Most people should forget about using them because they're expensive and a pain to repair. However, if you want the quick rundown, here it is …

1. The glue bond that holds the tire to the rim is broken by rolling the tire over the edge of the rim while pushing it with the palms or your hands or with your thumbs.

2. You have to find the leak, which isn't readily accessible because the tube is sewn inside the tire casing.

3. Once you find the leak, the base tape that covers the stitching has to be peeled back and the stitching around the leak has to be removed, opening as little of the tire as possible.

4. The tube is then patched or even replaced in some cases.

5. The tire is finally re-sewn using the original stitch holes.

6. Tubular cement is applied to the rim, and the sew-up tire is reinstalled.

I'm sure this doesn't sound like a ton of fun, so if you ever run across a used road bike with sew-ups, keep in mind that you'll probably want to build a new set of wheels for it.

A Breath of No Air

Before the invention of the pneumatic tire, cyclists had little to protect them from the bumps in the road except a hard rubber tire at best. They welcomed something so simple as an inner tube full of air. Thankfully, bicycles have come equipped with pneumatic tires for more than 100 years, and solid rubber tires have been banished to children's tricycles.

Well, what goes around comes around (ooh, bad pun), and some manufacturers have introduced new, slick versions of the solid tire. Air Free Tires, Inc. (1-800-771-9513; info@ airfreetires.com) offers a polyurethane tire made from an injected mold process that guarantees it for life against flats, dry rot, or mildew. The company claims that the air-free tires can last twice as long as conventional pneumatic tires and can be ordered according to your air pressure (psi) requirements. An English company, Greentyre (www.greentyre.com), also makes an airless tire. Both companies claim their tires are comparable in terms of weight to pneumatic tires (plus you don't have to carry a spare pump, patch kit, or tire-changing tools). Do these tires work? Let me put it this way: Despite marketing attempts, you see very few of these tires on the road.

Does this mean that tire technology won't evolve, possibly to materials beyond rubber? Absolutely not. Human invention almost mandates that someone in a lab or factory somewhere will tinker enough to come up with interesting materials that could be huge improvements over conventional tires. In the meanwhile, I'd hold on to the tire pump and repair kits.

The Least You Need to Know

➤ Tires are not all interchangeable, so be sure to know the size and type of tires on your bike.

➤ Clincher tires are by far the most popular and easiest to repair.

➤ Always carry a spare patch repair kit and inner tube when you ride (it beats walking because of a flat).

➤ Be sure you eliminate the cause of a flat tire before remounting the tube and tire.

➤ You can't avoid all flats, but careful riding, thorn-proof tubes, and tire sealants can help.

Chapter 8

Wheel Therapy

In This Chapter

➤ Straight wheels are happy wheels

➤ Hubs, the centers of attention

➤ True blue spokes

➤ Spin cycle

➤ Which wheel is for you?

Bicycles are very much about wheels. The term derives from two—hence "bi" in bicycle—wheels. From an engineering standpoint, wheels that get their strength from spokes under tension instead of compression are simply fascinating considering that they can operate under the weight of a bike, a rider, and a load that can range from a picnic lunch to racks full of chickens. On top of that, bicycle wheels also have relatively low rolling resistance (compare them to other wheels) and, with an added tire and tube, help to soften the ride.

A wheel should spin straight and true, and its spokes should be under proper tension to keep it that way. Hub bearings and cones should be kept greased and adjusted to move freely and keep you on your way. This chapter shows you the ins and outs of wheel maintenance and repair. After all, this is one time when you really do want to be spinning your wheels.

Give It a Spin

Wheels are pretty good about telling you that they have a problem or two. Listening will tell you if a spoke is broken (you'll hear a thunk against the brake pad) or if the hub needs to be overhauled (that fun grinding sound). Give it a spin and watch as the rim goes around the brake pads. It shouldn't bounce back and forth between them nor hop up and down like a jackrabbit. If it does any of these, it needs repair.

The parts of a wheel.

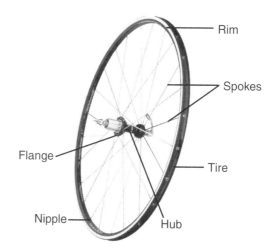

Loose spokes are spokes that will prematurely fatigue. Every time the wheel rotates, spokes are pulled and pushed; if they're too loose, they move too much and the metal breaks down. If there are too many loose spokes your wheel could cave in, which isn't exactly cheery news if you're careening down a nice, long descent on a paved road. Spokes that are too tight put too much tension on the wheel and can weaken it. Other wheel problems include wobbles, blips, and all kinds of hub troubles.

Wheels usually are repairable, although you might not get perfect results. Sometimes all you need is to get it usable enough to ride home. Other times, a minor wobble isn't the end of the world if it's on a commuter bike or an off-road model that you're going to use for rough riding anyway. In the latter case, you might as well use the wheel until it's completely toasted.

Derailed

Truing a wheel can be a frustrating experience, especially during your first efforts. You might even consider practicing on a junker wheel (in fact, you could buy a really cheap, beat-up bike to practice all your bike repairs). It's easy for things to get out of hand so watch your adjustments. It really does get easier with practice.

Hobbled by Wobbles

A wobbly wheel isn't the result of a bent rim or a broken spoke. Spokes pull on a rim in opposing directions because the spoke holes are almost always offset slightly to the left and right of the center line of the rim. If one spoke breaks, the rim will be pulled in the opposite direction, resulting in a wobble. A crash or other damage to the wheel actually can bend the rim, which also can cause a big wobble.

Blips

Rims get dented from running into curbs, rocks, and tree stumps. A blip isn't a big deal, but it can be annoying when you apply the brake and the brake pad bumps against it. Many can be repaired satisfactorily with a wrench or a pair of vise-grips (see the following).

Rim Repercussions

Clincher rims—it's almost assured that you have clinchers—are almost always made from aluminum on quality bikes. Cheap bikes and most bikes with some kind of internal hub gears (one-speeds, three-speeds, and so forth) usually have steel rims. Steel rims are heavier and usually not any stronger than aluminum rims. Also, steel rims don't stop as well with rim brakes as do aluminum rims because they don't dissipate heat build-up as well.

How will you know if your rim is damaged? You'll feel a bump in your ride or the rim will rub against the brake pad. You'll likely get a flat tire at the same time you dent your rim because any impact that will bend or distort metal will easily puncture an inner tube.

Bending Out Blips

You can ride with a bent or dented wheel (the wheel will still roll around), but it's a good idea to straighten it out if you can. Your braking will be more even for one thing (brake pads like smooth rims). For another, you won't have to adjust the brake pads outward to keep a blip in the rim from hitting one of them.

There are several ways to straighten out small dents:

➤ Remove the wheel from the bike and remove the tube and tire. Place the bent section of the rim inside the jaws of a vise and tighten until the section is flattened out.

➤ For dents facing out, use a large adjustable wrench or a vise-grips to tighten until secure, but not too taut, around the dent. Gently pull up on the handle as it faces you until you've minimized the dent. It's best if you can fit a piece of wood—exactly as narrow as an undamaged section of the rim—between the lips of the rim.

➤ More sizeable dents—those that truly distort the rim—sometimes can be removed, but there are no guarantees. With the wheel loose and the tire and tube removed, loosen the spokes around the dent and place the wheel dent side down. Put your foot on the dent and pull up on the opposite side of the rim and see if it improves.

You'll never end up with a new wheel with any of these repairs but you can end up with one that still has some life in it. Given the price and time to build a new wheel, this isn't a bad deal.

Bike Bites

If you do a lot of off-road riding, consider having a second pair of wheels built and ready to use in the event that you damage one of your regular wheels. You can always buy a really cheap second bike with the same size wheels, true them and overhaul the hubs, and use these as spares.

Bike Bites

If you want to keep your rim from getting scratched when straightening out a blip, wrap some tape or a rag around the jaws of the vise-grips first.

Extreme Damage, Extreme Repair

If you ride off road and you ride aggressively, chances are you're going to taco your rim someday. No, this isn't suddenly having a craving for Mexican food at which point you inexplicably start covering your wheel with refried beans, ground beef, and cheese in the mistaken belief that it's a taco. Rather, it's a really, really bent wheel that isn't going to go another inch until it's straightened out.

How do you do it? By using the age-old approach of aggression and catharsis (over the fact that you taco'd your wheel). Remove the wheel from the bike, grasp it with the bent section pointing down, and smash this section of the wheel against a rock or tree until it's straight enough to get you home. Don't worry about finesse; you're going to have to rebuild the wheel anyway. Just be sure you don't hit the spokes while doing this ... uh ... exacting repair.

Hubbub in the Hubs

Hub problems can range from the need for lubrication to a broken axle to a cracked flange. The same spokes that pull on the rim also are pulling on the hub flanges—and some cheap ones have been known to crack. A hub is a metal shell, usually aluminum, that is shaped to accommodate the following:

➤ An axle

➤ Some type of bearings

➤ The cones that fit against the bearings

➤ Washers

➤ Locknuts or a quick-release to secure the wheel to the bike frame

Most quality bikes come equipped with quick-release wheels, but not always. A quick-release axle is inherently weaker than a solid axle because it is hollowed out to accommodate the quick-release skewer. This usually isn't a problem, although you could be riding with a cracked axle and not know it.

A quality hub and all its details.

(Courtesy of Campagnolo)

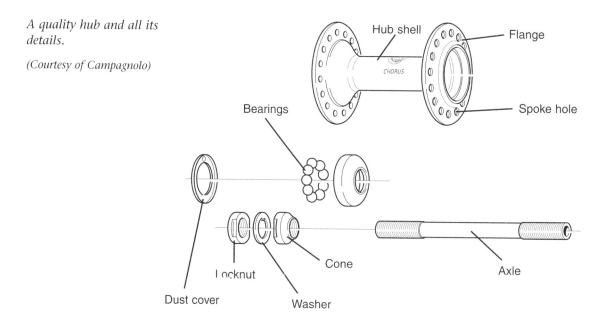

A quick release allows for tool-free wheel removal.

(Courtesy of Campagnolo)

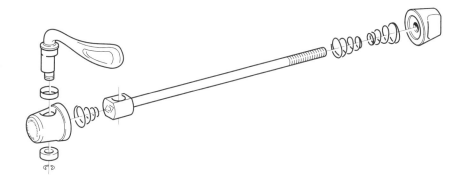

Hub bearings come in several flavors:

➤ Loose ball

➤ Loose ball in a cage

➤ Sealed mechanism

➤ Sealed cartridge

Loose ball bearings, as mentioned in Chapter 3, "Bike Details," are the oldest type; you don't see them much anymore. They are pressed into a slathering of grease and sit in the *hub races*. Ball bearings also can be held inside a cage, which is kind of a metal donut with openings for the bearings. A sealed mechanism (sometimes called a *sealed bearing*) refers to a rubber seal that covers and protects a bearing cage. In the not-so-old days, this function was taken care of by a metal dust cap on the end of the hub. A sealed cartridge bearing is a self-contained, modular unit of machine bearings that are protected by a plastic seal.

Regardless of the type of bearings you have, all hubs need periodic maintenance. As wonderful as sealed bearings can be, they are not as user friendly to work on as loose ball bearings.

The Spoken Word

Hub races refer to the surfaces inside of a hub in which the bearings sit. The cones push against the bearings at this point as the hub spins.

Hub Repairs

If a hub is cracked or a flange is broken near a spoke hole, you'll have to retire it and build a new wheel. Chances are you won't run into anything this extreme—well, unless you're an extreme rider—but you will have to adjust, lubricate, and overhaul your hubs once in awhile. Your maintenance schedule will depend on the type of riding you do and the type of bearings you have. If you hit the muddy trails every week and don't have sealed bearings, you're going to become really familiar with your hubs because you'll be tearing them apart regularly.

A wheel axle should be adjusted so the wheel spins freely, but without any noticeable play between the cones and the bearings. For the most part, cones and locknuts stay in adjustment unless you've been doing some really hard riding. It's easier to figure on overhauling your hubs rather than simply adjusting them unless you've done a recent overhaul and there still is some play between the axle and the hub.

Bike Bites

You can adjust most any hub with a pair of 13mm cone wrenches for the front wheel and 15mm wrenches for the rear (they come as a combination wrench with 13mm and 15mm ends). A pair of 17mm wrenches will adjust most locknuts more conveniently than will an adjustable wrench.

The Overhaul

Most new bikes come with some sort of seal in the wheel hubs. This doesn't mean that with a single seal they will be waterproof; it means that the seals will keep most dirt and water away from the bearings. However, the seal will leak if it gets enough exposure to water. A hub overhaul will allow you to check the condition of the bearings and give them some fresh grease. They'll move more smoothly and the grease will help repel any water that finds its way in.

An overhaul is not complicated. Follow these steps for the front wheel hub:

1. Remove one axle nut or the quick release that normally secures the wheel to the frame (be careful that you don't lose the springs that come with the quick-release skewer. Keep them on the skewer and loosely attach the adjusting nut to the threaded end of the skewer).

2. Lay the wheel down flat on a large rag.

3. Attach a cone wrench (see the following figure) to one side of the axle; with a 17mm cone wrench or a small adjustable wrench, tighten the locknut against the cone by turning clockwise (the locknut keeps the cone tight in place on the axle). This secures their placement on this side of the axle.

You'll need one set of cone wrenches for the front wheel and one pair for the rear to fit the different size cones.

(Courtesy of Park Tool)

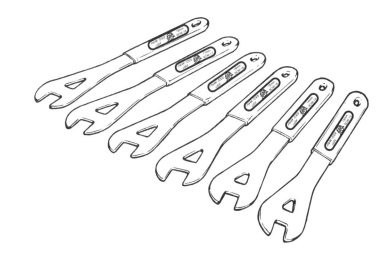

4. Flip the wheel over and attach the cone wrench to the other cone and loosen the locknut by turning it counterclockwise with the other wrench.

5. Loosen and remove the second cone. If it's too tight to remove with your fingers, place a cone wrench on the first cone to keep the axle from moving; then back off the second cone with another cone wrench by turning it counterclockwise.

Bike Bites

Some sealed mechanisms can be lubricated simply by lifting off the rubber seal on the hub and squirting grease into the hub. This isn't quite as good as disassembling and cleaning, but it's a good maintenance measure.

6. While keeping the axle inside the hub, completely remove the second cone.

7. Flip the wheel over again and slowly remove the axle and any seals or metal dust caps (the metal caps are gently pried off with a large screwdriver).

8. As the axle is removed, some loose ball bearings might come out with it.

9. For bearings in cages, note which way they come out (the balls almost always face in; the backs of the cages face out).

10. Remove any seals or dust caps from the other side of the hub and remove all bearings.

11. Soak loose ball or caged bearings, metal dust caps, the axle, and loose cone in solvent and spray the inside of the hub with WD-40 or other solvent and wipe clean.

With the hub disassembled, look for signs of wear or pitting on the cones, bearings, and races (see the following figure if you have sealed cartridge bearings). It can be hard to tell if a bearing is worn or not; consider replacing them, especially if you ride daily. Check the hub for cracks. When you're satisfied that everything is in good order, wipe everything clean and reverse your steps:

1. Put new grease inside the hub.

2. Place loose ball bearings into the grease, noting that the size and number (usually ten $^3/_{16}$" balls in the front hub) of the bearings are the same as those that came out. Add a little grease to bearing cages before inserting them into the hub and reinstall any metal dust caps by pressing them flat onto the hub.

3. Insert the axle into the hub. (If you have a sealed mechanism, be sure to put on the plastic seal on the side of the axle that still has its cone.)

4. Install the second cone on the hub, tightening it clockwise until it seats against the bearings.

5. Spin the axle and check that it moves smoothly. Try to move it up and down (it shouldn't have any play).

6. If the axle has up and down movement, place a cone wrench on each cone and tighten the second cone slightly. Remove the wrenches and check for play.

7. If the axle is too tight, put a wrench on each cone and back them off a bit in a counterclockwise direction.

8. When you're satisfied that the axle is properly set, place a cone wrench on the second cone and install the locknut, taking a second wrench to tighten it against the cone.

9. Test the axle again and adjust the cones and locknut as needed.

When doing a rear wheel, note that the right side of the hub has some additional spacers that must be kept in place. It also might be necessary to remove the freewheel or cassette to properly adjust the hub.

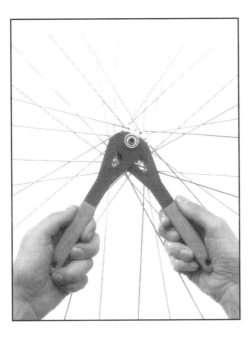

Cones should be adjusted until they move freely without any side play.

(Courtesy of Park Tool)

Some sealed cartridge bearings might not be serviceable at home. These hub assemblies are made with preset adjustments and require special tools to mess with them. Other sealed cartridges can be cleaned and greased by first wiping them clean and then lifting the edge of the plastic seal up with the blade of a knife. Spray the inside of the bearing with WD-40, wipe clean, add new grease, and push the plastic seal back on. Install the axle and adjust the cones and locknuts the same as you would for other bearings.

Freewheelin' Facts

The sealed bearings that come closest to living up to their name are found in bottom brackets. These units have more than one seal. Bearings submerged during a ride or ones that get hit by a garden hose during cleaning can still be contaminated even with these double seals. Traditional cup and cone loose ball bearings, which are even more subject to water and grit because they're not sealed, are easier to service and cheap to replace. However, they can degrade and form pits in the cones or cups, requiring complete replacement of these parts. Cartridge bearings can be easier to install, but more difficult to clean and lubricate as the seal has to be carefully removed.

Tried and True

A bicycle wheel might be a great piece of art and engineering, but it can quickly go from a Rembrandt to Art 101 if it's out of true. Every spoke is exposed to constant stress whether the wheel is stationary or moving. Poorly adjusted spokes can weaken, in turn weakening your wheel.

Bike Bites

One basic rim maintenance task is cleaning. Clean off road grime and oils with some spray cleaner and a rag. Very fine steel wool works, too. Don't use any heavy abrasives as they can scratch the metal.

Keeping a wheel straight and true takes patience, a good eye, and a knack. You might have the first two, but the third will take some time to develop. Mechanics speak of the sound spokes make when their fingers pluck them. They should sound like a musical note; not a dull thud. Obviously the correct pitch is dependent on the spoke length, type of spoke, and the wheel construction. Spokes usually need minor adjustments to keep a wheel true; a light hand here is better than an aggressive one.

Small Adjustments Only, Please

Spokes will have approximately the same tension throughout a wheel. By grabbing two spokes at a time on each side of the hub and squeezing them, you can tell if any are excessively loose. You also can tell by checking for wobbles in the rim by spinning the wheel between the brake shoes. If the wheel veers to one side or the other, this indicates that the spokes on the opposite side are not tight enough (a loose spoke allows the rim to drift in the opposite direction).

It's best to use a truing stand to mount your wheel and check its adjustment, but you can use your brake pads as an approximate guide. Placing a thumb on the brake pad will give you an even more precise guide. You're looking for two types of movement: side to side, or lateral and up and down, or radial. The wheel should spin evenly between them with no noticeable movement toward either pad. It also should not move up and down. If a wheel is moving up, it means this section of the rim has to be pulled down by tightening at least two spokes under that section of the rim.

Remember, you're only tightening the spokes in small increments; maybe up to half a turn with a spoke wrench. You might end up tightening or loosening more, but not until you have checked the progress from your first adjustment. If you attempt to tighten a spoke too much, you can end up stripping the nipple, in which case you'll have to remove it with a pair of pliers or vise-grips and replace it.

To adjust a loose spoke, follow these steps:

1. Spin the wheel and determine the type of adjustment that's required. Use the straight and true section of the rim as a reference point.

2. Mark this section of the rim with a felt marker.

3. If the rim is wandering toward the right, loosen the spokes in that section by turning them one-quarter to no more than half a turn; do the opposite if the rim wanders toward the left.

4. Tighten the spokes on the left side of the section that's moving to the right by one-quarter to one-half a turn.

5. Spin the wheel and check for trueness. Continue to adjust with smaller turns until the wheel is straight.

By loosening some spokes and tightening others, you will gradually pull the rim over in the direction opposite from where it is out of true; that is, where it is hitting a brake pad or the guide on the truing stand. Think small adjustments and small turns of the nipples; not big ones (unless a nipple is way loose). These things have a way of getting out of hand and you can throw the whole wheel out of true if you're not careful.

Derailed

Watch the direction in which you turn the nipples. They tighten in a clockwise direction as you're viewing them from the edge of the rim; that is, where the tire mounts. If they seem stiff and difficult to turn remove the tire, tube, and rim strip; give the wheel a spin; and spray all the nipple and spoke ends with spray lubricant.

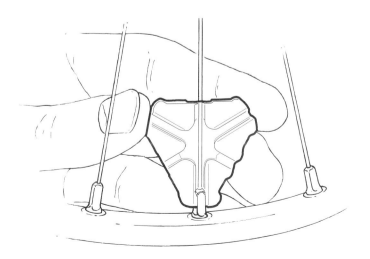

You can do some spot truing with the wheel mounted on the bike, using the brake pads as guides, but a truing stand is best for adjusting a wheel.

(Courtesy of Park Tool)

To test a wheel for radial adjustment, lay a small piece of wood or a pencil across the brake pads and give the wheel a spin. If it burps upward at any point, tighten at least two spokes to pull it down. Why two spokes? Because if you tighten only one, you'll throw the wheel out of true laterally and compound your problems. Tightening two will keep the lateral force even.

Spoke Spoken Here

You should replace broken spokes as soon as possible. Spokes come in all different lengths due to the myriad hub, rim, and *lacing* combinations. There are entire Web pages and sections of technical manuals dedicated to listing these spoke sizes. It's easiest to ask at your bike shop or take the wheel in and let them measure the spokes.

To replace a spoke on the front wheel, do the following:

1. Remove the wheel from the bike; then remove the tire, tube, and rim strip.

2. Poke the threaded end of the spoke through the hub flange so the hooked end of the spoke faces the opposite direction of the spokes on either side of it (if they face or are seated on the outside of the flange, your new spoke will face or seat on the inside of the flange, for example).

3. Examine how other spokes on that side of the hub are installed when their head faces the same direction as the spoke you're installing. Follow this pattern when you weave the new spoke toward the rim.

4. Push the threaded end of the spoke through the hole on the rim and put a drop or two of oil on the threads.

5. Hand-tighten the nipple to the threads and further tighten with a screwdriver.

6. Finish tightening the spoke with a spoke wrench and adjust until the wheel is true.

7. Reinstall the rim strip, tube, and tire.

The Spoken Word

Lacing refers to the pattern that spokes follow when they're installed. Some go directly from the hub straight to the rim (radial pattern); most others cross at least two other spokes (tangential pattern). Different lacing patterns give a wheel different riding properties.

On a rear wheel, you'll probably have to remove the cassette or freewheel if the spoke breaks on the right side. These spokes on the gear side will not be the same size as the spokes on the front wheel. Because the sprockets and longer axle prevent the wheel from being centered on the hub as it is up front, the wheel is dished or centered by being pulled over to the right side. These spokes are necessarily tighter than those on the left side; they also are shorter.

Spoke and Lace

The most standard lacing pattern is called *three-cross* because a single spoke will cross three connected spokes before it reaches the rim. Other patterns include two-cross, four-cross, and radial (zero-cross). Two-, three-, and four-cross patterns sometimes are called *tangenital* spoke patterns.

A three-cross pattern is used because it works well with the wheel's twisting forces of the rear wheel and makes for both a comfortable and a responsive ride. These forces are present because force is applied to the hub when the chain turns the rear sprockets and at that point the hub twists relative to the wheel rim. The spokes then carry the force from the hub and move the rim.

Tandems frequently have four-cross wheels because they tend to stand up better under the added weight. Some professional riders feel that a radial pattern on the front wheel, which is slightly lower in weight because of the shorter spokes, provides a competitive advantage.

The Least You Need to Know

➤ Minor rim damage usually is repairable with acceptable results.

➤ Major wheel damage might be repairable enough to get you home, but will call for a new wheel later.

➤ Sealed bearings are not ultimately waterproof, but more accurately water resistant; these bearings need maintenance the same as other bearing types.

➤ You should overhaul your hubs at least once or twice a year depending on the type of riding you do.

➤ Wheel truing is an art and a science that requires patience and a good eye.

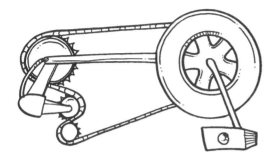

Chapter 9

The Power Train

> **In This Chapter**
>
> ➤ Pedal power
>
> ➤ Gears and stuff
>
> ➤ How derailleurs derail
>
> ➤ Whole lot of speeds
>
> ➤ Efficient riding

Bicycles are inherently efficient. They are made even more so by modern gearing, lightweight frames, and well-designed components. A new 27-speed isn't 27 times better or faster than a 1-speed cruiser, but it is a great improvement. The vast array of component and frame options available today ensure that even the most particular rider can have the ideal bike.

The basic functions of a bike are pretty apparent, but a little in-depth knowledge can lead you to an improved riding style and an even better choice of bikes for your type of riding. There's no point in working any harder than you need to when you ride. After all, the point is to enjoy yourself when you ride, unless you participate in international road races (in that case, you're voluntarily engaging in misery and you couldn't enjoy bike riding if you tried). For just about everyone else, this chapter will give you some insights for better use of your bike.

Powering Up

One of the biggest advances in early bicycle design was the development of the chain drive. A rider no longer had to directly pedal a wheel. A chain drive allowed all that leg power to be transferred to the rear wheel with a comfortable pedaling resistance for the rider. The introduction of gears allowed the rider to move more efficiently on flat roads, as well as up and down steep hills.

There's more to bike riding than simply pushing down on the pedals. A range of gears allows a rider to maintain *cadence,* or an efficient rate of pedaling. A cadence that is too slow or too fast results in inefficient riding. This isn't a big deal for a casual rider going short distances on flat roads; however, it makes a lot of difference to a racer or a rider on a long-haul tour. A wide range of gears enables you to maintain efficient pedaling without tiring yourself out unnecessarily.

Those Toothy Gears

Basically, combining the front chain rings with the rear wheel sprockets allow a rider to comfortably pedal on a variety of elevations. This means on a steep hill, you can choose a low gear that requires you to turn the pedals several full revolutions to turn the rear wheel

The Spoken Word

Cadence, the rate of pedaling, is measured in the number of revolutions per minute (rpm) of a crankarm or the rider's foot on a pedal. The cadence will vary depending on the terrain and gear choice. A 100 rpm cadence would be high whereas 60 rpm or less would be somewhat low, even if conditions called for it.

around once. When you get to the top of that hill and start heading down the other side, you can click into a higher gear, and the rear wheel will turn several times with every single revolution of the pedals. Multiplying the number of chain rings times the number of rear sprockets gives you the number of gears on the bike. Thus, 3 chain rings and 9 sprockets give you 27 (9 × 3) gears or speeds.

Think of your gears in terms of ratios. If the front chain ring has 54 teeth and the rear sprocket has 27 teeth, you have a ratio of 54 to 27, or 2 to 1 (two chain ring teeth for every single sprocket tooth); this is more simply stated as a ratio of 2. This means that for every time the chain moves the front 54 teeth one full revolution, the rear sprocket moves around twice and rotates the rear wheel twice. The larger the chain ring and the smaller the rear sprocket, the higher the resulting gear. The smaller the chain ring and the larger the sprocket, the lower the resulting gear. From a practical standpoint, think of it this way: The lower gears are closest to the bike frame, and the highest are farthest from the frame.

Another way of looking at this is to multiply your gear ratio by the size of your rear wheel. The resulting number will tell you how far your bike would have traveled had your crankarms been directly attached to a wheel of the same size. For example, say you have a mountain bike with 26-inch wheels, a 42-tooth front chain ring, and a 16-tooth rear sprocket. Your gear ratio and size would look like this:

$$42 \div 16 = 2.625$$

$$2.625 \times 26 = 68.25"$$

Freewheelin' Facts

Sheldon Brown, prolific online bicycle writer and service manager at Harris Cyclery, opines that gear ratios should include the length of the crank arms in the calculation. Sheldon has dozens of bicycle-related articles at www.sheldonbrown.com.

For every revolution of the pedals or crank arms when you're riding in a 42/16 gear, your bike will move the same distance as if your crankarms were connected to a 68.25" wheel. This is known as the *gear inch system* and goes back to the high-wheeler days when cranks were attached directly to large front wheels.

Comfortable, appropriate gearing enables you to depend less on muscle strength and more on your endurance, which generally is longer lasting than the former. It's also a lot easier on your knees. Cycling can cause knee problems, which can be brought on by a poor fitting between the rider and the bike or by strenuous, unnecessary pedaling.

Freewheelin' Facts

Internal hub gear systems have been available for almost 100 years, starting with the Sturmer-Archer three-speed in 1902. Derailleur mechanisms were available in the 1890s, but they didn't gain popularity until racers began to adopt them in the 1920s. Ten-speeds gained popularity in the 1960s and 1970s and have since been surpassed by 24- and 27-speeds. Some people have commented that such gearing is excessive; but in America, the more, the merrier.

Comfort is a relative term. A racer, with years of training and riding an ultra-lightweight bike, wants speed and high gears and often stands on the pedals when riding up hill. A casual rider doesn't want to work too hard and will use somewhat lower gears, including the *granny gear*. A touring cyclist wants the lowest gears to accommodate hills and a heavy load.

Ratio, Schmatio

Yes, gear ratios are important. You can find ratio calculators on the Internet and argue the minutia of gear selections forever. And you should take every advantage of a modern, multi-geared bicycle, even using a handlebar-mounted computer to display your cadence and make the best gear selection. In the end, you'll have plenty of gear combinations to choose from, and your body, ever inefficient as it can be at times, will choose the one it wants to use.

The Spoken Word

A **granny gear** refers to the smallest chain ring of a triple ring crankset. (It's uncertain whether grandmothers approve of this term or not.)

The type of terrain you normally ride will determine the most usable gear range. This doesn't entirely hold true for racers or competitive riders who are in top physical shape and use a very narrow range, even for hill climbing. Off-road riders generally have a narrower, lower gear range, as they rarely reach the types of speeds found on smooth road riding.

Derailed

If you decide to change your gears, either by replacing a chain ring or a rear sprocket, keep in mind that the chain might have to be replaced as well. Chains and gear teeth wear down along with the chain and an old chain can skip when used on shiny new components. If you install larger sprockets or chain rings, you might have to replace one or both derailleurs as well.

Connecting at the Pedals

The pedals are your point of contact with the drive train. You want a comfortable fit between your shoe and the pedal so you can get a full stroke every time you push. New clipless pedals, which lock into the pedal cage, allow you to pull up on the pedal with one leg while you press down with the other. This greatly increases your efficiency, as your legs are engaged during the entire pedaling cycle. Old-style toe clips, which secure the top of rider's foot, worked well for years, but it's more difficult to disengage quickly from this setup in case of an accident.

You're Suspended!

Suspension systems have some effect on your efficiency and certainly with your comfort. Every time a wheel dips or bounces, the frame does the same thing and takes you along for the ride. A suspension system absorbs some of the shock through a system of springs and shock absorbers.

Bike Bites

Be sure that the bike shoes you buy match the pedals on your bike. If you need some advice when adjusting the cleat to your natural riding position, ask an experienced hand at your bike shop. Everyone's foot is different, so you might have to experiment.

Freewheelin' Facts

Campagnolo is one of the best-known manufacturers of bicycle components. This Italian company was founded by Tullio Campagnolo, who is credited with inventing the quick-release wheel hub. The story goes that Tullio had to stop and change a tire during a race through the Dolomite Mountains in Italy. His hands were too cold to quickly remove the wing nuts and he lost his lead in the race. Instead of staying angry about his plight, he came up with a hollow axle and quick-release mechanism for bicycle wheels. Considering how many bikes this device is used on, it must have been quite a patent for Tullio.

May the Chain Be Unbroken

A bicycle chain is a terrific way to transfer energy from the front crankset to the rear cassettes or freewheel. Author Rob Van der Plas states in his book *Bike Technology* that a regularly maintained and lubricated chain delivers 95 percent of its input (that is, your pedaling efforts) as output (turning the rear wheel). The key, according to Van der Plas, is regular cleaning and the lubrication of the weather-exposed chain. Ignore these steps, and the efficiency can drop to 80 percent.

Chains can stretch as the pins and bushings wear out. A deteriorated chain will wear down the sprocket and chain ring teeth, and can break when you least want it to (not that you would ever want this to happen). The straighter the chain's alignment between a chain ring and a sprocket, the more efficiently the drive train functions. The greater the deflection—that is, the angle of the chain—the lower the efficiency. In fact, you should avoid the extreme deflection between the largest chain ring and the smallest sprocket and between the smallest chain ring and the largest sprocket.

That said, the correct length of a chain is such that it can comfortably function when shifted to the largest chain ring and the largest sprocket. Even if you really shouldn't use such an extreme gear, you need a long enough chain to accommodate this gear should you shift into it.

Freewheelin' Facts

Some three-speeds, found mostly overseas, come with closed chain guards that entirely encase the chain. They keep the chain perfectly clean and protected and keep the rider's pants clean. The guards come with a removable access cap for oiling the chain. These are really cool utility bikes and occasionally can be found at garage sales here in the States.

Shifters

Gear shifters have changed remarkably over the years. Some past models, such as certain stem shifters, were awful. Friction shifters, which are held tight by an adjustable nut or bolt, have been replaced with index shifters. The latter type of shifter automatically clicks into the chosen gear, taking any guesswork away from the rider. These shifters must match up with the cassettes, meaning you're looking at one manufacturer for both components.

Derailleurs

Without derailleurs, we would be stuck with either fixed gear bikes or internal hub gear arrangements, both of which limit the rider's options and comfort. Derailleurs not only move the chain from one gear to the next, but the rear derailleur controls the slack in the chain so the chain doesn't slip. As a rule, derailleurs are sold or are intended to be used with the same manufacturer's gear shifters.

Each derailleur has an interesting job:

➤ The front derailleur moves the chain, which is under tension, across two or three chain rings and, in better models, lifts and lowers the chain at the same time to accommodate the different sizes of chain rings.

➤ The rear derailleur shifts the chain across as many as nine sprockets and also moves back and forth, in line with the frame, maintaining some slight tension for smooth shifting.

These being bicycle parts, you can't just pop off your current derailleur and install a new one. Well, you can, but it might not work very well.

Up Front

Front derailleurs are attached to the seat tube either with their own clamp or directly to a braze-on threaded socket. The derailleur is installed so its *cage* is parallel to the chain wheels and just clears the top of the teeth on the largest chain wheel when shifted. Two screws control the *travel,* or movement of the cage. Without the screws, the cage could travel too far in either or both directions and throw the chain off the chain wheels before it has a chance to engage with the teeth.

Derailleur cages differ by their length and width, or distance, between the plates. Different styles are designed to handle a certain range of chain ring teeth; that is, the difference in the number of teeth between the largest and smallest chain ring. A derailleur set up for a touring bike can handle as much as a 26-tooth difference, whereas a racing derailleur might handle only half of that difference. The greater the capacity of the derailleur, the longer the derailleur's cage. Long cages won't shift as quickly as shorter cages, but a shorter cage won't work with a large range of teeth.

When purchasing a new front derailleur, keep the following criteria in mind:

➤ Gear range or capacity

➤ Compatibility with your current gear shifters

➤ Mounting and cable requirements

Some front derailleurs have a cable that attaches at the top and other that attach at the bottom. Others require that a short section of the cable run through cable housing before attaching to the anchor bolt; still others work only with an open, unsheathed cable. If you're not sure what your bike requires, take your old derailleur to your bike shop and buy a suitable replacement.

The Spoken Word

The front derailleur **cage** consists of two parallel metal plates held together with a cage screw. The chain runs through the cage and is moved from one chain ring to another as the derailleur shifter is moved.

Meanwhile, in the Back

A rear derailleur provides you with the bulk of your gear choices, anywhere from five to nine possibilities. Like its front counterpart, this derailleur comes with different cage lengths, which is the distance between the two pulleys that guide the chain. To determine a rear derailleur's capacity or the difference in the teeth range of the rear sprockets, do the following:

1. Add the number of teeth in the largest chain ring to the number of teeth in the largest rear sprocket.

2. Subtract the total teeth of the smallest chain ring and the smallest sprocket and subtract it from the preceding sum.

3. The difference will be the derailleur's capacity.

A rear derailleur must match up with your gear shift levers, especially if you're using index shifters. It was easier to mix and match when friction shifters ruled, but this isn't true with newer components. Like the front derailleur, the rear one also has adjustment screws to control its travel and the angle at which it sits.

Rear Gears

Rear sprockets or cogs range from a single cog found in fixed gear bikes and internal gear hubs to 9-speed cassettes (Campagnolo is now coming out with a 10-speed cassette). Another system of multiple sprockets, called freewheels, is still available; however, it is considered to be old technology and now is found only on cheap bikes. Both systems have a ratchet inside them that allow you to coast without the crankarms moving forward. They also allow you to pedal backward without engaging the gears.

Both cassettes and freewheels are attached to the hub. Freewheels are screwed on to a threaded hub, whereas a cassette body is incorporated as part of its hub. These hubs are not interchangeable. If you currently have a freewheel system and want to upgrade to cassettes, you'll have to build a new wheel.

New derailleur system bikes typically have either eight- or nine-speed cassettes. To accommodate these additional sprockets—remember, ten-speeds had only five sprocket freewheels or occasionally six—new chains are narrower as measured to the *sideplates,* or the outer portion of the links.

Component Groups

In the days of 10-speeds, riders tended to mix and match components based on the preferences and budget of the rider. At the time, Campagnolo, the Italian supplier, was considered the world's premier manufacturer of bicycle components. Many new bikes come with component groups; that is, many of the parts are made by the same manufacturer and made to work together smoothly. Both Campagnolo and Shimano make such groups that include everything from the headset to the hubs.

You get one neat, convenient, well-rated package with the assurance that everything will work in a coordinated manner. This is especially critical with gear shifters and derailleurs, brake levers and brakes, and chains and cassettes. On a new bike purchase, a group component set can make a lot of sense. The key to upgrading a drive train is to not mix and match components unless you're sure they're compatible. This means no Shimano shifters with old Suntour derailleurs unless you know they'll work together. Talk with a shop mechanic who's been around for a while. You'll get an earful of opinions, but should find out about compatibility.

When Drive Trains Won't Drive

I'll deal with specific drive train problems in later chapters. Most can be easily fixed with some select tightening and lubricating. Still, given the number of components involved, you can run into all kinds of pesky and annoying things that can go wrong, including ...

➤ Derailleurs out of adjustment.

➤ Shifters sticking.

➤ Chain skips or slips.

➤ Loose bottom bracket.

➤ Worn teeth on chain rings or sprockets.

➤ Bent pedal spindles.

Some of these problems are easily fixed with a quick shot of lubricant; others are more labor intensive. Like all the other moving parts on your bike, you want your drive train to be running at top efficiency. After all, you're the one doing the pushing.

An out-of-whack power train simply means more work for you. When your riding turns into a long stretch of work (think long ascents), you don't want to be wasting any of your precious energy and efforts. Remember, riding is supposed to be fun!

The Least You Need to Know

➤ Your drive train components work together as a group and cannot be mixed and matched on a whim.

➤ Gear ratios are important for your cycling efficiency and comfort, but in reality you won't use all the gear selections available to you.

➤ Maintaining a good cadence, or rate of pedaling, is less tiring in the long run than pedaling too fast or too slow during a ride.

➤ Derailleurs have to perform fairly complicated tasks, yet require only minor adjustments from time to time.

➤ You can buy an entire group of matched components from a single manufacturer, which ensures compatibility.

Chapter 10

Clean-Up Time

In This Chapter

➤ Cleaners, waxes, and polishes

➤ Saddle care

➤ Restoration tips

➤ Satisfactory storage

A bicycle is terrific when it's new and shiny, like just about everything else we buy and use. It's because we use them that they don't stay new and shiny very long, but that doesn't mean you can't keep your bike's appearance in top form with a little regular care.

The main ingredient in your bicycle is metal. Even composition frames have a lot of metal parts to deal with. These painted and unpainted metal surfaces are exposed to sunlight, rain, road grime, and general grit among other road and off-road menaces. They can pit your paint and alloy surfaces and cause corrosion aside from making your bike look cruddy. A beat-up-looking bike might be a badge of honor to a hardcore off-road rider, but not so to a recreational rider.

This chapter covers cleaning and storage of your bike. You might not clean it quite as often as you do your car or bathroom, but it's easy to do a thorough cleaning and polishing at least once a year during an overhaul. If you tuck your bike away for the winter, a tune-up and a bath will keep it ready for your first spring ride.

Metal Finishes

A bicycle frame and components will be made from a number of metals including steel alloys, aluminum alloys, and titanium. Most frame metals are painted, although some are chrome-plated. All of them will last longer and look better with regular attention. The automotive products industry has had this down cold for years and offers a plethora of waxes, polishes, sealers, and cleaners in every conceivable category and sub-category. Walk into any automotive parts store and you'll see shelves full of this stuff. In fact, these products are appropriate for your bike care as well. The order of events when cleaning your bicycle frame goes like this:

1. Wash the bike with a mild soap and warm water.

2. Thoroughly rub the frame with a mild liquid automobile *polish* or polish/*wax* mix using a clean cotton rag.

3. Wipe off the haze and excess polish with a clean cotton rag.

4. Coat the frame with a light coat of automobile wax.

The amount of work you'll have to do depends on the condition and age of your bike. Don't use automotive rubbing compound, which is too abrasive. It's better to use a milder cleaner and more elbow grease than a coarser cleaner that can scratch the paint.

General Cleaning and Gunk Removal

Unless you're doing all your riding on new, pristine roads in a planned community where it never rains, your bike will get dirty. Off-road bikes get really dirty. One state park near where I live even set up a bike stand and a hose for riders to rinse their bikes off after riding the trails (it's the northwest and those trails get muddy much of the year).

Not-So-Mean Cleaners

Traditional degreasers and solvents are petroleum based for a good reason: They work. It's a lot easier to clean the grease off a chain with kerosene or paint thinner than with, say, liquid laundry detergent. Still, for those of you who are concerned about using these admittedly less benign products, there are alternatives. Some people swear by citrus-based degreasers for their effectiveness and ease of use. Others swear at them for lack of performance. Some citrus solvents can soften or discolor some paints, plastics, and rubber so read the manufacturer's instructions and warnings before using a product on your bicycle. The advantages of citrus cleaners include the following:

➤ Biodegradability

➤ Can be rinsed with water

➤ Pleasant smell

➤ Easy on skin

Try a small bottle of your chosen cleaner before committing to the giant size. Ask your bike shop which citrus cleaner, if any, they use and try some of that brand. Bike shops aren't in the habit of using products that slow down their work and cost them money so you should be able to trust their recommendations.

The Spoken Word

Polish is a cleaner with a mild abrasive material that is used to clean metal and painted metal surfaces. **Wax** seals the surface after it's cleaned to protect it from weather and road dirt.

Bike Bites

If you want a convenient one-stop cleaning kit, look into Pedro's Super Pit Kit, which comes with a wash bucket; three different brushes for cleaning the drive train, components, and frame; sponge; polishing cloth; degreaser; chain wax; and frame polish. Go to www.bikeworld.com/pedros/pitkit.htm and take a look.

Detergent Degreasers Without the Jingles

Detergent-based degreasers generally are safe for paint, plastics, and rubber, but not quite as effective as the citrus-based products according to some manufacturers. Simply use your chosen degreaser straight and undiluted, pouring a small amount onto a rag; then wipe off the offending grease or oil. Do a second wipe with a rag dampened with water and wipe dry.

Polish Makes Perfect

Metal polish comes in paste, powder, and liquid forms. The liquid usually is the mildest and the easiest to use. Don't use the powdered on anything but the bare metal or chromed parts (and even then try the liquid first). You want to remove only the road grime and paint oxidation that soap and water cannot remove. You'll probably end up removing a minute amount of the oxidized paint (see if your rag changes to the same color as your frame), but this is okay. A wax/polish mix does some of both functions (cleans and seals), but doesn't do either as effectively as two separate products.

Polishing Practices

Polishing also includes unpainted, bare metal surfaces. Some small companies specialize in metal finishing and polishing. It is a bit of a science, requiring many steps, but the result is as brilliant a finish as the customer desires. Polishing involves buffing or otherwise rubbing metal with one or more abrasive substances. The finer the abrasive, the more refined (meaning shinier) the finish. If you really get into it, you can give your bike components a mirror-like appearance (which could look either very cool or very tacky, depending on your viewpoint).

For general machine polishing, you really need a bench-top grinder with polishing wheels and different abrasives. Bench-top grinders, so-called because they are portable and sit on top of a workbench, are nifty power tools and can be used for all types of polishing and grinding. Prices start at under $100 for very sturdy and dependable models. To machine polish a component:

1. Remove the component from your bike.
2. Apply a small amount of abrasive to the polishing wheel, starting with the coarsest.
3. Turn on the grinder and hold the part against the spinning wheel until you attain a satisfactory finish.
4. Apply finer abrasives and repeat.

This level of polishing involves very fine abrasives such as jeweler's rouge, tripoli, and white rouge. The abrasives come in a stick form. The edge of the polishing wheel is coated with the abrasive by rubbing the stick against the wheel as it spins. If it's easier to polish the component without removing it from the bike, or if you have a

Derailed

Don't clean and wax your bike frame in direct sunlight. Both products can dry to fast, making them too difficult to remove. Do the work in the shade and be sure that the metal has cooled off if the bike has been out in the sun.

Bike Bites

One low-tech tool for cleaning out the grime between rear free-wheel sprockets is a narrow wood dowel. Just place one end in a pencil sharpener to give it a sharp point and start digging. For the narrower spaces between cassettes, use a popsicle stick after clipping one end into a point with a pair of wire cutters.

chrome bike frame, a drill with a polishing attachment can substitute for the bench-top grinder. After the component has been polished, wipe it off with a clean cotton rag.

Wax Facts

Wax doesn't clean but seals the paint, protects it from moisture, and maintains the shine underneath. It comes in several forms: liquid, paste, and spray. Liquid wax is painless to use and does an adequate job. Just follow the directions on the bottle. Paste wax generally is more effective and will last longer than liquid products; however, no wax lasts forever. Carnauba wax is an old standby that gives excellent results, but is a little harder to wipe off than softer waxes. Spray waxes are okay for quick fixes but not for a long-lasting shine.

Freewheelin' Facts

The J.B. Brooks company began manufacturing leather goods in 1886 and added bike saddles to their product list as early as 1912. Raleigh Industries, known for their line of Raleigh bicycles, bought the company in 1958. Their peak production days were in the late 1950s and early 1960s, although most of their saddles were sold outside the United States. Brooks saddles require quite a bit of handwork and nearly 150 days from start to finish, including tanning time. These traditional saddles have many enthusiastic customers all over the world.

Derailed

Some cleaners and preservatives for vinyl and rubber found at auto parts stores are meant for exterior applications and won't be appropriate for a bike saddle that you're going to sit on. Buy a preservative meant for a car's interior if you want to treat a plastic saddle.

Leather Saddle Savvy

The traditional bike saddle or seat is made from leather; it has been mostly replaced by saddles made from plastic or synthetic materials. Leather saddles are terrific once they're broken in, but the key word here is "once." A thick, high-grade leather saddle will conform to a rider's anatomy as body heat softens the leather, but only after miles of riding and treatment. Additionally, a leather saddle is susceptible to weather, especially rain, if it's left uncovered.

Any standard leather treatment will protect a leather saddle, but products meant for things such as shoes and handbags might rub off on a cyclist's clothing during a ride. The one standard product that's been around for years is Brooks' Proofide, a leather dressing developed by the J.B. Brooks Company, manufacturer of the famous Brooks saddles. The dressing ingredients include natural oils and waxes, such as beeswax, that keep the leather soft and protect it from the weather. If your saddle has seen better days but is still salvageable, treat it with a good cream conditioner and cleaner before applying the Proofide.

Plastic saddles are easier to care for, of course. Simply wipe with a damp cloth and mild soap. Check out your local automotive parts store for vinyl preservatives if you want to add some shine to the saddle. You can try and patch a torn vinyl saddle with a vinyl repair kit, but this might be a short-lived repair be-cause of pressure on the saddle and weather exposure. Still it's cheaper than replacing an expensive saddle and worth a shot.

Tire Care

Tires should be scrubbed down periodically with a stiff scrub brush and mild cleaner. If you want to be really classy about it, go to an auto parts store and buy some tire dressing, which basically is a wax-type product that will give some shine to the tires. It's more for show than anything else, but you'll be a hit with the off-road crowd for at least two minutes before your tires get all caked with mud again.

Restoration Rules

Human beings have funny values when it comes to anything old that has the words "classic," "vintage," or "antique" attached to it, regardless of the item's mundane origins. This is just as true in the bicycle world as the antique furniture world. If you're simply inter-ested in spiffing up an interesting old bike (without going insane about the details), consider a few alternatives to painstaking replat-ing ("recoating" chrome and unpainted steel parts) and hunting down replacement parts for your original brake levers.

There are two basic ways to restore an old, classic bike:

➤ Duplicate all the original conditions, components, and colors.

➤ Modernize the bike with your choice of components and color schemes.

Derailed

Professional detailers disdain some popular automotive prod-ucts. A few are rumored to be poor choices for rubber and vinyl. If you have any concerns, go to a store that sells supplies to detailers and buy there; these suppliers can't afford to sell questionable products.

No Time for Refinement

Let's say you have an old, steel, crankset (crankarms and chainrings) that you want to keep, but it's rusted and has seen better days. If the bike is really old and interesting, you could justify removing the component and sending it out for cleaning and replating. However, if that is beyond your budget or interest level try the following:

➤ Remove the component.

➤ Attach a medium wire brush to your bench-grinder.

➤ Run the brush against the crankset until all the rust is removed and it's clean.

What if some of the metal plating has worn through? Run it against the wire wheel, clean it, apply a coat or two of wax, and keep an eye on it for future corrosion. Wipe it dry after a wet ride and don't worry about it. It's not the perfect solution, but it will do the job. Ab-rasive wheels will clean all kinds of rust off unpainted metal components.

Bike Bites

One Internet-advertised product that looks intriguing is the Vintage Bicycle Cleaning Kit from Menotomy Vintage Bicycles ($14.95 plus shipping at PO Box 2864, Acton, MA 01720, or e-mail Menotomy@aol.com). The kit includes a special cleaning and polishing oil for removing rust and cleaning paint and chrome. Photo examples of the kit's prowess are available at http://oldroads.com.

Rust to Dust

Rust doesn't have to be a serious problem if it's just some superficial corrosion, but it must be removed. On spokes, for instance, just take some fine or extra-fine steel or brass wool and rub the spoke until it's clean and rust free. For good measure, rub a bit of wax over the spoke and wipe off the excess. Rust on screw and bolt heads as well as nuts can be cleaned with a small wire or brass brush and then sprayed with lubricant or rubbed with a bit of light oil (wipe off any excess). Deeply rusted fasteners should be replaced as soon as possible.

Even cables with superficial rust on them can be wiped clean with fine steel wool, but plan to replace them as soon as time permits. Severely rusted cables can't be trusted and should be replaced immediately. A frayed cable should always be replaced as well.

Bike Bites

If nothing else, consider covering your bike with a sheet of plastic if it's stored outside during wet weather. The plastic can be stored on your bike's rack or inside a handlebar bag when it's not in use. It's not a terrific solution, but it will protect the bike.

Dry Storage Is Best

Bikes are kind of like people (no, I'm not anthropomorphizing here) in that they like to be kept out of the elements when they're not in use. (They might like to be kept out of the elements even when they are in use, but that really would be anthropomorphizing and I'm not going to go there.) It's easy to find storage space around most homes in a garage, basement, or utility room. Small apartments and condominiums can be a little tougher (especially if you don't have parking privileges) but you can improvise.

Dry, covered storage will keep your bike in better shape than being exposed to the great outdoors all the time. This is particularly true in dry, sunny climates as ultraviolet light breaks paint down and causes it to fade; salt air also will affect your paint. Additionally, leather saddles deteriorate in sun and wet conditions unless they're covered. Another advantage to indoor storage is that it reduces the chance of theft.

Your bike is to be used, not coddled, but that doesn't mean it should be abused or ignored. Keep it clean and covered up or stored away when you can and you'll get a longer, more serviceable life from it.

The Least You Need to Know

➤ Automotive cleaning and sealing products also work well on bicycles.

➤ An easy way to detail all your bicycle's metal surfaces is to do the job when you do your yearly overhaul.

➤ Even a rusted bike can often be renewed and made usable again when you use the right tools and cleaners.

➤ A high-quality leather saddle can last for years with proper care and protection.

Part 3

Bigger Repairs

Eventually, you'll have to disassemble the major components of your bike if you expect to do your own overhauls. As important as brake, derailleur, and cable adjustments are, for example, there are other moving parts whose bearings need to be cleaned and lubricated regularly, especially those on off-road bikes. All that mud and grit and water have to go someplace, and it might go inside wheel hubs, headsets, and bottom brackets. Even sealed bearings aren't entirely immune to water infiltration and should be checked periodically.

Bigger repairs mean your bike will be out of commission until the component is disassembled, checked and repaired, and reassembled. These are not lengthy jobs, but they must be done carefully. You'll be dealing with some of the dirtier components—the chain comes to mind—but they also are in the most need of cleaning and lubricating. Built-up grime makes for a less efficient machine and more work by you every time you pedal. You can think of all this maintenance as making your riding easier and extending the life of your components.

If your bike hasn't been overhauled in some time or it's a used bike with an unknown history and creaky parts, you'll be amazed at how much smoother it will run after you've taken apart all the bearing components and reassembled with fresh grease. Even lower-quality bikes will improve, sometimes dramatically. Good-quality lubricant, new bearings when needed, and careful adjustments will give you winning results every time.

Don't worry about whether you're getting the adjustments right or not. Your bike will let you know if you have to back off or tighten up a little. It won't pass any judgment on your work; it just might refuse to move! These chapters will help to keep you moving along and keep the friction down.

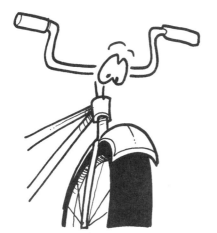

Your Bike's Steering System

Your bicycle's steering system isn't very exciting. It doesn't bring to mind the life-and-death functions of your brakes; nor does it provide the speed and thrill of cranking up through your gears as you race a car down a hilly road (hey, I can't recommend it but we all try it once in awhile). Still, the bike has to go where you want it to go and if you can't steer it, you're going to have big problems.

Like other components on your bike, the steering is dependent on bearings and the cups in which they sit (the headset). You want a bike that's easy to steer; not one that's stiff, too loose, or locks up on you. Usually, we just kind of lean on the handlebars and ignore the headset and the fork. Your steering system must be maintained just like the rest of your bike. It's easy for water and grit to get washed up into the bearings. On top of that, these bearings feel every bump and rut in the road and can become damaged. This chapter shows you how to overhaul your headset so you can steer yourself straight.

The Front End

The shortest of all your frame tubes is the head tube, so it's easy to ignore. It houses all the steering apparatus including the stem and handlebar, the headset, and the steerer tube (the threaded end of the fork to which the headset attaches). Your stem and handlebar are your bike's steering wheel, but perhaps with more choices in style and type than you would find in a car.

Most road bikes come with some form of dropped handlebar. The three types of dropped bars are the *randonneur, road,* and *criterium.* They differ by the degrees of their curves.

Mountain bikes never come with dropped bars, but they do come with various types of upright bars. An off-road rider assumes a riding style different from a rider who's touring or racing on a paved road. A mountain bike's steering system also takes a lot more abuse and has to be made of tougher stuff than a traditional road bike's components.

The headset contains two sets of bearings that allow the fork and handlebar to pivot around and turn. The bearings sit between individual cups and races (the part of the headset where the bearings sit); one race on the fork and one inserted into the top of the head tube. A stem that is inserted into the top of the fork (the steerer tube) secures the handlebar itself.

Unlike other bearings in your bike, the headset bearings are loaded *axially;* that is, in line with the steerer tube (analogous to an axle in this case) rather than *radially,* or perpendicular to it, like axle bearings. You find the latter in the wheels, pedals, and crankset. This means every bump in the road is transferred to the headset bearings. Because these bearings stay in one position most of the time—you don't change direction all that often when you're riding—they are prone to pitting from all these impacts in the same locations.

> **Bike Bites**
>
> When choosing drop bars, find a pair that's approximately as wide as your shoulders for easier, more comfortable cycling. If the handlebars are too narrow, the rider's breathing can be constricted. Women or others with narrower shoulders will want narrow handlebars.

Every part of a headset comes together for smooth steering and control of your bike.

(Courtesy of Campagnolo)

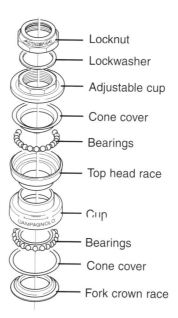

- Locknut
- Lockwasher
- Adjustable cup
- Cone cover
- Bearings
- Top head race
- Cup
- Bearings
- Cone cover
- Fork crown race

Headset Hassles

Headset problems include looseness, tightness, and pitted bearings or races. You can test your headset adjustment by lifting the front of the bike off the ground (or putting it in a bike rack) and trying to move the fork back and forth at the fork crown (at the top of the two fork blades or tips). If you feel any play, the headset is too loose. Now try turning the fork around at the crown. If it's too tight, you'll feel it, at which point you'll need to overhaul the headset.

A headset can come loose from aggressive off-road riding or if it's simply out of adjustment. However, they're easy to check and not too difficult to repair. A tight or grinding headset should be taken apart so you can check the condition of the bearings and races. Also make sure to keep your headsets cleaned and lubricated.

Threadless or Threaded?

Headsets come in one of two types: standard threaded and threadless. A threaded headset is traditional and is still seen on new bikes. It attaches to the threaded steerer tube at the top of the fork. A smooth, threadless steerer tube accommodates a threadless headset, which clamps to the tube.

With both types, the length of your bike's fork and steerer tube will determine your choice of headsets. In some cases, a long tube can be compensated for with various spacers or additional washers for the headset to fit properly. However, this will not work if the headset requires more threading on its own. A short fork can limit the brands of headsets that will fit your bike; each type of headset requires its own type of stem.

Derailed

Threadless headsets don't offer the same range of smaller height adjustments that threaded headsets do. If you're considering changing over your fork and headset to threadless, first check one out on a set-up bike for height and comfort.

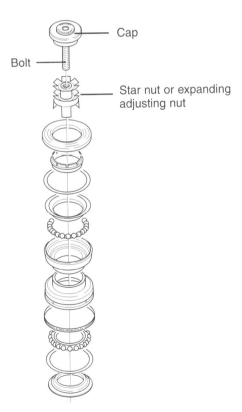

Cap

Bolt

Star nut or expanding adjusting nut

A threadless headset attaches using an Allen bolt and expanding nut.

(Courtesy of Campagnolo)

Overhauling a Threaded Headset

A threaded headset will have either loose ball bearings, ball bearings in a retainer, or some form of sealed bearings. Some of these are not serviceable and have to be replaced. The overhauling procedure for all three bearing types is pretty much the same:

125

1. Put the bike on a rack or otherwise get it off the floor to a comfortable working height.

2. Remove the front wheel.

3. Release the front brake cable.

4. Remove the stem from the steerer tube.

5. Carefully let the handlebar hang loose on the top tube (you can wrap it with a rag or old towel to be sure it doesn't scratch the paint).

6. Using a headset spanner wrench (an open-ended wrench made for removing headsets) or a large adjustable wrench, remove the locknut by turning it counterclockwise.

A headset spanner wrench fits securely around the locknut for easy removal.

(Courtesy of Campagnolo)

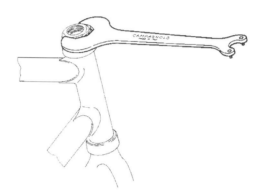

7. Remove the washer (you might need to slip a large screwdriver blade under it and pop it up).

8. Remove any brake cable hangers or reflectors.

9. Remove the adjustable cup by slowly turning it counterclockwise with a wrench. Be sure to hold on to the fork, as this is the last fastener holding it in place.

10. After the adjustable cup is removed, slowly remove the fork. If you have loose ball bearings, cup your hand around the races on the fork so they don't go rolling all over the floor.

Hold on to the fork while you remove the headset, otherwise it will fall out!

(Courtesy of Campagnolo)

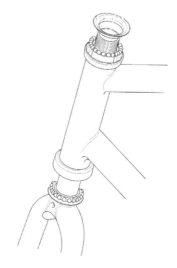

With the fork and bearings out, examine the races and cups for pits. If they're damaged (and this is a bike that you like) replace the headset (see the following page). For a cheap knockaround or commuter bike, you can get away with cleaning the bearings and packing them with lots of grease. To reinstall the fork and headset, do the following:

1. Clean all the bearing, race, and cup surfaces.

2. Install new bearings (you can replace loose balls with a retainer) and pack them in grease; also fill the cups with grease.

3. Place the bearing retainers into the cups with the exposed balls—not the metal ring—facing the cups.

4. Grease the fork race and the top race, and lightly grease the steerer tube and the threads.

5. Insert the fork into the head tube and attach the adjustable cup by turning it counterclockwise and tightening the cup until the fork turns easily and has no side play.

6. Install any brake cable hangers or reflectors along with the washer.

7. Place the headset spanner wrench on the adjustable cup and screw on the locknut, tightening it against the cup until it's snug. Test the fork once again for free movement.

8. Lightly grease and reinstall the stem. Install the handlebars and brake cable and check the headset again for adjustment.

Bike Bites

If you have loose ball bearings, replace them. You should have enough to fill each cup with some space left over for movement. When installing the adjustable cup, tighten it until it's close to the top head race and then turn the fork for the last few turns so you don't disturb the placement of the bearings. If they get bunched up, reinstall them.

If your headset needs only a minor adjustment, simply hold a spanner wrench against the adjustable cup, loosen the locknut, and tighten or loosen the cup as needed. When you're satisfied with the headset adjustment, tighten the locknut until it's snug against the cup.

Threadless Headset Overhaul

Threadless headsets are a slightly different world from their threaded counterparts. The stem holds the bearings and other removable parts in place. There is no threaded adjustable cup or locknut. These headsets need relatively little adjustment but they do require servicing from time to time. To overhaul a threadless headset, do the following:

1. Put the bike in a rack and remove the front wheel and front brake cable.

2. Loosen the stem bolts.

3. Loosen the top bolt that tightens the star nut, which initially secures the stem to the fork. Remove the top cap and, while holding on to the fork, remove the stem from the steerer tube by loosening the Allen bolt(s) that secure it.

4. Lay out all the pieces of the headset you remove in their proper order on a rag or paper towel.

5. Clean everything, replace any bearings in retainers, and grease the new ones along with the races and cups.

6. If the cups or races have to be replaced, go to a bike shop and let them install these components (they have the tools for the job).

Bike Bites

New threadless headsets and stems are more convenient and stronger than traditional quill stems, which tighten against the inside of the steerer tube, and threaded headsets. If you're looking for threadless headsets that will handle tough cycling conditions, try the Chris King brand. It's gotten plenty of praise from hard-riding off-road cyclists.

7. Reinstall the fork and the other parts, reversing the order in which they were removed.

8. Tighten the center bolt in the top cap enough that the fork turns freely without any play.

9. Tighten the other two Allen bolts that secure the stem and reinstall the brake cable and wheel.

Always check your work after the stem and handlebars have been installed for final adjustment. Loosen or tighten the top cap bolt as needed. When you're satisfied with the adjustment, tighten the stem bolts.

Installing a New Headset

Replacing a headset at home without special tools used to install the cups can be an iffy proposition; consider having a bike shop press the cups and races into the head tube and fork. Take your bike to your mechanic to be sure the headset you're purchasing will fit it correctly. Finally, if you choose to install a threadless headset, bear in mind there are some limitations regarding stem adjustments.

Stems

There are two types of stems: *quill* and *threadless*. In mechanical terms, "quill" refers to a hollow shaft in which a second shaft is enclosed, which pretty much defines the older quill-style stem. This is an L-shaped stem with an expander bolt, which holds it tight inside the steerer tube. These stems are made in both alloy and steel models.

A threadless stem is quite different and fits only in a threadless headset. It is a stronger stem and has three fasteners to attach it to the steerer tube. These are increasingly standard on both mountain bikes and road bikes.

Derailed

There's a reason the steerer tube and quill stems get a light coat of grease: The grease protects them from corrosion and makes the stem easier to remove. If a stem is sticking, try tapping the top of it with a block of wood and hammer after the bolt is loosened. If it's still stuck, shoot some Liquid Wrench, a popular anti-seize solvent, down the tube and let it sit overnight.

Stems can be adjusted for height and handlebar angle. When buying a new stem, check that the diameter of the new stem is the same as the old one and be sure the length and height of the stem are suitable to your reach and riding style. The traditional rule for measuring stem length is to place your elbow against the front end of the saddle (the saddle must be positioned first) and extend your hand toward the stem. Your fingertips should just reach the front end of the stem.

However, this measurement might or might not fit your purposes. For instance, a shorter stem can give an off-road rider more steering control in an upright riding position. Like frame size and crankset length, stem dimensions can require some experimentation on your part.

Getting a Handle on Handlebars

Handlebars vary in style and width. This is one bike component that doesn't have any ball bearings (you probably are wondering by now if there is any such animal) and whose installation and adjustment are fairly straightforward. The stem secures the handlebar with one or more stem bolts that tighten around the center of the bars.

You can adjust the handlebar height and the angle at which it sits. To adjust the height of a quill-style stem, follow these steps:

1. Place the front wheel of the bike between your legs and hold it securely.

2. Turn the stem's expander bolt counterclockwise two or three turns.

3. If the stem remains tight inside the steerer tube, it might be that the wedge at the bottom of the bolt hasn't dropped down. To loosen it, place a small block of wood on top of the head of the bolt (you just loosened it) and tap it with a hammer.

4. With the stem loose, twist it back and forth a few times (if necessary) to pull it up a bit from the steerer tube until you've reached the desired height.

5. Tighten the stem bolt and give the handlebar a twist while still holding the wheel between your legs. If the stem moves, it needs to be tightened further.

Derailed

When raising a quill-style stem, pay attention to any marking on the stem that says "Minimum insertion" or something to that effect. You need at least two inches of stem inside the steerer tube; any less, and the bike will be unsafe.

Threadless Adjustment

Threadless stems don't give you as much leeway when it comes to height adjustment because the stem clamps directly to the top of the steerer tube. Adjustments sometimes can be made with the various spacers that come with different models, but if you really need more height, you might need a taller stem.

Lubricate the steerer tube and press the stem firmly against the head- set cone.

(Courtesy of Campagnolo)

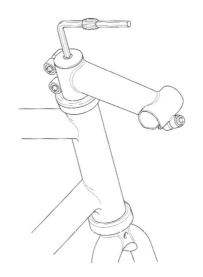

Tighten the adjusting bolt until the fork moves freely, but without play.

(Courtesy of Campagnolo)

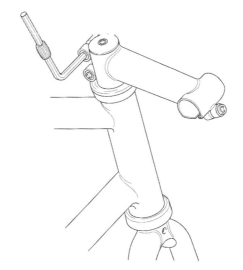

Align the stem and tighten the fixing bolts.

(Courtesy of Campagnolo)

Handlebar Angles

Once you've chosen the handlebar style that best suits your riding needs, you should determine the angle that's comfortable for you. Dropped bars should be angled so you can easily hold on to the ends of the bars. With mountain bikes, you want the angle of the bars to match the angle of your wrists. With any type of handlebars you'll know soon enough whether they're positioned correctly—especially if you get sore. With all styles of bars, you want the saddle or seat to be installed and adjusted first so you can adjust the bars according to your seated position.

Freewheelin' Facts

Aero handlebars allow an rider to lean forward more and provide an added extension to rest hands and elbows. In this position, the forearms help support the rider who is riding almost parallel to the ground with elbows tucked in. Two models are available: *dedicated Aero bars,* which are a single unit and *clip-on bars,* which attach to existing drop bars. Aero bars come in various models; some are longer than others for a fuller stretch. Pads on the bars add to the rider's comfort. Aero bars usually are used on road racers and, to a lesser extent, on touring bikes.

Installing Handlebars

Handlebar installation seems pretty self evident: Loosen or open up the stem, insert the bars, and tighten the stem. True, but there's a little more to it than that. Way back in the old days, you had to finagle the bars through a quill-style stem, turning them repeatedly to move them through the center collar. Many new stems come apart at the collar (also called the *handlebar ferrule* or *central ferrule*), so twisting and turning are no longer necessary.

To install new handlebars in a standard quill-style stem, do the following:

1. Loosen or remove the binder bolt.
2. Insert the handlebars into the collar and begin moving them through, turning and twisting as needed (if they stick some, spray them with WD-40).
3. After reaching the collar or ferrule of the handlebars, turn them to the appropriate angle and tighten the binder bolts; wipe off any excess WD-40 if used.

Bike Bites

It can be easier to install the handlebars with the stem removed from the bike if the stem doesn't have a removable clamp. This is especially true of drop handlebars in which the fit inside the stem's collar might be tight. With the stem removed, there's less chance that you'll bang up the frame when moving the handlebars around.

If you have a newer stem with a removable clamp, simply remove the two binder bolts by turning counterclockwise; then insert the bars, hand-tighten the binder bolts, and adjust the angle of the handlebars. Tighten the bolts with an Allen wrench after you've positioned the bars to your satisfaction.

If the old handlebars have to come out, you'll need to remove both brake cables, one brake lever, any tape or padding from one side, and probably the bar end plug (the stopper that fits inside each open end of the handlebars) on that same side. With these items removed, the handlebars can be slipped out from the stem.

More to Install

Once your new handlebars are installed, you have to install the brake levers, some models of gear shift levers, any handlebar wrapping, and the end plugs. On mountain bike bars, you'll want to install grips at the ends of the handlebars. (Brake lever installation is covered in Chapter 6, "Gimme a Brake!")

Derailed

Before you tape your handlebars, be sure the brake levers are positioned where you want them. You don't want to be retaping because they're in the wrong place. Also, install any brake and shifter cables that run under the tape. Secure the cables to the handlebars with electrical tape so they stay put during the wrapping. Some handlebars have grooves or channels in them to accommodate brake and gear cables.

Taping drop-style handlebars is trickier than it looks. Your first attempts probably won't be terrific, but they should be acceptable. Pick a tape color or pattern that appeals to you. Try to dress up the bike a bit; you can always change it later (and get more practice taping at the same time).

To tape drop bars, follow these steps:

1. If they are old bars, remove all the existing tape and clean off all adhesive.

2. Cut a small piece of tape to cover the clamping bands that secure the brakes to the handlebars. Place one piece of tape over each band to cover it (you might have to hold the tape while wrapping the bars).

3. Start at the top of the bar where it tapers down from the thicker middle section inside the stem and wrap the tape once fully around the bars so the end of the tape is covered.

4. Continue wrapping, pulling the tape taut to keep it stretched, and overlap it by roughly half its width.

5. When you get to the brake levers, fold the hood covers up and out of the way and wrap the tape around in a figure eight, making sure to cover the first half-inch or so of the brake lever nearest the handlebars.

6. Tuck the end of the tape inside the end of the handlebar (only one layer of tape should be inside).

7. Install the bar end plugs.

This is more a learning-by-doing job than many of the others. Not all mechanics agree on the best approach (some start at the ends of the handlebars; some start in the middle of the bars, working their way toward the end). Tape is relatively inexpensive, so you can always redo your work if you're not satisfied with the results.

Get a Grip

Handlebar grips are installed on mountain bikes or any other bike with upright or flat bars. Traditionally, one-speed bikes, children's bikes, and bikes with internal hub gearing (three-speeds, for instance) all had these types of bars. The grips cover the ends of the handlebars and provide a solid, comfortable surface for the rider's hands and, to a lesser extent, act as shock absorbers. A grip should install with some resistance, but not so much that you can't slip it all the way onto the handlebars. If a grip resists too much, you can lubricate it with water, soapy water, or rubbing alcohol. If the grips are too loose for your handlebars, spray the bar ends with hairspray, which will act as a mild adhesive.

Slipping a narrow screwdriver under them and spraying with soapy water or WD-40 can loosen hard-to-remove old grips. If the grip has a hole in it, blow some compressed air into it. This can blow off the opposite grip. With that grip off, put the air hose nozzle in the open end of the handlebar and repeat for the first grip.

The main thing with any grip or handlebar tape is that they be both comfortable and give you a good surface to grab on to, especially in wet weather. If you're replacing your existing equipment, experiment with different products at your local bike shop. You might decide, for instance, that a softer, more shock-absorbing product is more to your liking than some harder or less forgiving materials.

Bike Bites

Handlebar tape comes in vinyl, cotton cloth, leather, and cork versions; almost always with an adhesive backing of some kind. Pre-formed foam inserts also are available and are used for their shock-absorbing properties. Cork is tough to keep clean and can tear if stretched too much. Leather isn't at all common, although some riders swear by it.

Derailed

Never use grease, silicone, or oil as a lubricant for installing grips. This defeats the purpose of a tight fit, as any of these will make the grips too loose. The last thing you want is to pull off a grip during an off-road ride.

The Least You Need to Know

➤ Your steering system is easy to ignore but needs yearly maintenance like the rest of your bike.

➤ You can always change or adjust your handlebars and stem for a more comfortable riding position.

➤ Stem and headset sizes vary so be sure any new replacements are the same size as your existing components.

➤ An out-of-adjustment headset can be a safety hazard and needs to be repaired promptly.

Chapter 12

Bottoming Out

In This Chapter

➤ Bottom bracket overhauls

➤ Chain ring repairs

➤ Choosing your bearing type

➤ One size doesn't fit all

➤ Old-style cranks

Your crankset and the bottom bracket that houses it are the beginnings of your drivetrain. This is where your leg power connects and is converted to spinning wheels. A bottom bracket contains a spindle, two cups, and bearings in various combinations. Like all your bike's moving parts, the bottom bracket components need to move freely and be protected from grit and water.

Your crankset has to stand up to a great deal of stress; not just from a rider pushing on it, but also from a rider standing on it. During tough off-road riding, chain rings and crank-arms can bend, spindles can crack, and the adjustable cup can come loose. Riding on paved roads isn't anywhere near as traumatic (nor as much fun), but even this type of riding mandates that some attention be paid to the crankset.

As a rule, you don't adjust so much as to overhaul a crankset and bottom bracket. New, one-piece, sealed bottom brackets are not even serviced; they are just replaced. They have a pretty good working life, but are more expensive to replace than old-style loose ball bearings. (Technology really does bring great advancements to bicycle design and comfort, but you'll be spending more money to make use of it.)

The Spoken Word

Cotter is a fourteenth–century term that refers to a wedge, key, or bolt that is fitted or driven into an opening to keep two separate things together.

Overhaul Time

A bottom bracket should be taken apart, inspected, cleaned, and greased at least once a year. A crankset, unless its components are damaged, needs only to be cleaned, and have its chain rings and crankarms tightened once in a while. You will have one of three types of cranksets on your bike: one-piece steel, *cottered* steel, or *cotterless* alloy.

One-piece steel cranksets, called *Ashtabula* cranks in the United States, combine the crankarms and the axle into a single-piece, continuous crank assembly. The cups are pressed into the bottom bracket shell with an adjustable race and lockring on the left or nondrive side. The race is reverse threaded, that is, it tightens to the left and loosens to the right. Overhauls are fairly simple, but these are not terribly efficient cranksets. You'll find them on some BMX bikes, kids' bikes, and old Schwinns, especially the Varsity series. These cranksets almost always have ball bearings contained in a cage or a retainer.

The simplest version of a crankset is a one-piece Ashtabula model.

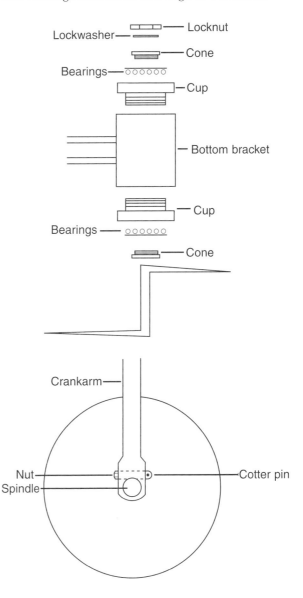

Cottered cranksets used to be standard on introductory model 10-speeds, but are seen today only on the most inexpensive bikes.

136

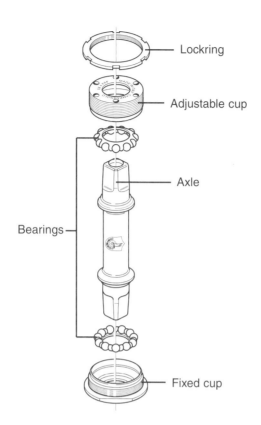

Lockring

Adjustable cup

Axle

Bearings

Fixed cup

Alloy cotterless cranksets are the standard for most new multi-speed bikes.

(Courtesy of Campagnolo)

Cottered steel cranksets are a step up but are rarely seen anymore, except on older 10-speeds. This crankset consists of a steel spindle, steel crank arms, and steel chain rings. The crankarms attach to the spindle with *tapered cotter pins,* which are forced into a hole in the crankarm and rest against a cut-away section of the spindle. This means that all the movement of the crankarms is transmitted to these small pins. Ball bearings in these cranksets will either be loose balls or housed in a cage.

With a cotterless crankset, the crankarm has a greater contact area because it's pressed directly onto the end of the spindle and secured with a nut or bolt. Cotterless components are now pretty much the norm on any decent bike. Older models come with loose or caged bearings; most new ones come with some form of sealed bearings. Each type is disassembled with its own tools and rules.

Attacking an Ashtabula

Unlike other cranksets, Ashtabula cranks don't require any special tools to disassemble them. All you need is a large wrench or channel-lock pliers to loosen them up, but you will need to remove the left-side pedal first. To overhaul these one-piece cranksets, follow these steps:

1. Remove the left pedal by turning it clockwise with an appropriate-size wrench.
2. Turn the large locknut on the left side of the bottom bracket clockwise. Remove it by sliding it down the left crankarm.

Derailed

Bottom bracket dimensions and threading vary. You have to know the width of the bottom bracket, as this will affect the length of the spindle. Threading can be English, Italian, French, or even Swiss on some older French and Swiss bikes. If you're not sure, take the old bottom bracket components to a bike shop and ask a mechanic.

3. Remove the keyed washer.

4. Remove the cone by turning it clockwise (all of these are left-hand threads). If it has notches or grooves in it, you can loosen it with a large screwdriver by pushing the tip of the screwdriver against it.

5. Remove the retainer of ball bearings and slide the cranks out through the right side of the bottom bracket, removing the right-side ball bearing retainer as you go.

6. Clean the bearings, cups, and cones and wipe the entire assembly clean.

7. If necessary, replace any damaged components including the cups, which can be forced out from the inside by hammering a large screwdriver or punch against them, working your way around the edge of the cup. To install new cups, fit them onto the bottom bracket and pound a piece of scrap wood against them until they're set.

8. Rub some grease into the bearings, grease the cups, and press the exposed ball side of the bearing retainers into the cups.

9. Install the crankarm/axle from the right side.

10. Install the left-side cone, adjusting until the cranks turn freely without any play and secure the washer and locknut (the cone and locknut tighten by turning to the left).

11. Check for adjustment again and back off or tighten the cone as needed, followed by tightening the locknut.

Bike Bites

Conversion kits are available to upgrade a bike with a one-piece crankset to a more modern cotterless set. You have to decide if the rest of the bike is worth the upgrade.

Realistically, if the bike is an old clunker, it might not be worth replacing pitted cups or cones, but rather just repacking them with a ton of grease until you replace the bike altogether.

Cottoning to Cottered Cranks

Overhauling a cottered crankset calls for a little less finesse than a cotterless crankset. The cotter pin can be removed with a special *cotter pin press,* which forces the pin out. This is a tool that you do not—and will not—ever own unless you're in charge of repairing hundreds of cottered cranksets as some kind of penance. This is a shop tool, but you can do the job using a hammer and punch if you do it carefully. Figure on replacing the pin with a new one.

Here's how you do the job:

1. Unscrew the nut on the threaded end of the cotter pin until it's just above the end of the threads.

2. Place a block of wood under the crank arm (a length of pipe will work as well and it will catch the cotter pin).

3. Hit the cotter pin hard! If you don't, and have to hit it repeatedly, you can bend the end of the pin.

4. Remove the nut and washer, and hammer the end of the cotter pin again; if it doesn't fall out and is stuck inside the crankarm, take a large punch or nailset and hammer the end of the pin again.

5. It's best to remove both pins and crankarms, but sometimes you can get away with just removing the chainwheel side assuming there's room to tighten the adjustable cup properly.

6. With the cotter pins removed, slide the crankarms off the spindle.

7. Remove the lockring on the left-side adjustable cut by turning it counterclockwise.

8. Remove the adjustable cup, spindle, and ball bearings.

9. Clean the bearings, spindle, and cups, replacing any damaged components.

10. Grease both cups (you'll have to do the fixed cup from the outside using your little finger). If you have loose bearings, place half inside the adjustable cup.

11. Place a ring of grease on the cone-shaped race (outer edge) on the long end of the spindle and carefully place the bearings in the grease. Add more grease to the outside of the bearings.

12. Slowly place the spindle in the bottom bracket and push it against the fixed cup, giving it a spin to make sure that the bearings are still in place.

13. Hold the spindle straight from the outside of the bottom bracket on the right side, and then install the adjustable cup.

14. Tighten the adjustable cup until the spindle spins freely without any up-and-down play.

15. Hold the cup firmly with a wrench and install the lockring, tightening it against the cup.

16. Check again for adjustment and back off or tighten the cup and lockring as needed.

17. Slide the right-side crankarm onto the spindle and insert a new cotter pin, lining up its tapered side with the slot in the spindle.

18. Place a block of wood under the crankarm and hammer the pin into the crankarm (it will be easier than when you remove it). Don't worry; you cannot hammer it so hard that it will fall through, but it must be in as far as it will go.

19. Attach the washer and nut to the threaded end of the cotter pin and tighten (be careful; it's easy to strip these threads).

20. On the left-side crankarm, insert the pin in the opposite direction of the first pin (when you turn the cranks with the right-side pedal up and the left pedal close to the ground, one cotter pin head should be facing the rear wheel, and the other should be facing the front wheel).

It's a good idea to replace the cotter pins when overhauling a cottered crankset. The idea is for the crankarms to be at 180 degrees to each other. A bent or worn pin can affect this separation and consequently affect your riding. Also, once your locknuts are installed, tighten the locknuts, securing the cotter pins after your next few rides.

Derailed

Cotter pins are not all the same size; the thickness varies. Be sure to take your old pins to your bike shop to get an exact replacement. And don't be tempted to grease them a bit before installing them: This can affect the fit of the crankarms.

139

Cotterless Crank Clues

Cotterless crankarms are wedged onto the tapered ends of an alloy spindle in a much more civilized fashion than cottered cranks using cotter pins. The arms are fixed to the spindle with either a bolt or a nut. The following instructions are applicable only for cotterless cranksets with serviceable bearings. Sealed cartridge bottom brackets, which are replaced and not overhauled, will be discussed later in this chapter.

Derailed

Off-road riding can be tough on bottom brackets. If your cranks seem wobbly, you might have a cracked spindle. Any ride or jump that can bend your cranks probably will damage your axle as well. A cracked spindle should always be replaced.

Each manufacturer of cranksets also offers a crankarm extractor built specifically for its products. It is best to use these rather than a universal extractor, although the latter will work in a pinch. The problem is that you never know if your crankset will be the one that doesn't quite match up with a universal extractor; if it doesn't quite match up, you can have problems.

You do not have to remove the pedals to overhaul the bottom bracket. You will need some or all of the following depending on your bicycle's equipment:

➤ A crank extractor

➤ A large adjustable wrench or open-end wrench

➤ A lockring spanner

➤ A pin spanner

Here's what you do to overhaul a standard (but slowly disappearing) cup and cone bottom bracket:

1. Place a rag under the bottom bracket to catch any loose ball bearings that might fall out.

2. Remove any dustcap covering the end of the crankarm fixing nut or bolt. Some older dustcaps are metal and unscrew; some are plastic and need to be carefully pried off with a small screwdriver.

3. Remove the bolt or nut under the dust cap using either an Allen wrench, your crankarm extractor (most have one side for removing a hex bolt), a crankarm bolt spanner, or a socket wrench.

4. If you remove a bolt, be sure to remove the washer as well.

5. With the bolt or nut removed, take your extractor and screw the internal, central pin counterclockwise until it has retracted inside the extractor.

6. Carefully thread the end of the extractor onto the crankarm, hand-tighten, and then tighten with an adjustable wrench until the extractor has been set against all the crankarm threads.

7. Tighten the extractor with a wrench while holding on to the crankarm. As you do this, the pin will push against the spindle and force the crankarm off.

8. With both crankarms removed, loosen and remove the lockring on the left side with a lockring spanner.

9. Remove the adjustable cup on the left side with a pin spanner.

10. Remove the spindle and bearings.

11. Soak the bearings in solvent and clean everything, checking for damage and wear and tear.

12. Grease both cups and install the bearings in the adjustable cup (remember, if they're in a retainer, the exposed side showing the bearings goes in first).

13. If the bearings are in a retainer, rub some grease on them. Put more grease on the cone-shaped race on the long end of the spindle and insert the bearings, adding a little more grease to the side that will sit in the cup.

14. If the bearings are removable sealed bearings, take a small knife and pry up the outer plastic seal, wipe the bearings with a rag dipped in solvent, grease, and reattach the seal.

15. Insert the spindle into the bottom bracket. (Note: The section of the spindle with the greatest distance between the end and the bearing race goes in first. If you're not certain, just be sure any numbers or letters on the spindle would be readable if you could see through the bottom bracket while sitting on the bike.) Hold the right side of the spindle as it comes out of the fixed cup and install the adjustable cup on the left side until it's hand-tight.

16. Tighten the cup with a pin spanner until it's tight and the axle moves freely without any up-and-down play.

17. Hold the cup with the spanner and install the lockring, tightening it against the cup.

18. Check again for movement and adjust the cup and lockring if necessary.

19. Put the right crankarm on the axle and insert the nut or bolt, tightening it with the same tool you used to remove it earlier.

20. Tighten both crankarms, check again for adjustment and play, and then install any dustcaps.

You do not want to grease the ends of the axle when installing the crankarms. This is one place where grease can cause problems, so be sure to install them on a clean, dry axle.

Bike Bites

Grease doesn't just keep things spinning smoothly; it also protects parts from water. Grease acts as a water barrier and inhibits corrosion. Usually, the more grease, the better.

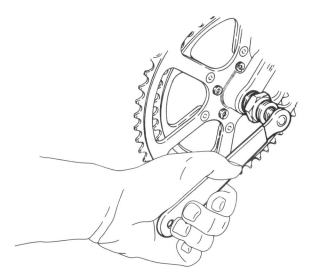

There's no way around it: You need a crank extractor to disassemble a cotterless crankset.

(Courtesy of Park Tool)

Sealed Bottom Brackets

More and more new bikes are coming with some type of sealed bottom-bracket cartridges. These can give you years of service-free riding and are replaced as complete units. They are calibrated to fit standardized bottom brackets and are not difficult to install. Not only that; the fixed cup comes attached, and the unit is fully adjusted at the factory.

You will need a special removal tool from the manufacturer. Simply install the unit from the fixed cup or right side, tighten the cup until it's fully screwed into the bottom bracket, and install and tighten the adjustable cup, making sure to follow the manufacturer's instructions. When you can no longer tighten the adjustable cup, do one final check for adjustment, and your installation is finished.

Sealed cartridge bottom brackets are pretty simple to adjust.

(Courtesy of Park Tool)

Upgrades

There's a world of difference between an inexpensive, cottered crankset and a moderate-quality, alloy cotterless crankset. The latter is a worthwhile upgrade to an older bike that you enjoy riding. Keep these points in mind when you consider upgrading your bottom bracket:

➤ One-piece Ashtabula cranks can be replaced with a conversion kit.

➤ Remove all the old components, including the fixed cup.

➤ Check that the crankarms are the same length as your old ones.

➤ Decide if you want a double or a triple chain ring.

➤ Decide if you want the same chain ring size (number of teeth) as your old crankset.

Derailed

If you do switch to a triple chain ring from a double, be sure your front derailleur can handle the third chain ring. Some less expensive derailleurs will not travel the additional distance satisfactorily.

You'll have to remove the fixed cup when updating a crankset unless the new component is compatible with your existing cups. Check with your bike dealer; most likely, you'll have to remove both cups. Some lockring spanners actually are combination tools with the other end used to install and remove fixed cups, but this can be a difficult job to do at home. Fixed cups are just that—fixed—and fixed big time so they stay that way. They can be tough to get out with a wrench, and there's always a chance the tool will slip. Bike shops have a special fixed cup tool that makes life a lot easier. Consider having a mechanic remove the old fixed cup and install the new one.

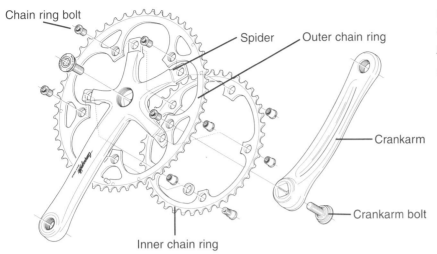

Chain ring bolt

Spider　　Outer chain ring

Crankarm

Crankarm bolt

Inner chain ring

Cranksets come apart easily so individual components can be replaced.

(Courtesy of Campagnolo)

Another consideration is the profile of the crankarm, or its angle as it leaves the bottom bracket. Older crankarms form roughly a 90-degree angle, whereas newer ones will have a bend or two. Matching a crankset with the wrong-size bottom bracket will make for some uncomfortable riding.

Chain Ring Checks

Most chain rings on cotterless, and even steel-cottered, cranksets are removable. The chain rings attach to the right crankarm with small chain ring bolts through a *spider,* or series of short arms that extend out from the crankarm. Because they're removable, you can …

➤ Remove the chain rings and repair bent teeth.

➤ Change the chain rings to those of different sizes.

➤ Replace damaged crankarms without the expense of replacing the chain rings.

Chain rings can be replaced by removing the bolts and sliding the chain ring off (you'll have to remove the crankarm to replace the smallest of the triple chain rings). These bolts should be tightened periodically as part of your bike's general maintenance. A bent tooth can be straightened out by bending it with an adjustable wrench or by removing the chain ring, placing it on a metal surface, and carefully pounding it flat with a hammer. It also might straighten out if placed in the jaws of a vise.

Chain rings and cranksets in general are pretty tough and long-lasting under most normal riding conditions. Riders who put a lot of miles on their bikes or crash a lot off-road are a different story. Like any other component, normal maintenance and replacement when needed is one more step to keep your bike in good shape.

Bike Bites

Chain rings can accumulate a lot of greasy gunk. Wipe them down with a rag or old toothbrush and some solvent every few weeks or after a particularly messy ride. Clean and lubricate the chain at the same time.

Derailed

A new chain and new chain rings will wear down at a more or less consistent rate with each other. If you replace the chain and not the chain rings, the chain might skip over the worn teeth when changing gears. The same is true if you replace a chain ring or a rear sprocket and keep the old chain.

143

The Least You Need to Know

➤ You should plan to overhaul a bottom bracket without sealed bearings at least once a year.

➤ Whenever replacing crankset parts or upgrading to a new crankset, be sure you're buying parts that have the correct threads and measurements for your bike frame.

➤ Sealed bottom-bracket cartridges, which are common on new bikes, cannot be serviced; they are simply replaced.

➤ Bottom brackets are particularly susceptible to water infiltration, so always cover them with plenty of grease.

➤ When overhauling, it's a good idea to replace the bearings.

Chapter 13

Chain Gang: Pedals and Chains

In This Chapter

➤ Pedals styles

➤ Pedal anatomy

➤ Chain conflicts

➤ Clean chains are happy chains

➤ When stretching isn't healthy

A chain is the true workhorse component of your bicycle. The only time it gets a rest is when you're coasting. Otherwise, about half the links are under constant pressure as they are pulled through the front chain rings; the other half go slack as they head back toward the rear sprockets. The chain also is pushed back and forth from one chain ring and sprocket to the next and is expected to perform flawlessly. On top of that, because it needs plenty of regular lubrication, the exposed chain is a target for gunk, especially during off-road riding.

We tend to pay attention to chains when they break or start skipping during shifting. Skipping can be caused by the chain itself or the condition of the gear teeth. Breakage comes with age and one too many pounds of pressure during one too many rides.

Pedals are very low-maintenance components. They tend to keep going and going and generally need only routine cleaning and lubricating. They're also easy to remove and replace because you don't have to remove anything else to get at them and all you need is a wrench. If they're really inexpensive pedals, it's easier to replace them than to repair them. This chapter will show you how to do both.

Chain Facts

Chains come in two different sizes: $\frac{1}{8}$" and $\frac{3}{32}$". These measurements refer to the nominal distances between a chain's inner link plates. The chains are sized to fit over chain ring and sprocket teeth. One-speeds and bikes with internal hub gears come with $^1/_8$" chains; derailleur-equipped bikes come with variations of a $^3/_{32}$" size. I say "variations" because older 10-speed bikes have chains with a wider outside measurement than newer, cassette-equipped bikes. The latter have more rear sprockets than the old five-sprocket freewheels and consequently require a narrower chain to fit them. Both chain sizes are removable for cleaning, servicing, and replacement, but each removes differently.

When replacing a chain or installing a new link, you must know the size of the existing chain so your replacement has the same dimensions. If the new chain is too wide on the outside, it might not shift properly. There are even differences between chain widths that can accommodate 8-speed cassettes, as well as 9- and 10-speed cassettes. If you're uncertain about your chain size, take your current chain or bike to your local bike shop for assistance.

Bike Bites

There are different styles of chain tools, but the simplest and most portable is a simple screw-type mechanism that forces a thick pin against the chain pin when a screw-drive mechanism is turned. These tools are inexpensive and indispensable to anyone doing bike maintenance.

Keep It Clean

A chain is easily the dirtiest component on a bicycle—you wouldn't even have to count the votes for this one. Every pin, plate, and roller (the components of each link) are exposed without protection to the elements. A thin layer of lubricant helps a chain move freely, but also attracts dirt. Riding off-road can really rub the mud in from wet trails.

There are several ways to clean a chain, from a simple wipe to removing it and soaking it in solvent. Some of these cleaning processes include the following:

➤ Place the bike in a rack or otherwise raise the rear wheel off the ground so you can spin the cranks. Dip a rag in solvent and wrap it around the chain as you run the chain through the solvent, wiping away the worst of the buildup.

➤ With the rear wheel off the ground, turn the crank and spray the moving chain with a solvent such as WD-40 (really soak it, but don't spray into the freewheel or cassette bearings) and wipe with a rag, repeating as necessary.

➤ For a really dirty chain, soak it with spray solvent as you turn the crank, but place an old toothbrush or small nail brush over the tops and undersides of the links where the chain runs over the rear sprockets. Do a final wipe with a rag dipped in solvent. The solvent and gunk will spatter and drip, so keep some rags nearby and some old newspaper on the floor.

After cleaning the chain, lubricate it with light oil or any of the many special chain lube products available from bike shops. If using oil, use a light touch with the oil can and wipe off any excess from the sideplates (you need to concentrate only on the rollers, pins, and inner plates). You can be more liberal with many chain lube products because they don't attract as much dirt as oil does.

When Chains Come Off

A $^1/_8$" chain comes with a master link; a U-shaped spring clip keeps it in place. The chain is disassembled by sliding a screwdriver under the clip, prying it off, and pulling the link apart. Another type of master link has the outer plate held tight by two pins with grooves in them. This type of master link is removed by slightly bending the adjoining links with your hands until the plate slips past the grooves and can be pulled off using your fingers or a screwdriver. A master link will be thicker than the other links on the chain, which makes it easier to find.

A $^3/_{32}$" chain is removed by using a chain tool that does one of two actions, depending on the brand of chain:

➤ It pushes out a reusable pin, which can later be pushed back in to connect the chain links.

➤ It pushes out a special pin, which must be replaced and cannot be reused.

At every overhaul, the chain should come off for a good cleaning and lubricating; removing the chain is pretty simple. To remove a reusable pin from a chain and subsequently remove the chain itself, do the following:

Bike Bites

Line up your chain tool so it pushes the pin away from the bike frame instead of toward it. This will make it much easier to reinstall the chain later.

1. Shift onto the lowest front chain ring.

2. Push the rear derailleur cage forward, letting some slack into the chain, and lift the chain off the chain ring. Let it rest on a rag between the chain ring and the seat tube.

3. Place any link on the slot in the chain tool and line up the chain pin with the tool's pin (see the following figure).

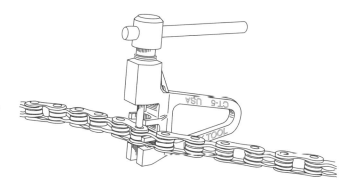

Removing a chain requires an inexpensive, but specialized, chain tool.

(Courtesy of Park Tool)

4. Turn the screw mechanism and push the chain pin out, but do not push it all the way out of the chain.

5. When the chain pin has cleared the inner plates but is still inside the far outer plate, pull the chain out of the tool.

6. Bend the chain gently until the inner plates clear the pin.

7. Holding on to the link with the loose pin, gradually pull the chain off the bike. Once the chain is off, it can be thoroughly cleaned.

Removing Special Pins

With some chains, you can remove any pin to disassemble the chain. In others, particularly newer chains with mushroom-shaped pins, you must look for a single black link or pin that is both removable and reusable (see the following figure). Shimano, among other manufacturers, uses a special pin that is removed and then discarded; only a Shimano special pin replacement part should be used to reassemble the chain.

The Campagnolo perma-link is an example of a single link constructed for removing a chain.

(Courtesy of Campagnolo)

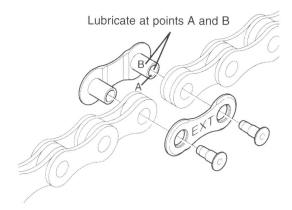

Lubricate at points A and B

Chains with special pins are disassembled the same way as a reusable pin. The main difference is that a special pin is pushed all the way out of the link and then replaced with a new special pin. If this sounds like a nuisance, you're right; if you happen to be short a special pin, you're stuck. They are necessary because of the design of the chain and its pins.

Hi-Tech and Low-Tech Cleaning

If you had plenty of money, you could buy an ultrasonic chain cleaner that combines solvent and vibrations to really get all the grit out. Of course, for the price of one of these machines, a home mechanic could regularly buy new chains for about the next 400 years. You can settle for low tech instead and still get good results.

To clean a chain removed from the bike, follow these steps:

1. Wipe the worst of the mud off with a rag.
2. Place the chain inside an old baking pan or bucket used exclusively for parts cleaning.
3. Cover the chain with solvent such as kerosene and let it soak. You can also clean it with a good citrus-based cleaner.
4. Wearing gloves, pick up the chain, letting the solvent run off, and place it on a section of newspaper.
5. Scrub the chain with an old toothbrush, wipe off with a rag, and place in a container of fresh solvent.
6. After it's soaked and the remaining grime has loosened, remove the chain and wipe it dry.

One variation on this theme is to place the chain and solvent inside a large can or plastic container with a cover, shake vigorously, and then soak the chain elsewhere in clean solvent.

Reinstalling the Chain

Once the chain is cleaned (along with the rear sprockets and front chain rings), you can reinstall it by reversing your removal steps. Run one end of the chain through the cassettes or freewheel and guide it through the rear derailleur. Bring the other end through the front derailleur and hang it between the smallest chain ring and the seat tube. Bring the ends together by slightly bending the link section with the pin sticking out of it and sliding the inner plates inside it, hooking the pin into the hole on the inner plate. Push the pin all the way through using the chain tool, being careful not to push it too far out. Check that the end of the chain pin is approximately level with the surrounding pins.

If you have a Shimano chain with a special pin, align the plate holes in the two sections of chain and push the pointed end of the replacement pin in with your fingers. Push the pin in the rest of the way using a chain tool (you'll want both sections of the pin to pass through the link). After the pin is fully inserted, snap off the section of the pin that's sticking out of the link by grabbing it with a pair of pliers and bending it. File down any remaining rough edge.

Derailed

When reassembling a master link with a spring clip, the open end of the clip faces backward, and the closed end faces (or travels) forward. Remember, the chain is pulling forward; you want the pressure to be against the closed end, not the open end, as there is a slight chance it can loosen the link.

When Chains Go Bad

Chains have their share of problems, but they are remarkably long-lasting given their job and the grime they have to put up with. Some chain problems include skipping, roughness, link stiffness, and being worn out.

Chains skip when they can't grab on to gear teeth and get fully seated. One cause is a worn-down chain ring or sprocket. Put your bike up so you can run it through the gear combinations and watch how your chain behaves. If it skips or jumps only at one particular spot, make sure the teeth are still sharp and defined. A worn sprocket or chain ring should be replaced. Why would one wear down more than the others? Despite all the gear combinations available, most riders will use certain gears for much of their riding, leaving others relatively unused.

A chain that skips in all gears might have a stiff link (see the following figure), which is easily rectified. Run it through the gears and follow the chain as it skips. Find the wayward link and gently bend the adjoining links against its pins. This will loosen up the pins a bit and allow the link to rotate freely around them. Lubricate the chain and run it through the gears again.

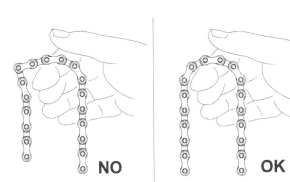

NO   OK

A stiff link makes for choppy riding, but it is easily repairable.

(Courtesy of Campagnolo)

If your chain is running rough, it can simply be worn out and need replacement. The pins wear down through use and the chain can loosen (a condition referred to as *chain stretch*) and then skip. Remember, as the chain wears down the gear teeth also are wearing out. Eventually they will have to be replaced, too.

A maintained chain will last longer than one that's ignored. Give it a quick clean and lube after every dirty, wet ride and at least once a month during cleaner conditions.

Missing Links

You can't toss just any new chain on to replace your old one. It has to be the same width and the same length unless you're changing your gearing as well. Earlier we discussed how width is determined by the space between the rear sprockets and the front chain rings. Some manufacturers, such as Shimano, sell power train systems whose chains, gear teeth, and derailleurs match up perfectly.

Bike Bites

Keep any extra links from a new chain as spares. In the case of a stiff link that won't loosen up, you can always remove two links and install two of the spares. Also, if you change to lower gears with more teeth, you'll want those links to lengthen the chain.

The length of the chain must match up with the gearing as well. If you have too many links your shifting will be sloppy and inefficient; too few and you won't be able to shift into some gears—and even if you can, the chain will be under way too much stress and will wear down prematurely. Follow this guideline when determining the correct chain length:

1. Shift the front derailleur to the largest chain ring.
2. Shift the rear derailleur to the largest sprocket.
3. If the chain works in this gear combination, its length is okay.

Crossing the chain at such an extreme angle—largest chain ring/smallest rear sprocket—is one extreme gear combination that you should never use—the other is the smallest chain ring and the smallest sprocket—because it puts too much pressure on the chain. You want the chain long enough to handle these gears in case you ever inadvertently shift into one of them. When the chain is crossed on the largest chain ring/smallest sprocket, you should be able to pull the chain away from the large chain ring at a distance roughly equivalent to half a link or so.

Bike Bites

There is an add-on component that's kind of the front derailleur's equivalent of a spoke guard. Anti-derailment devices, such as the 3rd Eye Chain Catcher, clamp to the seat tube and prevent the chain from dropping off the smallest chain ring. These devices allow some fudging when it comes to adjusting the front derailleur for some tough gear combinations.

Slipping and Sliding

A chain that drops between the chain rings and the seat tube or doesn't shift properly in the rear actually might be in perfect condition. The problem can be the derailleurs, which can be out of adjustment. Think of the chain as a dumb component, subject to the whims of flashier derailleurs and gears. It goes where it's told, and if the front derailleur travels too far inward, the chain goes along for the ride. Check your derailleur adjustment (see Chapter 15, "Derailleur Systems, Part 2") along with your chain.

Meddling with Your Pedals

Bicycle pedals range from dirt-cheap hard rubber block to high-end platform road models. They all do the same thing: provide a place to put your feet and activate the power train. On the surface, this looks pretty simple, but there's a lot to it given the demands of different riding styles. You don't want to be careening downhill in some off-road paradise of tree stumps and boulders only to have your foot slip off a pedal. Riders who do a lot of standing on their pedals for sprints and off-road riding need dependable, properly fitted pedals. The pedal has to match the choice of biking shoe as well.

Your riding style will determine your choice of pedals. A leisurely ride down the beach on an old three-speed calls for an inexpensive rubber or steel pedal and a pair of flip-flops on your feet. If you're training for a road race across Death Valley, you'll want the lightest, newest clipless pedals and shoes to match. Regardless of the type of pedal—rubber block, rattrap, quill, or platform—the basic construction is pretty much the same and includes …

➤ A metal, rubber, or nylon platform where the rider's foot sits.

➤ A spindle or axle that goes through the center of the platform.

➤ Two sets of bearings around which the platform spins.

Rubber block pedals are found on children's bikes and three-speeds. They cannot be serviced, but are easily replaced. Nylon pedals are some improvement over rubber-block ones (but not by much), which often are replaced when found on cheaper, derailleur-equipped bikes.

Bike Bites

If you're a recreational rider or take long road trips, be sure your biking shoe is comfortable for walking as well as cycling. This can always be accomplished with standard toeclips, but not always with cleats.

Rattrap pedals have simple, rectangular metal platforms and either cannot be serviced or aren't worth servicing. They're generally found on low-end derailleur-equipped bikes. "Rattrap" is an old name that refers to toeclips, which hold the riders foot in place on the pedal. A rattrap pedal is one to which toeclips can be attached. A quill pedal also has a metal platform or cage, but is of higher quality than a standard rattrap. Quill pedals are almost always serviceable and more durable than cheaper rattraps.

Moving up in the pedal echelon, platform pedals offer more space for your foot and are performance oriented. Some platform pedals—called *clipless* pedals—are designed to fit special cleats that fit on the bottom of biking shoes; others are more universal in the shoes they can accommodate.

Campagnolo clipless pedals are one example of modern performance pedals.

(Courtesy of Campagnolo)

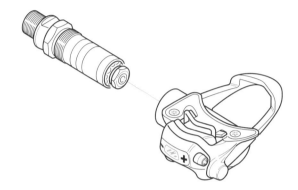

Toeclips: Old Technology That Works

Toeclips are clever devices that attach to quill pedals and platform pedals and contain your bike shoe while you ride, almost like a cage for your foot. Toeclips secure your foot to the pedal and increase your riding efficiency by allowing you to pull up on the pedal in addition to pushing down on it.

Toeclips come with single straps that pass through a buckle and tighten around your shoe. A clipless pedal has the same advantages of a toeclip, except that the bike shoe itself locks onto the pedal rather than slipping inside the toeclip. Your shoe and cleats must match up with the specific brand of clipless pedal you purchase. Mountain bikes and new road bikes typically have clipless pedals.

Clipless Concerns

A clipless pedal is constructed to hold a cleat securely and allow you to remove your foot expediently. This is really important during off-road riding when you might have to make a quick exit from your bike. Your shoe clips should be in good shape (carry an extra pair of shoes or sandals if you have to do a lot of walking); replace them when they are worn down. Your new cleats have to be compatible with the pedal design. Unless you have experience installing and locating cleats on a bike shoe, have the work done at your bike shop.

If you have clipless pedals, be sure your shoe cleats are tightly secured to the shoes with their screws. Adjust the tension on the pedals as needed. Clipless pedal tension determines how easily you can remove your foot from the pedal. The factory tension level probably is set at a minimum, which might be too loose for your standards. Tension adjustment should be kept to a minimum, so tighten slowly, a quarter turn or so at a time. As with any new component, read the manufacturer's instructions in the owner's manual before messing with the pedals.

Bike Bites

Before you start tearing into a pedal, be sure that the pedal isn't simply loose; make sure it's tightened completely into the crankarms. Check your cleats, too. If one or both of them are loose, you could mistake a cleat problem for a pedal problem.

Pedal Problems

Pedals will let you know when they need some attention by getting noisy or difficult to rotate. Pedals should be cleaned and greased with every major overhaul. Off-road riding will move your schedule up to at least twice a year, although sealed bearings are increasingly used on mountain bike pedals to withstand the mud and the dirt that can get into loose ball bearings.

A pedal with loose ball bearings that doesn't move smoothly probably needs to be cleaned and lubricated. If enough grit gets into the bearings, they might need to be replaced. Once you've torn the pedal open, you might as well replace the bearings if they've given you even a hint of trouble. Older pedals typically will have loose ball bearings.

To overhaul a loose ball pedal, follow these steps:

1. Remove the pedals from the crankarms using a pedal wrench or cone wrench.

2. To loosen the left-side pedal, turn the wrench clockwise. Turn the drive side pedal counterclockwise to loosen it.

Bike Bites

It can be easier to loosen the locknut on a pedal spindle if you put the other end, the one where you attached the cone wrench to remove it from the crankarms, inside a vise. Wrap a rag around the spindle threads or squeeze it between two blocks of wood. Once the locknut is loose, remove the pedal from the vise so you don't lose the ball bearings.

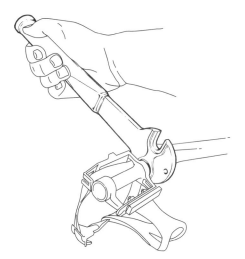

Removing a pedal.

(Courtesy of Park Tool)

3. With the pedal removed, take off the dust cap at the end of the spindle (you can do it with either an Allen wrench, channel locks, or a screwdriver if it's a pry-off type).

4. There is a locknut under the dust cap that secures the position of the cone underneath it the same way a wheel hub locknut works with a hub cone. Remove the locknut and its washer by holding the other end of the spindle with a wrench. Use the ends of an adjustable wrench or carefully use needle-nose pliers (depending on how much room you have to maneuver), loosening the nut counterclockwise.

5. Hold the pedal over a tray or plastic container and remove the cone with your fingers or with the blade of a screwdriver, turning counterclockwise. Count the bearings and dump them into the tray or container (they might have to be removed with a tweezers).

6. Pull the spindle out along with the remaining bearings.

7. Check all the bearing surfaces for pitting and wear and replace any damaged parts and bearings.

8. Clean all surfaces of old grease and grime.

9. Repack both sets of bearings in a bed of grease within each bearing race and insert the spindle (don't turn it—you can loosen the bearings).

10. Install the cone and tighten it until it's just short of touching the bearings.

11. Hold the cone with one hand and turn the spindle with the other as it tightens against the cone (this prevents the second set of bearings from dislodging while the cone tightens against them).

12. Tighten the cone until the spindle moves smoothly but shows a trace of play.

13. Install the washer and locknut.

14. Hold the cone with a cone wrench and tighten the locknut against it.

15. Make sure that the spindle can move freely and doesn't have any play. If either condition exists, adjust the cone and locknut accordingly.

16. Install the dust cap.

Bike Bites

Cone adjustment is an art form. You can get the cone just right only to have it move slightly when tightening the locknut. Be prepared to back the cone off slightly during the final adjustment, whether you're overhauling a pedal or any other component with bearings.

Bike Bites

Sealed bearing pedals aren't all that serviceable by a home mechanic. Take these to your local bike shop and inquire about repairs and maintenance.

If you don't have a cone wrench that can reach the pedal cone, you'll have to hold the cone with the end of a screwdriver while you tighten the locknut. In this case, leave the cone a bit loose because it will tighten some as the locknut is secured. After the pedal is reassembled, put a small amount of grease on the spindle threads and screw it into its crankarm. Remember to tighten the drive-side pedal, turning it clockwise; turn the left-side pedal counterclockwise to tighten.

Pedals are pretty unassuming and go unnoticed. Maybe that's because they spend so much time under our feet. Like every other moving part on your bike, the smoother they move, the less work you have to do. That in itself is a positive motivation to keep them maintained.

Derailed

Be sure that any replacement pedals have the same threading as your current pedals. If you try to force an Italian threaded pedal onto an English threaded crankarm, you'll ruin the softer alloy threads in the crankarm. If you're uncertain of the threading, either check with a shop or slowly tighten the new pedal to the crankarm. A lot of resistance is a signal to stop and check the threading.

The Least You Need to Know

➤ Chains are not interchangeable and every power train requires a specific size of chain to operate properly.

➤ As the dirtiest part of your bike, the chain needs regular cleaning and lubrication for smooth running.

➤ Chains and gear teeth wear down together, so replacing one but not the other can cause some problems.

➤ Pedals come in various styles and are adaptable to different riding shoes; clipless pedals must be carefully matched to your shoes.

Chapter 14

Derailleur Systems, Part 1

In This Chapter

➤ Working principles

➤ Design features

➤ Shifter styles

➤ Adjusting shift levers

Multiple gears on a bicycle exist to help the rider confront any riding conditions. If human beings could put out a greater amount of power—say, a couple hundred horsepower, just to pick a nice, round, impossible number—we could get along quite well with single speed bicycles. Because we can only pump out so much horsepower, the different gears help us make the best use of it. Multiple gears also make the ride more enjoyable.

A derailleur system, as opposed to internal hub gears, provides the greatest range and number of gears—up to 27 distinct gears on modern bikes. We tend to think of derailleurs as modern components, but patents were filed as early as 1890s for an array of front and rear gear-changing components. They were awkward, but they were a start.

This chapter will take you through the design and function of front and rear derailleurs. They're not difficult to maintain and tend to keep to themselves once they're installed and adjusted. Like everything else on your bike, your derailleurs and shifters will need to be tuned up from time to time.

How They Work

Derailleur systems are made up of three components: gear shifters, cables and housing, and the derailleurs themselves. Gear shifters come in many shapes and sizes, all of which perform the same job. Left to its own devices, a derailleur will drop into a position that puts the least amount of tension on it. A gear shifter secures one end of a cable that maintains tension on a derailleur and shifts it around from one chainwheel or sprocket to another. Moving the shifter in either direction changes the gears for the rider.

Freewheelin' Facts

One of the earliest developers of derailleur systems was Paul de Vivie, a Frenchman born in 1853. In 1905, he tested a two-speed derailleur he named the Cyclist. M. de Vivie was a strong advocate of bicycling and derailleur engineering. It is said that to convince bicycle racers that multi-geared bikes were an improvement over single-speed racing bikes, he challenged a champion racer to race along a mountainous route against a young woman riding a three-speed. The race took place, and the woman won. There's nothing like an attack on a male ego to spur along innovation.

Derailleur designs and dependability have improved over the years, but derailleurs all perform the same functions. A front derailleur has to force a chain back and forth across two or three chain rings. The rear derailleur must move the chain among five to nine rear sprockets and maintain chain tension among the different-size sprockets. Adjustment screws limit the movement of each derailleur so the chain doesn't move beyond the chain rings or the sprockets.

When Push Comes to Shove

Derailleurs work as the rider pedals the bike. The chain rings or rear sprockets must be moving for the derailleurs to move the chain. When a derailleur moves, the chain, which is happily moving along in one gear, is forced off at an angle to mesh with the teeth of another chain ring or sprocket.

Chains on derailleur-equipped bikes run at different angles as they are moved from gear to gear. This leads to more wear and tear on the pins, rollers, and plates than you'll find in the straight chain drives of single- and three-speed bikes. This is one of the reasons chains wear out faster in derailleur systems than in fixed-gear or internal hub–gear bikes.

The front derailleur is mounted on the seat tube and has a moving metal cage that runs vertical to frame. As the shift lever is moved back or forth, the cage moves the chain to an adjoining chain ring. The rotating teeth of the chain ring catch the chain as it meshes with the teeth.

The rear derailleur has a different sort of cage; it contains two rotating pulleys that guide the chain. This cage runs parallel to the sprockets and maintains enough tension in the chain to keep it from slipping off the sprockets. Like the front cage, the rear one keeps the chain from wandering around on its own.

The Shifters

The first component in the derailleur system is the gear shifter; there's a shifter for every style and taste. Some are attached to the frame on the down tube and others can be found in different locations on the handlebars. Modern index-type shifters are the standard on new bikes and the most accurate when it comes to shifting. Instead of feeling your way around looking for gears, index shifters automatically click to the chosen gear.

Down tube friction shifters, which are mounted on the down tube and whose levers stay in adjustment by the simple tightening of a bolt, are pretty much a thing of the past, but they are elegant in their simplicity. When the bolt loosens from prolonged use, simply tighten it up some, and you're back in business. Down tube shifters are secured to the down tube in one of the following ways:

➤ An integral clamp wraps around the tube.

➤ The shifters bolt directly to down tube bosses, small threaded braze-ons that are a permanent part of the frame.

These shifters are the easiest to adjust, but not the easiest to use. The friction bolts on cheaper shifters must be adjusted with a screwdriver. Others have some form of finger-adjusted wing or D-ring bolts that can even be adjusted as you ride. Higher-end models are pretty good about staying taut without needing much attention.

Freewheelin' Facts

One old-style front derailleur changer was a pull-and-push–type plunger mounted on the bottom of the seat tube. The rider had to reach down toward the crankset to change gears. This was hardly the most convenient arrangement.

Friction Shifter Fits

If you still have smooth working down tube shifters and you're comfortable with them, there's no reason to replace them. The only maintenance these shifters need is an occasional shot of lubricant and a tightening. If they are particularly gunked up, do the following:

1. Push the shifter lever forward and loosen the cable anchor bolt on the derailleur.

2. Remove the cable from the small opening in the shifter where it is seated.

3. Unscrew the mounting bolt and remove the bolt, shifter, and any washers and spacers, noting their order.

4. Lay the pieces out in order on a rag and wipe them clean with a rag dipped in a small amount of solvent.

5. Reinstall the shifter pieces in reverse order and hand-tighten the mounting bolt (give it a good twist), pushing the shifter all the way forward.

6. Install a new cable (see the following figure) and stretch the cable by running through the high and low gears and moving the shifter back and forth a few times.

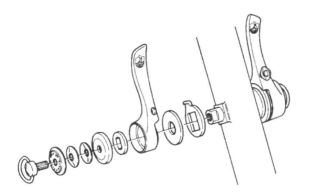

Down tube shifters are still available, but not as popular as they were in the days of 10-speed bikes.

(Courtesy of Campagnolo)

159

7. Move the shifter all the way forward; if necessary, loosen the cable at the derailleur and pull it until it's taut. Don't go crazy here; it needs only to be snug.

8. Adjust the tension in the mounting bolt so the shifter moves smoothly but doesn't slip around once it's moved to one gear or another.

When all your adjustments are done, give each shifter a squirt of spray lubricant. If you're installing new shifters, they will either attach directly to brazed-on bosses or, if they come with an integral clamp, they will be installed directly above a small stop brazed to the top of the down tube.

Cable Connections

Derailleur cables run from the shifters to individual anchor bolts on each derailleur. The routing of the cables varies with each bike. Cables can be routed through ...

Bike Bites

Before installing down tube shifters that come with their own mounting clamp, wrap a single layer of handlebar tape around the tube. This protects the paint from the clamp. Replace the tape any time you remove the shifters for maintenance.

➤ Braze-ons just above the bottom bracket.

➤ Braze-ons under the bottom bracket.

➤ A clamp-on guide for both cables that attaches to the bottom of the down tube. If your bike has a clamp-on guide, a small piece of cable housing will run from the guide to the derail-lelur. The housing is needed to hold the cable in an even curve and be able to operate the derailleur.

To install down tube shifter derailleur cables, do the following:

1. Place the shifter in the forward position.

2. Thread the cable from above until its end fitting is seated in the opening in the shifter.

3. Run the cable the length of the down tube to the cable guides at the bottom bracket.

4. Guide the cable to its respective derailleur.

5. If your system calls for a section of cable housing to be installed between the cable guide and the derailleur, grease the section of the cable that will run through the housing (there is a cable stop on the chain stay as opposed to a cable guide).

6. Thread the end of the cable through the housing (if required) and through the anchor bolt of the respective derailleur.

7. Pull the cable end with needle-nose pliers and tighten the anchor bolt.

8. Move the levers back and forth a few times to stretch the cable.

9. If the cable is too loose (the derailleur won't immediately move when the shifter is pulled back), push the shifter all the way forward, loosen the anchor bolt, and give the cable a tug with the pliers.

10. Tighten the anchor bolt and test the derailleur adjustment again.

Derailed

Some really awful, cheap bikes once came with stem shifters and the derailleur cables entirely encased in cable housing. If you have one of these and can possibly justify keeping it, just junk the shifters and install a pair of used down tube shifters. Anything will be an improvement!

11. Cut the excess cable off, leaving two inches or so past the anchor bolt. If you have one, place an end cap on the cable.

Cable Conundrums

A sticky cable can hang up a derailleur. Sometimes a cable will stick because the housing is full of grime or the cable is rusty. Other times, the cable housing loop at the rear derailleur is too short and the cramped cable prevents smooth shifting. A little attention paid to the cable routing will go a long way toward smooth shifting.

Bar End Shifters

Bar end shifters were popular on some racing and touring bikes before the introduction of shifters integrated with brake levers. A shifter located at the end of the handlebars allows the rider to keep both hands on the handlebars while changing gears. The drawback to this model of gear shifter is that the longer cable makes for somewhat slower shifting.

Bar end shifters encase the derailleur cables inside cable housing from the shifters to the first cable stop located on the down tube. These stops are either brazed to the down tube or are a clamp-on style that attach where down tube shifters normally would be installed. The cable housing runs along the underside of the handlebars where it is wrapped with handlebar tape. Often, the housing runs until just past the first bend in the bar and then is routed toward the cable stop. If the housing does not run along the handlebars for this distance, the cable won't be rigid enough to shift properly.

Bike Bites

On mountain bikes, depending on the type of derailleur, the cable can enter from either the top or the bottom of the front derailleur. Be sure you understand the routing before you install the cable.

Bar end shifters are convenient and normally seen on road and touring bikes.

(Courtesy of Campagnolo)

To install bar end shifters, take the following steps:

1. Run the cable housing by measuring a length of it from the end of the handlebar to the first cable stop on the down tube. It will need enough loop to allow the handlebars to steer without restriction.

2. Start the housing flush with the end of the handlebar, running along the bottom, and tape it with a piece of thin tape, such as electrical tape, to secure it.

3. Wrap a single layer of electrical tape around the cable housing in a couple of other locations to secure it.

4. The body of the shifter has an expander-type plug that fits inside the handlebar. Insert this into the end of the handlebar, align the cable hole with the cable housing (it

161

should point straight down), and turn the hex bolt inside the body counterclockwise with an Allen wrench until it's tight.

5. Place the lever into the wide slot in the shifter body and line it up so the pivot bolt can be pushed through the body and the shifter.

6. Tighten the bolt through the recessed nut on the opposite side of the lever body.

7. Move the shifter up and down a few times and place it in vertical position by pushing it all the way forward (it will be pointing down).

8. Lightly grease the cable and thread it through the slot on the shifter and through the cable housing.

9. Connect the other end of the cable to its respective derailleur and run through the gears to stretch the cable.

10. When you're satisfied with the adjustments, install the slotted locknut with a large screwdriver to the end of the pivot bolt.

11. Wrap the handlebars with new tape.

Freewheelin' Facts

Gear-changing systems originated with James Watt, who patented a two-speed transmission for steam carriages in 1784. Hundreds of patents for gear changers in machines and bicycles were applied for in the late nineteenth and early twentieth centuries. These included internal hub gear systems—both two-speeds and three-speeds—and external derailleurs. The most enduring three-speed from these times is the English Sturmey-Archer hub.

Integrated Shifter/Brake Levers

Integrated shifter/brake levers (see the following figure) are terrific and expensive, and found on both road and mountain bikes. These are index shifters that usually come with thumb and finger controls—one for shifting into higher gears and one for downshifting. The advantage for a competitive rider is the ability to shift while climbing and standing on the pedals, as the rider's hands normally are resting on the brake levers at this time. A racer can shift to a lower gear as needed to match leg power to the ascent. The drawback is that if one component in the shifter/lever breaks, you have to replace the entire unit. Because usually they come in pairs, you have to buy two of them for the one that you need. Rider complaints have influenced manufacturers to bring back the old system of separate gear shifters and brake levers and get away from integrated units.

Installation instructions vary depending on the manufacturer of the shifter/lever. The following guidelines will get you through most installations, but always follow the printed instructions that come with your component:

1. Examine your lever for a section of the plastic cover plate that is attached with a screw over the approximate location of the cable end.

2. Remove this cover plate.

3. Place the shifter in the lowest gear and insert the cable.

4. Run the cable through its housing and connect to the derailleur.

5. Reinstall the cover and run through the gears a few times.

6. Tighten the cable at the derailleur if necessary and run through the gears again.

7. If fine-tuning is needed to tighten the cable, use the barrel adjuster.

8. While the cover plate is off, lightly spray the interior of the lever with lubricant.

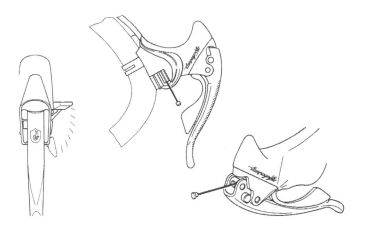

Combination brake/shift lever are really convenient for competitive road racers.

(Courtesy of Campagnolo)

Mountain Bike Shifters

Mountain bikes have introduced a lot of new bike technology and design; gear shifters are no exception. Twist-grip shifters, different types of thumb shifters, and shifter/lever units are all available on mountain bikes. You would have to have a really old mountain bike to find down tube shifters.

Twist-grip shifters combine handlebar grips with a shifting mechanism. Thumb shifters are located either below the handlebar or above it depending on the manufacturer. Some shifters must be replaced when one of their components breaks, but all can be serviced for cleaning, lubrication, and cable replacement.

Twist-Grip Shifters

You don't find twist-grip shifters as often as other types. Some riders like them for their convenience; others think they put too much stress on the wrists. These shifters get dirty. Muck and dirt seep inside; they also can be tough to shift and can slip out of gear. Sometimes it's simply a matter of lubricating or replacing the cable. Other times the mechanism has to be disassembled and cleaned and lubricated.

Twist-grip shifters differ by manufacturer and age. Some older models require disassembling before installing the cable. Others are simpler to work with. For these newer models, do the following:

1. Place the shifter in the forward position.

2. Open the cap that covers the end of the cable.

3. Remove the old cable, noting how it sits in the shifter.

4. Lightly grease or oil the new one and install.

5. After connecting the cable to the derailleur, run through the gears a couple of times and adjust the cable for any slack (if necessary) using the barrel adjuster for fine-tuning.

All Thumbs

There are a number of thumb shifters made for mountain bikes. New versions are index shifters; older ones can be either friction or ratchet style. For those not integrated with the brake levers, maintenance is pretty much the same. To install a new cable, do the following:

1. Remove the old cable by turning the anchor bolt on the derailleur counterclockwise.

2. Pull the cable from the derailleur and any housing; then pull it out of the shift lever.

3. Push the lever in the forward-most position and install the new cable so it's seated in the shifter.

4. Lightly grease the cable and reroute it to the derailleur, attaching it at the anchor bolt by pulling it taut with a needle-nose pliers.

5. Stretch the cable by running the derailleur through all the gears a couple of times.

6. Check the cable for adjustment. If you have too much slack, loosen the anchor bolt and pull the cable taut again.

7. Do a final adjustment check by running the derailleur through the range of gears.

If the shifter has to be removed for cleaning or replacement …

1. Remove the handlebar grip.

2. Loosen the bolt that secures the shifter's clamp to the handlebars.

3. Slide the shifter off the handlebars.

Bike Bites

If you disassemble the shifter for cleaning, keep track of the parts, especially if you have an older friction shifter that will involve various washers. Place the parts on a rag or paper towel so you can note their order.

Chain, Chain, Chains

The bike chain transfers power from the crankset to the rear cassettes or freewheel. A modern 27-speed bike will have a narrow profile $3/32$-inch chain. Any replacement chain must be the same size as the original, otherwise the new chain might not work properly.

For a chain to work smoothly with your derailleurs, it should be kept clean and lubricated and must be long enough to shift to all gear combinations. (Chains are covered in Chapter 13, "Chain Gang: Pedals and Chains.")

No single component on your bicycle stands alone. Each depends on—or is in some way tied to—another to make the whole package work. The chain, derailleurs, cables, and gear shifters all work together (at least they should) as major components in your power train. Regular maintenance will keep all of them running smoothly and keep you on the road.

The Least You Need to Know

➤ Derailleurs don't stand alone, but are part of a system that includes the gear shifters and derailleur cables.

➤ There are gear shifters for every taste and riding style; the newest index shifters are the smoothest operating yet.

➤ The chain might look like a dirty mess, but it's a critical part of the drive chain and shouldn't be ignored.

➤ Many shifting problems are centered with the cables and their adjustment, not the derailleurs themselves.

Chapter 15

Derailleur Systems, Part 2

In This Chapter

➤ Finding the right size

➤ Shift fits

➤ Tweaking and tuning

➤ Replacement and installation

Derailleurs are fairly self-contained, as long as you don't smash them up in an accident or toss the bike down on its right side. They're very exposed to the elements, just like the chain, so they do need regular cleaning and lubricating to keep them happy. This is one time when internal hub gears—a three-speed, for instance—have the upper hand because they never get dirty and can get by with a few drops of oil from time to time.

As your bike shakes and vibrates, especially from off-road riding, the different adjusting screws that limit the travel of a derailleur can move a bit and need tightening. Dirt gets into the pulleys or other moving parts and can make shifting mushy and uneven. Often the problem lies with the cable or the shifter, not the derailleur itself. This chapter will take you through derailleur adjustments, installations, and appropriate component selection for your bike.

Sizing Up

Derailleurs vary in quality, price, and capacity. The last term indicates the range of chainring teeth or sprocket teeth that the derailleur can comfortably move around while it brings the chain along with it. If you change any of your gearing without accounting for your derailleur capacity, your current components might not handle the additional teeth. Conversely, if you have large capacity derailleurs and you change to higher range (fewer teeth) cassettes, your rear derailleur will shift more slowly than one designed for a higher gear range.

Quality is another issue. Some derailleurs of the early 10-speed days left a lot to be desired. They worked, but were awfully stiff and imprecise, especially some French models. Suntour, a Japanese component company, came out with greatly improved, moderately priced derailleurs that were vastly superior to these clunkers.

Derailleurs also differ by their cage dimensions. The greater the difference in teeth from one chain ring to the next, the longer and wider the front derailleur cage needs to be for efficient shifting. The same is true for the rear derailleur. For this reason, touring bikes, with their wide gear range, usually have derailleurs with long cages. The rider is expecting smooth, but not necessarily fast, shifting. A racer, on the other hand, needs quick shifting. With a higher gear range (thus fewer teeth on the chainrings and sprockets), racing derailleurs work quite well with shorter cages.

The Spoken Word

A **spoke guard** is a metal or plastic disc that sits between the freewheel or cassettes and the spokes. It acts as a barrier to an errant derailleur that might otherwise travel into the spokes and ruin itself and the wheel.

A Shift Too Far

Derailleurs are adjusted to control their travel, or how far they move the chain from one gear to the next. The adjustments differ with every bike and every set of chainwheels and cassettes. It's particularly critical that the rear derailleur is properly adjusted, because it can travel into the spokes if the adjustments are off. The result isn't just a missed gear, but a bent derailleur and a ruined wheel. A *spoke guard* usually prevents this damage, although hardcore riders, especially racers, tend to remove these. Each derailleur also has adjustment screws that limit their travel.

Front Derailleur

The front derailleur (see the following figure) moves the chain across the front chain rings. It attaches by means of a clamp or by bolting directly to a boss or socket that's brazed to the seat tube. The derailleur's cage is parallel to the chain rings. It should be positioned on the seat tube so the cage just clears the teeth of the largest chain ring (manufacturers usually recommend a 2mm clearance). If the derailleur is mounted too high, it won't shift properly.

An out-of-adjustment front derailleur will reveal itself in one of the following ways:

➤ It can overshift and fall off the large chain ring.

➤ It might not shift far enough to the right; therefore, the chain won't mesh with the large chain ring.

➤ It can overshift in the opposite direction and fall between the small chain ring and the frame.

➤ It can undershift and fall between two chain rings.

It's not the end of the world if the chain falls off the large chain ring, because you can always stop and put it back on manually. However, when a chain drops between chain rings or between the small chain ring and the frame, it can be a real job pulling it out. This is especially true with new triple chain rings, which have narrow clearances.

The front derailleur has to perform when the chain is under a lot of pressure. This makes shifting difficult when a rider is pedaling hard. Even an index shifter can be a little uneven under these conditions.

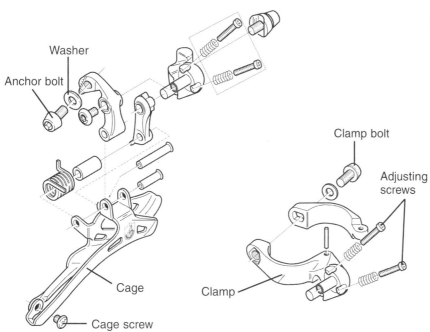

Washer

Anchor bolt

A front derailleur has to move a chain sideways as well as up and down with every shift.

(Courtesy of Campagnolo)

Clamp bolt

Adjusting screws

Cage

Clamp

Cage screw

Adjusting the Front Derailleur

You can't completely adjust one derailleur without adjusting the other, as they affect each other's positions to some extent. If your front derailleur is falling off one or more of the chain rings or isn't shifting all the way onto a chain ring, do the following:

1. Look at the derailleur from above to be sure the cage is aligned with the chainwheels. If necessary, loosen the bolt securing the derailleur to the seat tube and adjust the cage.

2. Make sure the cage just clears the top of the teeth on the largest chainwheel.

3. Find the two adjusting screws for the high and low ranges of the derailleur.

4. Place the derailleur and chain over the smallest chain ring and on the largest rear sprocket.

5. Turn the low-range adjusting screw until the chain just clears the inner (closest to the frame) side of the cage when it's in the lowest gear. The low-range adjusting screw is nearest the frame on older-model derailleurs, but its position might be reversed on new models. (See the following figure.)

6. Shift up to the larger chain ring and then back again a couple of times and check the derailleur setting.

In the low setting, the outer side, or *plate,* of the cage pushes the chain onto the smallest chain ring just enough without pushing it off. The position of the inner plate will prevent it from overshooting the chain ring and dropping off.

Derailed

Your drive chain should be in perfect tune if you're going to be shifting while standing up on your pedals and doing ascents. This puts the most pressure on the front chain rings and the chain and creates the most difficult shifting environment. It's especially hard with old derailleur and friction shifter systems.

169

Front derailleur travel adjustments are usually small turns of the high- and low-range adjusting screws.

(Courtesy of Campagnolo)

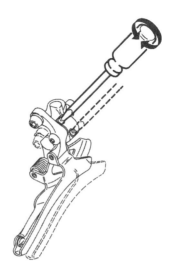

Shifting to the High Ground

High-range adjustments to the front derailleur are as simple to do as low-range adjustments. Turning the head of a screw is a pretty basic repair that anyone can do, and if you over- or under-tighten, you can redo the repair with a twist of a screwdriver.

To adjust the front derailleur for its high range, do the following:

1. Move the derailleur and chain into the highest gear (largest front chain ring, smallest rear sprocket).

2. Set the adjusting screw so the chain clears, but just about rubs against, the outer cage plate.

3. Run the derailleur through the front chain rings and check its adjustment.

Derailed

New component groups—including a crankset, derailleurs, cassettes, and gear shifters—are built to work together smoothly. If you have shifting problems, make sure the chain rings and cassettes are lined up properly. It could be that your bottom bracket needs to be faced off (milled and finished flat with the sides parallel to each other) or your frame has an alignment problem. Make sure the chain rings aren't bent or otherwise deformed and that the bottom bracket isn't loose.

Remember, some gears just aren't meant to be. This includes any gear with the chain at an extreme angle (largest chain wheel to the largest sprocket or smallest chainwheel to the smallest sprocket). What if you've adjusted the cage travel correctly, but the performance leaves something to be desired? Run the derailleur through the chain rings and observe the distance between the cage and the chain. If it looks as if there's more space than the chain needs, use a pair of pliers or a small adjustable wrench to slightly bend or toe in the front tips of the cage plate. This will be a slight bend inward to redirect the chain in the direction you need it to move.

New component systems are so precise that toeing them in might adversely affect their performance. Every component—in this case, the derailleurs, chain rings, chain, and rear sprockets—are designed to work together with a minimum of adjustment. Retrofitting new derailleurs to an existing set of chainwheels is an exception and might require the cage to be toed in some since the chain rings aren't part of the derailleur's component group.

Just a Trim, Please

Sometimes, regardless of how you fuss and adjust, the chain can rub against the front derailleur cage. This can happen as you change gears with the rear derailleur and the angle of the chain changes. On old 10-speeds, this is a common occurrence and can be rectified by trimming or slightly moving the front derailleur back or forth until the chain clears it. This is simple to do with old friction shifters where such minute adjustments require only a slight move of the shifter.

Modern index systems are so exciting that trimming is called for only if the cable stretches and the derailleur goes out of adjustment. In that case, you can trim it during a ride by turning the cable barrel adjuster near the gear shifter. When you get home, tighten the cable as needed and return the barrel adjuster to its closed position. If you have to trim, do so; otherwise, the chain can cut a groove into a cage, and the derailleur will no longer shift properly.

Cleaning and Lubing

Unless it's really decrepit and hasn't been cleaned in a few seasons (not very likely, but you might end up with a bike that's been in storage for a long time), most front derailleurs can be cleaned in place and lubricated. It's easiest to just wrap a rag around the frame and give the derailleur a healthy shot of WD-40. Scrub it with an old toothbrush, spray again, and wipe the derailleur off with a clean rag. Lightly oil the moving parts or use an appropriate spray lubricant.

If the derailleur needs to come off, do the following:

1. Move the gear shifter forward, loosen the anchor bolt at the derailleur, and pull the shifter cable out.
2. Remove the chain and clean it as well.
3. Unscrew the bolt that secures the derailleur to the seat tube (it will either bolt directly to the frame or use a clamp).
4. Remove the derailleur and clean and service as needed.
5. Reinstall the derailleur, cable, and chain.

When all the components have been reinstalled, check the derailleur for adjustment by running it through the gears several times.

Bike Bites

Sometimes the best thing to do when a chain rubs against the cage plates is to widen the cage slightly. A washer can be slipped in under the bolt that holds the spacer at the narrow end of the cage. However, some cages do not have this bolt and cannot be opened.

Derailed

If you hear your chain rubbing intermittently against the front derailleur cage, say every revolution or so of the pedals, you might have a bent chain lring or a loose bottom bracket spindle that's moving back and forth as you pedal. Be sure to address this as soon as possible so you don't ruin the derailleur cage.

Bringing Up the Rear

Rear derailleurs (see the following figure) also come with different size cages. The length of the cage is the same as the distance between the pulleys. A longer cage can handle a greater difference in the number of teeth between the largest and smallest rear sprockets. The shorter the cage, the faster the shifting, which is why you'll see these types of derailleurs on racing bikes. Touring bikes, with their wider gear range, sport longer cages.

Older-style rear derailleurs stay in a fixed position; the cage moves and adjusts as the gear selection changes. Newer derailleurs have both a pivoting body and a pivoting cage, allowing for a greater capacity, or number of sprocket teeth it can handle.

A rear derailleur attaches to the frame in one of two ways:

➤ It bolts directly to a hanger that is brazed and/or bolted to the wheel dropout (the opening at the end of the stays) at the end of the seat and chain stays.

➤ It comes attached to a separate bolt-on hanger that attaches itself to the wheel dropout.

The bolt-on hanger attachment is pretty cheap and comes on equally cheap bikes. It's not unheard of for the hanger to come loose, so occasionally make sure this bolt is tight and secure. Derailleurs that attach directly to the frame are found on every quality bicycle.

All derailleurs have at least two adjusting screws: one for the high gear range and one for the low. Newer derailleurs with dual pivots (both the cage and the body) have a third screw that adjusts the angle of the derailleur. Like the front derailleur, the one in the rear must match up with its index shift levers for the system to work properly. The gear spacing clicks (the movements of the gear shifters) are specifically designed to match the derailleurs that come with the component groups. The clicks correspond with the distance from one sprocket to another.

A rear derailleur is a complicated component that holds up surprisingly well.

(Courtesy of Campagnolo)

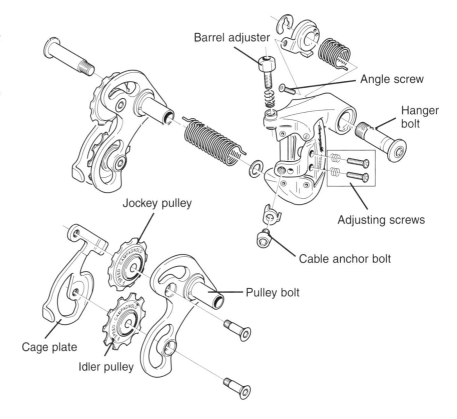

172

When It's Out of Whack

Unless you've been in an accident or have been dropping your bike down on its right side, it's unlikely that your rear derailleur will be bent. However, it's not a bad idea to give it a quick check just to be sure. The pulleys should line up straight. If the cage is crooked or bent, take it to your shop and have them straighten it out with one of those special tools you'll never be able to justify buying for yourself. Consider replacing cheap derailleurs when they bend. You might be able to do some minor straightening yourself if your derailleur bolts to the dropout with a hex bolt by inserting an Allen wrench and bending as needed. This doesn't always work, but it's worth a try.

There Are Limits!

The rear derailleur's adjusting screws actually are limit screws (see the following figure). They don't move the derailleur; rather, they limit its movement to the left and right. Loosening an individual adjusting screw allows the derailleur to travel farther; tightening it shortens the movement. Some derailleurs will label the screws "H" and "L" for high and low, respectively.

To set the adjusting screw for the low gears, do the following:

1. Shift the chain on the smallest chain ring.

2. Slowly shift the chain to the largest sprocket (you don't want to find out the hard way by shifting quickly that it's out of adjustment and is headed for the spokes).

3. If the chain won't make the jump to this sprocket (or barely makes it) loosen the low-gear adjusting screw until it shifts smoothly to the sprocket.

4. Tighten the low-gear adjusting screw if the derailleur starts to go into the spokes.

5. Run through the gears a couple of times and check the low gear adjustment.

To adjust for the high gears:

1. Shift the chain to the smallest rear sprocket and the largest chain ring.

2. Tighten or loosen the high gear adjusting screw as needed until the derailleur smoothly shifts into high gear.

Run both derailleurs through all the gears several times and adjust as needed. Remember, the cross gears shouldn't be used for riding, but for testing the shifting the length of the chain.

Bike Bites

New index shifters and their corresponding rear derailleur come with barrel adjusters to fine-tune the cables. This is especially important with index systems because they depend on very precise adjustment. The adjusters are a convenient way to take slack out of the cable after it stretches.

Derailed

An out-of-adjustment rear derailleur can cause big problems. If it goes into the spokes, it can not only ruin itself and the wheel, it also can bend the dropout where it attaches. This isn't a regular occurrence, but it takes only one time to make it a painful lesson.

Rear derailleur adjustments can be done with a simple screwdriver and a few good turns.

(Courtesy of Campagnolo)

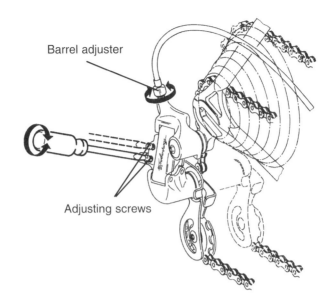

What's Your Angle?

Many new derailleurs have a third adjusting screw. This screw adjusts the angle of the derailleur itself and the height of the *jockey* (upper) *pulley*. The tighter the screw, the farther the derailleur cage is from the cassettes. Set the angle adjustment using the largest rear sprocket as a guide. You want it loose enough to shift quickly, but not so much that the cage runs into the sprocket. Often, the derailleur body simply needs to be parallel to the chain stay, but this isn't a given, so adjust it as needed.

Cleaning and Feeding

A rear derailleur can get pretty gunky, and gunk affects performance. For a quick cleaning, remove the wheel, spray the derailleur heavily with WD-40 and clean with an old toothbrush. Spray again and wipe with a clean rag. Install the wheel and spray the derailleur liberally with an appropriate lubricant. Oil is okay to use as well, but nowhere near as convenient or as thorough as a spray.

To remove the derailleur for a more thorough cleaning, take the following steps:

1. Remove the wheel from the bike.
2. Loosen the anchor bolt and pull the cable out from the derailleur.
3. Remove the chain and clean it as well.
4. Loosen the hanger bolt (this will require either an adjustable wrench or an Allen wrench) and remove the derailleur.
5. Soak the derailleur in solvent and scrub it with an old toothbrush, finally wiping it with a clean rag.
6. Leave it on the rag and thoroughly lubricate, allowing the lubricant to soak in before wiping off the excess.
7. Reinstall the derailleur, chain, and cable, pulling the cable taut with a pair of pliers.
8. After the components are installed, check for adjustment by running through all the gears.

Click, Click, Click …

Index shifting systems come with a barrel adjuster on each gear shifter and one on the rear derailleur. These are important for fine-tuning both derailleurs so they match up with the click stops. Each stop corresponds to a gear. You cannot depend on the barrel adjusters for major adjustments to the derailleurs, only minor ones. For this reason, it's important that the derailleurs are aligned correctly and the cables are taut before messing with the barrel adjusters. When you do use barrel adjusters, think in terms of half turns, not several full turns.

A Sense of Attachment

With indexed systems, everything matters—even how the cable it attached to each derailleur. Check for a groove in the body of the derailleur near the anchor bolt or a washer with hook on it to guide the cable in. Run the cable so it sets in the groove or is clasped under the hook on the washer before tightening the anchor bolt.

Other Adjustments

Remember that not all shifting problems originate with the derailleurs. They don't stand alone and are affected by other components. You also should check the following in addition to your derailleurs:

➤ The derailleurs should have the capacity to handle the range of gears offered by the chain rings and sprockets.

➤ The cables are taut.

➤ The chain has proper length and its condition is satisfactory.

➤ The chain rings are not bent and that none of the teeth are chipped.

➤ The alignment of all the components in the drive chain is correct.

You can adjust and adjust your derailleurs to no end, but sometimes the problem is more elusive. If all your fine-tuning still leaves you with unsatisfactory results, start snooping around for other reasons for the problem. You might not like what you find, but at least you'll have some answers.

The Least You Need to Know

➤ Derailleurs today are quite specialized and must match up with their shifters, chain rings, and sprockets for clean shifting.

➤ Index systems require precise fit and alignment and little—if any room—for error.

➤ For the most part, derailleurs stay in adjustment and primarily need regular cleaning and lubrication.

➤ It's critical that the rear derailleur is adjusted properly so the cage doesn't end up in the wheel spokes and cause a lot of unnecessary damage.

➤ If the derailleur cage is too short to shift through the gears, you need a larger-capacity derailleur.

Chapter 16

Cassettes and Freewheels

In This Chapter

➤ Same job, different systems

➤ Minimum maintenance components

➤ Tinkering with the gearing

➤ Removal and replacement

Internal gear hubs have been around forever, most often in the form of a three-speed. They are fairly complex, but extremely low maintenance (just give them a few drops of oil now and then, and they're happy). Before the mass introduction of ten-speed, derailleur-equipped bikes in the 1960s, three-speeds were the fastest wheels around for most riders. Like one-speeds, a three-speed bike has only a single cog or sprocket. Increasing the number of sprockets with different numbers of teeth increases the gear combinations available to the rider.

Then came the freewheel, a combination of at least five sprockets all attached to a central body, which in turn attach to the rear wheel hub. The internal parts of a freewheel include a pair of *pawls,* which engage the internal gear teeth when you pedal and disengage, allowing the bike to coast when you stop pedaling. Each sprocket has a set amount of teeth, which, when combined with the front chain rings, offer a range of gears for all types of riding.

Freewheels are still used today, but are a dying technology that is being replaced by cassettes. There are certain advantages to cassettes, such as ease of removal and sprocket replacement. Unlike freewheels, which screw on to the hub, cassettes attach to a hub, which has the cassette body integrated into its design. I'll discuss both components in this chapter.

Cassette Capers

Cassette systems (see the following figures) incorporate the hub rather than simply using it as a point of attachment. One advantage of this is that it moves the placement of the hub ball bearings farther out; therefore, the axle is better supported. One problem with freewheel

The Spoken Word

A **pawl** is a spring-controlled catch that is designed to wedge into or catch the teeth of a ratchet wheel to push it forward or prevent it from going in reverse. A ratchet wheel is a toothed gear meant to move in one direction.

systems is that the bearings are closer together near the flanges, the same way they are in the front hub, but the axle is longer than the axle in the front because it has to accommodate the freewheel sprockets. This puts more stress on the axle; freewheel systems have been known to bend or even crack under particularly hard riding conditions.

Cassettes incorporate the ratchet feature as part of the hub body itself. This means you can replace the sprockets separately if they wear out rather than replacing the entire mechanism. This offers certain cost savings, especially if you wear out your sprockets regularly.

You can buy individual sprockets or an entire set (the cassette), the latter being the way they're usually sold. You can change an individual sprocket if you want to change your gearing, but think it through first. If you go to a lower gear you can affect your derailleur, chain length, and shifting. Be sure you're not duplicating an existing gear ratio. Manufacturers of cassettes offer fairly wide ranges of gearing, although you might want some specific gears to complement your riding strengths and abilities.

The Campagnolo cassette is an example of modern-day gearing technology.

(Courtesy of Campagnolo)

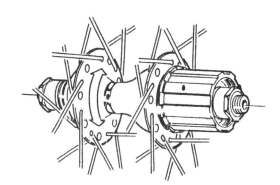

The Campagnolo cassette body is integrated into the rear hub rather than attaching to it like a freewheel.

(Courtesy of Campagnolo)

Campagnolo sprockets offer plenty of gear combinations.

(Courtesy of Campagnolo)

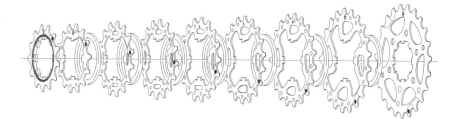

Pulling Them Off

A cassette usually is secured to the wheel by a lockring that is unscrewed in a counterclockwise direction. Some older models are secured with the smallest or smaller two cogs. Removing either type requires special tools (of course!), but they're worth having around for when you want to overhaul the rear hub and will need to remove the cassette. Broken spokes on the drive side also require that the cassette be removed before they can be replaced.

Remove your rear wheel and look closely down the center of the cassette. If the sprockets are splined (have grooves), you have a cassette held in place by a lockring. To remove this cassette, follow these steps:

1. Remove the rear wheel from the bike.

2. Remove the quick release and place the lockring remover inside the splined section of the cassette.

3. Place a chain wrench (also called a chain whip) around a mid-range to low-range sprocket with the handle facing the crankset and an adjustable wrench around the remover with its handle facing left.

4. With the wheel standing up, push down on both tools, moving the adjustable wrench around at least a half-turn, and the lockring will loosen.

5. Remove the adjustable wrench and, holding on to the chain wrench, loosen the lockring by hand.

6. Pull the cassette and remove it from the hub.

If your cassette does not have a lockring, you'll have to attach a second chain wrench to the smallest sprocket and push down on it in a counterclockwise motion. Once this sprocket is loose, the others will slip off.

Soak the cassette in solvent and scrub it with an old toothbrush to remove any grime from between the sprockets. Wipe off the cassette body with a rag dipped in solvent, then wipe dry. Drip some oil into the cassette body, let it soak in, and then oil again. When reinstalling the cassette, lightly oil the cassette body and align the cassette before sliding it on. Secure with the lockring.

Bike Bites

One way to keep your chain and sprockets clean with or without the use of solvents is by using Park Tool's GearClean Brush. This handy brush has long, tough nylon bristles to clean the narrow spaces between sprockets and is good anywhere grime collects, particularly on derailleurs and brakes. Dry brushing will get the worst of the dirt out, and your components will last longer. A small brush such as this fits easily in a bike pack, too.

Cleaning Caveats

Some mechanics (my tech editor, for instance) don't believe in solvent-cleaning the internal works of either freewheels or cassettes. They feel that solvents wash out the factory grease that, left to its own devices, will serve the component quite well and that you will be hard pressed to replace it with oil. There's something to be said for this opinion, and as long as your freewheel or cassette is spinning freely without the sound of grit inside the bearings, I say go ahead and clean the sprockets, but go easy on flooding the body with solvent.

Derailed

When replacing sprockets, use those made by the same manufacturer for your specific cassette: They are not interchangeable from one maker to another.

Sprocket Replacement

Once the cassette is removed from the hub, it's relatively simple to replace an individual sprocket; just be sure you keep all the sprockets and spacers in order. Some cassettes are held together with bolts that pass through all the cogs and spacers. The bolts are used strictly to keep things orderly and will have to be removed to separate the sprockets.

Freewheels

Freewheels were the standard technology on older 10-speeds. In these, the rear hub is threaded to receive the threaded freewheel cluster. Removing a freewheel requires a freewheel puller or remover, a small tool that fits into the notched or splined freewheel body such as the one shown in the following figure.

Notched freewheel puller.

(Courtesy of Park Tool)

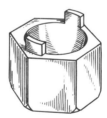

Different manufacturers vary their designs from each other just enough that different tools often are required for their removal. Notched freewheels are a little more precarious to remove, as the puller has a tendency to slip out when pressure is put on it. To remove a freewheel, do the following:

1. Determine which puller your freewheel requires and remove the wheel and quick release or axle nuts.

2. If you have a notched freewheel, insert the notched puller and secure it by installing the axle nut or quick release (without the springs) and tightening (but not too tight) one or the other against the puller.

3. Holding the wheel upright on the floor, place a large adjustable wrench on the puller and turn it counterclockwise.

4. When the freewheel initially loosens, remove or loosen the axle nut or quick release and continue removing the freewheel.

5. Remove the axle nut or quick release and finish unscrewing the freewheel, pulling it off the hub.

A freewheel can be tough to remove, especially if it's been on the wheel forever and the threads weren't greased before installation. Splined freewheels offer a much better grip on the puller and less slippage when they're being removed. (See the splined freewheel puller shown in the following figure.)

Splined freewheel puller.

(Courtesy of Park Tool)

The main reasons a freewheel is removed include …

➤ Spoke replacement.

➤ General cleaning and lubricating.

➤ Installation of a new freewheel.

➤ Changing out a sprocket.

➤ Overhauling the hub.

When a spoke breaks on the freewheel side, it's best to remove the freewheel to get at the hub. In a real emergency on the road, you can curl the spoke up and poke it through, as it will straighten out once the nipple is tightened—but I'd avoid doing this if you can. You'll probably never change out a sprocket because it's simpler to just replace the freewheel altogether. Besides, if you have an old one, you probably won't find any sprockets for it.

Bike Bites

Some mechanics will place the freewheel puller inside the jaws of a vise and place the wheel on top of it, turning the wheel instead of the puller. This actually gives you quite a bit of leverage and can be a useful technique against reluctant-to-be-removed free-wheels.

Cleaning and Lubing

Freewheels, like chains, can get pretty gritty (well, thanks to the chain, actually). You can do a quick cleaning with the wheel on the bike by spraying it with a solvent such as WD-40 and wrapping a rag around a paint stirrer or popsicle stick and placing it between the spinning sprockets. This isn't as thorough as removing the wheel and going at the freewheel with a toothbrush, but it will do until you can pull the wheel.

To flush out the bearings and pawls—do this only if you hear grit mixed with the bearings—place the wheel flat on a rag and spray WD-40 or other solvent inside the freewheel body (the section the sprockets spin around when spun backward). For a really thorough cleaning and lubricating, do the following:

1. Remove the freewheel from the wheel hub.

2. Soak the freewheel in solvent such as paint thinner or kerosene.

3. Scrub the sprockets with a toothbrush and soak again in clean solvent.

4. Put the freewheel on a rag and let the solvent drain out.

5. Wipe off any remaining solvent with a rag and oil the freewheel body, allowing plenty of time for the oil to drip into the bearings.

6. Give the freewheel a few spins to distribute the oil and then wipe off any excess. Oil again, spinning the freewheel, and allow the excess to drip onto a rag, giving it a final wipe before reinstalling.

You'll know if your freewheel needs attention by the sound when you spin it backward. If it's gritty and rough, it needs cleaning and lubing. To reinstall the freewheel, coat the wheel hub with grease and carefully turn the freewheel onto the threads.

Disassembling and Servicing a Freewheel

Don't. That's simple enough. Freewheels are labor-intensive to disassemble, and the internal works generally last a long time when left alone. If the sprockets start wearing out, replace the entire unit. This is not an example of throwaway culture, by the way—it's just intelligent decision making.

Freewheels might become harder to find as the bike world increasingly goes to cassettes. When freewheels were popular and the only game in town, there were a number of free-wheel manufacturers, but that is no longer the case. If you want to stick with your older freewheel system and hubs, consider stockpiling an extra freewheel or two as future replacements.

Derailed

Be sure any new freewheel has the same thread pattern as your wheel hub. As with pedals or any other threaded bike component, trying to force one type of thread over another (Italian over English, for example) can ruin the component made from the softer metal. If you're not sure about your threading, ask your bike mechanic. Almost all Japanese freewheels are English-threaded.

The Least You Need to Know

➤ Freewheels and cassettes look alike, but they are different technologies and are not interchangeable.

➤ It's unlikely that you will find replacement sprockets for older, out-of-production freewheels; you're better off replacing the entire unit instead.

➤ For best performance, the rear sprockets should be cleaned at least as often as the chain.

➤ Cassette systems offer more support to the rear axle and easier sprocket replacement than freewheel systems.

➤ When upgrading from a freewheel to a cassette, the entire rear wheel will have to be rebuilt as each system requires a different type of hub.

Part 4

Specialty Areas

Some bicycle repairs and projects can be complicated and challenging, but still doable by an average rider. Keeping a wheel straight and true is one such challenge and a test of one's patience, but it's a worthwhile exercise if you really want to test your skills. You might even find that you have a talent for it (there are some mechanics who are known for their wheels).

Other repairs, such as frame alignment, require more specialized tools than the average rider will ever invest in, as well as plenty of knowledge gained only by years of experience. It's one thing to practice straightening out the fork on an old three-speed using homemade tools, but quite another to risk it on your high-end, full-suspension mountain bike. One attribute of knowledge is realizing when to go to a higher source; in this case, that source is a good bike shop.

I'll also cover saddles and seatposts. You have to sit somewhere, and you want that somewhere to be comfortable. From traditional leather saddles to new synthetic materials, a good saddle makes all the difference between a comfortable ride and a miserable one (comfortable is better).

In the appendixes to follow, you'll find a glossary for quick reference, as well as some guidelines for buying a new or used bike.

Chapter 17

Saddle and Seatpost

In This Chapter

➤ All saddles are not created equal

➤ Adjustments for comfortable riding

➤ Micro-adjusting seatposts

➤ Fitting the seatpost

Once upon a time in the old days of bicycling, there were few choices of saddles and seatposts. Leather was the standard saddle material, and the saddle quality and cost varied as much as any other components. Although plastic and synthetic saddles rule today, it's hard to beat a good leather saddle after it's been broken in.

Saddles differ by more than the material used in their construction. Some are ultra-narrow; others are extremely wide and include springs for shock resistance. Unique designs have developed over the years, such as slung canvas (something like a hammock for your personal seat) and dual pad saddles (one pad for each half of your seat), but some of these are considered novelties and aren't big sellers.

Seatposts have evolved into components that can be minutely adjusted to your measurements and riding style. Older styles with clunky adjustments have fast become a thing of the past. This chapter introduces you to various types of saddles and seatposts. It also shows you how to install both and adjust the saddle for your riding comfort.

Saddle Selections

Narrow leather and plastic saddles are the most traditional type. They are designed to allow the rider's legs to move near the edges of the saddle, yet rub against them as little as possible. This makes them especially appropriate for racers. Wider touring saddles often are considered to be more comfortable and aimed at longer, more leisurely rides. These rides entail more upright riding, which places more pressure on the saddle (and the rider as well, which is more to the point).

A softer saddle won't necessarily yield a more comfortable ride. A cheap padded saddle will offer little support. An excessively stiff plastic saddle will never give or soften and won't be appropriate for much but competition riding. A thick, "hard" leather saddle eventually will soften and conform to the rider's anatomy as it is broken in. Traditional riders often prefer a leather saddle and will go to all kinds of lengths to break them in. Plastic versus leather has been an ongoing discussion among bike riders and manufacturers for years.

Leather

Traditional bike saddles in all price ranges were made from leather stretched over the saddle frame. Cheap leather saddles left a lot to be desired and would give up the ghost if left untreated and exposed to a few rainstorms. Good-quality leather saddles, such as those made by Brooks, will last for years if properly maintained. The break-in period can be lengthy for the thicker, more expensive leather saddles, but the comfort is well worth the price and the wait.

Some riders prefer wide, spring-supported leather saddles made specifically for touring. These saddles are narrow in the front (to avoid chafing) and wide in the rear for extra support and comfort during upright riding. Unlike plastic, leather has natural breathing properties that help keep the rider cool during rides in hot weather. (See the following figure.)

Bike Bites

Use a well-broken-in saddle for any long road trips. You don't want to end the first day sore and chafed and have only more of the same to look forward to. Some riders soften leather saddles by applying multiple coats of Neat's foot oil (look for it at a shoe store or cobbler's shop) months before using the saddle.

Narrow and wide leather saddles should satisfy almost any rider's anatomy.

(Courtesy of Brooks Saddle)

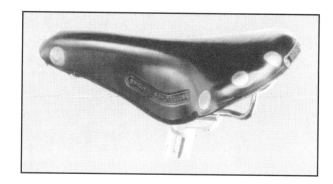

Living in a Plastic World

Plastic saddle design varies by manufacturer. The plastic base of the saddle attaches to a metal or titanium frame. More comfortable models might have different thickness of plastic and flex some when ridden for shock absorbency. Plastic saddles, some of which have leather covers, come in a variety of styles, including those that are split or otherwise have openings to keep pressure off the groin area. Because one size hardly fits all when it comes to saddles, these designs have had only moderate success.

This Isn't Hair Gel

The gel in some modern saddles actually is a type of thick foam. Some riders prefer this padding because it gives them firm support and doesn't collapse or flatten as cheaper foams do. Like all other saddle types, gel construction is strictly a matter of preference.

Freewheelin' Facts

Several years ago, a number of articles were written about a suspected connection between frequent bicycling and male impotence (there's nothing like the risk of impotence to put a crimp in a guy's bike riding). The problem appeared to be too much sitting on hard saddles, compressing vital arteries and nerves. As a result, saddle manufacturers introduced new designs to relieve this pressure, including saddles with V-shaped wedge cuts in the rear and others with grooves cut lengthwise down the middle.

It's a Cover-Up

Padded saddle covers, both homemade and manufactured, are available to add some comfort and protection to your saddle. However, they can disguise the fact that your saddle doesn't fit you properly, is the wrong size, isn't broken in properly, or is simply cheap. You're better off buying a saddle that works on its own without a cover. An exception, of course, is a thin plastic cover used to protect leather saddles from wet weather.

Seating Arrangements

The height and adjustment of a bike saddle are critical to the comfort and efficiency of the rider. The seat should be high enough so a seated rider can place the ball of one foot on one pedal in its lowest position and have a slight bend in the knee. This gives the rider enough leverage against the pedal without hyper-extending the knee. To find this position, do the following:

1. Rotate the crankarms until one of the pedals is as close to the ground as it can get.

2. Sit in the saddle and place your heel on this pedal.

3. Adjust the saddle height by loosening the seatpost bolt and moving the seatpost up and down until your heel sits flat on the pedal and your leg is fully extended.

4. Place the ball of your foot on the pedal and make sure there is a slight bend in your knee.

A saddle that is too low is not only uncomfortable; it puts too much stress on your knees when you ride. It also puts less weight on your legs and more on the saddle, adding to the rider's discomfort. This kind of riding can lead to pain and injuries if it goes on for too long.

The tilt or angle of the saddle also is important. Usually, the best position is parallel with the top tube. If the nose or front end is

Derailed

If you're having trouble reaching the handlebars, but your bike fits you heightwise, don't move the saddle into an extreme position to accommodate your reach. First, look into buying a shorter handlebar stem or different handlebars. If that won't work, look into a bike frame with a shorter top tube.

Bike Bites

A pair of seamless bike shorts, either padded or lined, can greatly add to your riding comfort and reduce chafing. Buy a pair that's comfortable, not simply fashionable.

tilted downward, the saddle doesn't give adequate support and the rider depends more on arms and shoulders pushing against the handlebars. This can cause soreness and numbness in the hands, arms, and shoulders. On the other hand, if you tilt the nose up, your groin will register complaints in no time.

Finally, a saddle has to be positioned over the pedals so you can get the best use of your leg power as you turn the cranks. Your right knee should line up approximately with the center of a pedal when the drive-side pedal is in the three o'clock position, and the left-side pedal is in the nine o'clock position.

Major saddle manufacturers often make saddles designed for women, as men's saddles can prove to be too narrow for a woman's wider hips. As with all saddles, comfort is the main issue; if a woman's saddle suits you, by all means, change your current saddle. Don't put up with compromised riding when something as simple as a new saddle can solve the problem.

Derailed

Some seatposts are secured with quick-release devices instead of seatpost bolts. These are really handy for quick adjustments—but also handy for someone to swipe your saddle off the bike. Think twice before installing a quick-release on anything but a mountain bike, whose riders sometimes adjust the height according to the riding conditions.

Taking It in the Shorts

Discomfort isn't always due to the saddle or the saddle's positioning. Your clothing and laundering habits make a difference, too. Biking shorts lined with natural chamois can help avoid chafing. Some riders skip using underwear, preferring the feel of the chamois. This is okay, but regular laundering is a must. You don't want a lot of bacteria building up in your shorts. Bring along extra shorts for long road trips.

In case of actual saddle sores, keep your skin clean and dry and consider changing saddles. If the problem is a stiff leather saddle that isn't broken in yet, and you're several days into a tour, cover the saddle with anything that will cushion it somewhat—a towel or a T-shirt, for instance—and kick yourself a few times for not testing the seat before you started your trip. (I once made this mistake riding from Boulder, Colorado, to Seattle, and I never want to repeat the experience again.)

Seatposts

Saddles mount onto a seatpost, which in turn fits inside the seat tube. The seatpost also allows for height adjustment of the saddle. Old-style seatposts are simple steel or aluminum pipes with one end narrower than the other. A saddle is secured to these pipes with a separate clamp consisting of a bolt running through two sets of washers that wrap around the undercarriage of the saddle (see the following figure). Sometimes these washers are serrated, so they'll hold the saddle more securely.

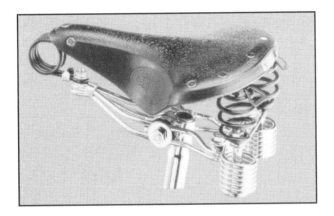

A basic pipe-style seatpost and even more basic saddle clamps.

(Courtesy of Brooks Saddle)

Modern seatposts come with attached clamps, are of a cleaner design, and offer a wider range of adjustments. Built-in clamps allow saddle adjustment by loosening one or two bolts, which secure a pair of grooved blocks that hold the saddle tight. Two-bolt designs allow for very small adjustments to the position of the saddle. (See the following figure.)

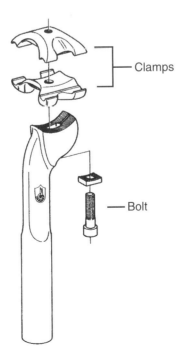

Clamps

Bolt

A modern one-piece seatpost that allows for lots of adjustments.

(Courtesy of Campagnolo)

189

Installing Seatpost

Before you install any seatpost, follow this simple rule: Grease it. If you use plenty of grease (you don't have to go crazy with it), the seatpost will be easier to adjust for height and it won't get stuck in the seat tube. Seatposts are not easy to remove once they decide to stay put (see the following section). While we're at it, keep another rule in mind: No hammers. If you need a hammer to get the seatpost into the seat tube, your seatpost is the wrong size and you should stop what you're doing and install one that's the correct size.

Most seatposts have a horizontal mark on them that says "Minimum insertion"; you must heed this instruction. It means the seatpost has to be installed with a minimum amount of it inserted inside the seat tube. This is a safety issue and should not be ignored. If you want to raise the seat beyond this insertion point, buy an extended seatpost.

The seatpost doesn't stay put without some help in the form of a seatpost binder, which tightens the lug at the top of the seat tube. This can be a standard hex head bolt, an Allen bolt, or a quick release. Modern, quality bikes have Allen bolts, whereas older bikes or cheap new ones come with a hex head bolt. Quick releases are more often found on mountain bikes because they allow the rider to change seat positions for long downhill riding.

When you loosen your binder bolt, check the threads for corrosion and wear. This bolt rarely gets used, but it does get exposure to rain and dirt, just like the rest of your bike. If it's difficult to remove it, clean the threads with a wire brush and lubricate the threads before reinstalling.

Derailed

Some old pipe-style seatposts can drop down the seat tube during installation if they are so narrow that they don't fit snugly inside the tube. To avoid having to retrieve the seatpost, attach the saddle first, then tighten up the seatpost binder bolt.

Derailed

Don't use a vise-grips or channel locks on a seatpost unless you're going to be trashing it, because these tools can deform a seatpost. You might be able to get away with wrapping a rag around the post first to protect it from the tool's jaws. Saddles are safest for removing a stuck seatpost.

Removing an Almost Permanent Seatpost

A seatpost can get stuck inside the seat tube for various reasons, such as lack of grease, rust and corrosion, the wrong size post. You can avoid all these problems by greasing the correct size seatpost before you install it. If you buy a used bike with an existing post, you could be inheriting someone else's problem. To remove a really stuck seatpost, try one of the following:

➤ Loosen and remove the seatpost bolt and twist the saddle back and forth until the post loosens.

➤ Use a large, flat screwdriver to *gently* spread out the seat lug seam; then twist and pull the seatpost.

➤ In the case of a badly corroded steel seatpost inside a steel seat tube, dribble some penetrating oil down the side of the post so it soaks between it and the seat tube (for aluminum seatposts, try plain ammonia).

➤ If the crankset has been removed from the bike, you can plug any openings in the top of the seatpost, invert the frame, and squirt a lot of oil into the seat tube—enough to fill the top 12 inches or so—and let the oil soak in overnight before trying to remove the seatpost.

➤ As a last resort, cut the tube off with a hacksaw, leaving an inch or so sticking out of the seat tube; take a hacksaw blade and carefully cut the inside of the seatpost lengthwise (the shavings will fall down into the bottom bracket, so be sure the crankset has been removed first).

This last approach isn't much fun, but it's either that or heating the seatpost with a torch and running the risk of blistering the paint. Keep in mind that the more you twist the post when removing it (or installing it, for that matter), the more scratches it will have from rubbing against the seat tube.

Like every other bicycle component, seatposts don't rest on their design laurels. If a regular, stiff seatpost isn't to your liking, you can install a suspension seatpost for added comfort. Models differ. Some act on a telescoping mechanism; others use proprietary linkage systems. Neither one can simply be popped inside the seat tube like standard seatposts. There are clearance and adjustment issues, but they can definitely soften a ride on an otherwise stiff bike.

The Least You Need to Know

➤ Saddle selection is highly individual, so weigh your selection carefully.

➤ Good-quality leather saddles are very comfortable, but only after a long break-in period.

➤ Think twice before buying a new saddle design.

➤ Saddle adjustment is as critical to your comfort as the saddle itself.

➤ Modern, one-piece seatposts are lightweight and allow for multiple saddle adjustments.

Chapter 18

Frame Affairs

In This Chapter

➤ Clean and lean

➤ A case of the bends

➤ Facing and tapping

➤ Add-ons

A dictionary would define a frame as an underlying or supportive structure that has something built on or around it. That pretty much defines a bicycle frame, the added components of which are bolted, tightened, and secured. The frame accommodates these attached parts by supplying the dropouts, tube openings, threaded bottom bracket, and braze-ons.

The main enemies of a quality frame are paint chips, rust, and excessive twisting and bending. Some of these problems can increase with cheaper bikes. A mediocre brazing or welding job combined with bad geometry and cheap tubing can make a bike literally come apart at the seams.

Additionally, a frame is an anchor for nonessential, but useful bike toys such as racks and lights. There are also mounting and clearance considerations. I'll cover add-ons and ailments in this chapter.

Frame Fitness

A bike frame should have intact paint, strong welds, and proper alignment. This doesn't mean it has to be flawless, without a scratch or a dent. It does mean that it has to ride straight and be safe. Even the best frame can break if the conditions are right, but that doesn't mean the frame is defective. Off-road riders know this fact well; for that reason, warranties on mountain bikes are somewhat restrictive and can be loaded with disclaimers. Warranties typically cover only the original purchaser and do not extend to normal wear and tear.

You Can Fix This?

A steel frame can almost always be repaired, even to the point of replacing an entire tube. An aluminum frame or a composite frame is less likely to be repairable. What can a shop repair? All kinds of things, including ...

➤ Bent or cracked frame tubes.

➤ Failed joints.

➤ Bent derailleur hangers and braze-on brackets.

➤ Bent forks.

➤ Realignment.

Some frames are worth repairing and repainting more than others, even after factoring in emotional attachment. Before having a frame repaired, you should factor in a few things, such as:

Derailed

Index shifters are very sensitive to derailleur alignment. If you have a bent derailleur hanger, the shifting might not work properly. The hanger should be in line with the cassette or freewheel sprockets.

➤ Will the bike be safe after the repair is completed?

➤ Can I ride the bike as is, possibly for less demanding rides?

➤ How much is the bike worth?

➤ How much would it cost to replace the frame and transfer all the components to a new frame?

➤ Is a used bike a better value than repairing this one?

➤ Do I like this bike enough to go through this expense and trouble?

The last one is completely subjective. Collectors, if they really fancy a particular bicycle, will spend way more time and money to restore it than it is objectively worth. It's the same reason some homeowners spend money restoring a beat-up old house rather than demolishing it and building a new one. If you like your bike and have a long history with it, go ahead and repair it.

The Usual Suspects

A frame doesn't simply decide that it's tired of being taken for granted and ridden in lousy weather, then snap just to teach you a lesson. Well, it might, but you'll have to consult with your neighborhood exorcist on that one. Bicycle frames give way for two basic reasons: metal fatigue or big-time trauma.

Bike Bites

Before you spend a lot of money repairing your favorite been-with-you-through-thick-and-thin bike, put it aside for a while. Hang it up in the garage or store it in the basement and ride something else. Let some time pass and then decide if you really want to spend a lot of money on extensive frame repairs.

If you stress any frame joint to or beyond its normal limits over a long enough period of time, the metal will fatigue. A hairline crack can become a bigger crack—and then bigger still. Lug joints and tube sections with braze-on brake bosses are good places to check for this type of crack. Clean the paint and inspect closely. A thin, rusty line is a dead giveaway and should be looked at.

Big-time trauma is one too many jumps off 15-foot overhangs or other off-road pranks. Some riders who do this type of riding will retire their mountain bikes every two years or so before they disassemble on them during a jump.

Paint It Yourself?

Bicycle frames are painted under highly controlled conditions—and the paints that manufacturers use don't come out of spray cans from an autoparts store. Does this mean you should never attempt to paint a bike frame yourself? Not necessarily, but you won't get the factory results if you do it yourself.

I have painted utility-quality, used bike frames and had perfectly serviceable results, but I never would have passed them off as professionally painted. Still, it's a good way to clean up an old bike if you want to invest the time. To paint a bike frame:

1. Remove all the parts except the bottom-bracket fixed cup and the headset cups (the fork can stay attached).

2. Scrub off all the dirt and grease with a strong degreasing detergent and rinse and dry thoroughly.

3. Completely sand and degloss the original paint with a light grade of sandpaper (150 or heavier if you have paint chips to feather out).

4. Wipe off all the dust with a tack rag or a clean rag dipped in paint thinner.

5. Cover the fixed cup, the headset cups, decals, and any chromed sections of the frame with masking tape.

6. Hang the frame up by running a long dowel through the head tube and tying the ends to the ceiling using bailing wire.

7. Spray the entire frame using a can of high-grade automotive primer in several light coats, allowing each one to dry before spraying on the next. Wet sand with 400 grit paper between coats.

8. When the primer has dried, test it for adhesion by trying to scrape off a small section of it with your thumbnail. Lightly wet sand with 600 grit paper.

9. If the primer is adhering tightly, apply a light coat of high-grade automotive spray paint. Don't attempt to cover the primer completely in one coat; instead, apply several until all the primer is coated.

10. Sand with 600 wet/dry sandpaper (a very fine sandpaper that can be used with water for even finer sanding) between coats.

11. Apply enough coats of paint to develop some build-up, but avoid runs and drips.

When the paint has completely dried, remove the masking tape. You can eventually apply a light coat of automotive wax for additional protection, but the curing time of the paint varies with each type and manufacturer. Inquire about cure time with your paint supplier.

Be careful when reassembling your bike. A spray can paint job scratches more easily than a factory paint job. A shop that specializes in frame painting will sand between paint coats and apply a final clear coat or two over the paint.

Derailed

It's not a good idea to take a bike frame to a "hot tank" dipping operation for paint removal. These tanks are primarily water with a caustic additive. Steel frames will corrode once the paint is removed and the frame gets wet.

Bike Bites

If you're not too particular about color, you might strike up a deal with a body shop to spray out your bike frame when they spray paint a car. Do your own preparation work and priming to keep the cost down.

You might choose to strip all the original paint off the frame before repainting. You can do this chemically with methylene chloride paint remover. Follow the directions on the can and rinse the residue with lacquer thinner and coarse steel wool.

Every Frame Has Its Limits

I don't care how much you paid for your full-suspension mountain bike; it isn't indestructible. As the original owner, you can expect a warranty to cover manufacturer faults, but not normal wear and tear. The bike also should be used according to its design limitations (no off-road riding with a Colnago, a sleek Italian racing bike, for instance). Always read the warranty that comes with your bike so you don't void it with your riding or unauthorized modifications.

Derailed

Methylene chloride paint remover and lacquer thinner are hazardous to skin, eyes, and lungs. Wear gloves, long-sleeve pants and an old sweatshirt, and a respirator if working indoors.

When Hangers Hang Loose

A home mechanic can sometimes straighten out a rear derailleur hanger, but it must be done carefully. Too much pushing or pulling can weaken a joint, and you can be worse off than when you started. Here's what you do:

1. Remove the derailleur.

2. Reverse the rear wheel with the sprockets on the left side of the bike and install it or use a spare axle bolted in place (this prevents the stay from moving).

3. Use the largest adjustable (crescent) wrench that will fit over the hanger and slowly bend the hanger out. Don't pull too far; the hanger should be parallel with the rear sprockets after the wheel is installed.

Parts Can Bend, Too

If your frame can bend and crack, so can your various components. You don't want to be depending on split or extremely bent parts for your cycling safety. Follow these guidelines with damaged parts:

1. Replace a seat post if it's bent or cracked.

2. Replace bent or cracked stems.

3. A mild bend in a handlebar won't render it unusable, but severe bends call for replacement.

4. You can injure your knee from riding with a bent pedal axle or crankarm; replace these right away (repairs are uncertain with these parts).

5. Replace the fork if the steerer tube is bent (fork blades can sometimes be straightened and aligned, however).

6. Bent wheels should be rebuilt and bent derailleurs often replaced, especially if you're using index shifters.

Bike Bites

Some bikes come with certain sections of the frame chrome-plated (other frames are entirely chrome-plated). There is some advantage to having chrome plating on the dropout faces and rear stay faces where the wheels attach, as the paint in these areas can wear off easily. Some shops will do this plating on painted frames.

Alignment

An alignment check by a shop that does frame repairs will check for bends in the down tube, twisting in the head tube, alignment of the rear triangle, and bends in the fork blades. The mechanic will use special tools that you'll never have at home. There are various ways to check with string, but you still need tools for much of the straightening. If it's a frame you like, take it to the shop.

Rear alignment should be done by experts with tools such as this one.

(Courtesy of Park Tool)

Packing It with You

There's no point in carrying books, groceries, or other items in a backpack when your bike can carry them for you. All you need is some kind of rack and packs (panniers); there is no shortage of either at bicycle shops and mail-order firms. Racks are made to fit every type of bike regardless of the frame geometry, but you still need to choose the correct one for your bike.

The earliest form of carrier was a simple metal or wicker basket attached to the handlebars. These actually are pretty convenient, but can make for tougher steering and handling if you carry a lot of weight in them. Large baskets are still used in urban areas by some bicycle-delivery services. You can use a basket if you want, but the alternatives are a big improvement.

Rack 'Em Up

Bike racks are good things on road bikes, even if you're not touring. With a rack and a couple of bungee cords, you can carry home some groceries, books, or a box of bike components. In other parts of the world, bicycles have racks that look like they're made from steel girders and are used to haul just about anything.

Long-range tours can require front and rear racks to carry a rider's gear. When choosing a rack, check for durability and load thresholds, clearances, and mounting procedures and hardware. Some racks are designed for lighter duty than others, so be sure to discuss your needs with your bike shop. You want a rack that clears the

Derailed

Always test your racks and packs with a full load before starting a long tour or ride. You want to be sure that the bike is stable and doesn't present any handling problems.

pedals with sufficient room so your feet won't knock against either the rack or your panniers. There is a rack and mounting system for every bike style and frame design.

Pack Rats

You can mix and match racks and panniers to your heart's desire. Some long-haul, world travelers will load up every inch of a bike while others might practice what some once referred to as "California touring" (the rider carried a sleeping bag and a credit card and little else). The types of bike packs or panniers include the following:

➤ Panniers that attach to a front or rear rack.

➤ A rack pack that sits on top of your rack.

➤ A frame pack that fits under the top tube in the frame triangle of the bike.

➤ A wedge pack that fits under the seat.

➤ A handlebar bag.

Pack purposes can be broken down into commuter or day-to-day use and touring needs. Consider the following when choosing a pack:

➤ The amount of stuff you carry every day such as bike tools, clothing, and food

➤ Weather conditions

➤ The smallest size pack that will fulfill your storage needs

➤ Whether the pack is removable, so you can tote your stored items with you when you park and lock the bike

The simplest thing to do is simply strap a box or a crate to a rear rack with bungee cords. It won't be elegant, but it will do the job.

Let There Be Light

Biking lights range from barely visible to very impressive. A front light not only lights the road for the rider but, like a rear safety light, allows drivers and pedestrians to notice you. Because you never know what kinds of conditions you might get caught riding in, you're better off investing up front in a high-quality set that will stand up to all kinds of weather conditions and provide plenty of illumination.

Derailed

Reflectors are no substitute for a good lighting system. Lights are visible far earlier than reflectors and allow pedestrians to see you.

When choosing a lighting system, consider the following:

➤ Battery power versus generator power

➤ The type and number of bulbs

➤ Attachment to the frame

Many cyclists prefer battery-powered lights as opposed to generator power because the latter causes a drag on the wheel. Generator manufacturers claim that modern systems are a great improvement over past generations of generators, but at least in the United States, cyclists aren't buying the argument. We like our batteries because they don't impede performance. In addition, generator systems are dependent on a moving wheel to maintain light. If you stop, the light stops (except for those models that incorporate batteries with the generator).

At low speeds, generators don't produce much light; at high speeds, a rider can burn out the bulbs. Stick with batteries—preferably rechargeable ones.

Battery systems offer a number of options for attaching the lights. Some are secured to the fenders; others to seatposts or even the bike packs. You want to be sure the attachment hardware will fit on your particular bike. Detachable lights give you the added benefit of being useful wherever a low-beam flashlight might be needed.

Freewheelin' Facts

There are some generator systems that are built in to the wheel hub. The best known is the Sturmer-Archer Dyno-Hub, which has been found on some old three-speeds in the United States. The Dyno-Hub usually was used in the front wheel, but some were built into three- and four-speed hubs as well. These systems typically consist of a stationary armature or coil. This coil is secured to the wheel axle with a donut-shaped magnet that spins around it as the wheel turns. This creates the electromagnetic current that runs the lights. These hubs are heavy and not terribly efficient, but a fun part of bike history.

Fenders

If you live in mostly rainless Death Valley, it's safe to say you won't need to bother with fenders. Here in the Northwest, they're a good idea for at least one of your bikes. Fenders primarily keep mud and grit from being washed on you and your clothes. They also keep a lot of this grit from getting into your bike's moving parts and your headset.

The best fenders are full-length with either plastic or aluminum mud flaps, but not all bikes can accommodate these. In some cases, there isn't enough clearance or there are no eyelets for attaching the fender struts. A fender has to clear the brake arms and the tires. Clip-on fenders also are available, but they don't do as good a job as full-length versions. When buying fenders, take your bike to your bike shop if you're unsure about fitting and clearance.

Pumped Up

Bicycle pumps can be attached to pump pegs on the frame or with mounting hardware that comes with the pump. It's hardly worth the effort or expense to have pegs brazed to the frame unless you're having a lot of other work done, too. Some older three-speeds and ten-speeds have pegs that will accommodate only cheap pumps. With these, you're better off buying a quality pump and installing it on a different frame tube.

Bike Bites

I found a couple of sources for straightening out old fenders at www.bicycletrader.com/archives/20classifieds. The service includes removing dents and reshaping metal fenders.

199

Kickstands

You mostly see kickstands on kids' bikes, even though they're a good idea for adult bikes, too. However, no one will install them because, well, your bike will look like a kid's bike. A kickstand simply allows you to keep your bike upright without depending on a wall or tree to lean it against. The best ones are rear-mounted kickstands, although they are kind of clunky and add some weight to the bike. Mostly, though, they violate the cool factor, so we don't use them.

With all these accessories, you can turn your bike into a real workhorse, and some people in other parts of the world do just this. They will haul tools, groceries, and other worldly goods around on heavy, three-speed bikes. You probably won't go to this extreme, but the option is to carry all the goods you need for a commute into town or a trip across country, and carry them in style.

The Least You Need to Know

➤ A bent frame isn't a lost cause, but it might not be economical to repair it.

➤ Steel frames generally are repairable, whereas aluminum and composite ones often are not.

➤ On a bicycle frame, a home paint job will never equal a factory paint job.

➤ Before you buy any add-ons such as fenders or racks, make sure your frame can accommodate them and that it has sufficient clearances.

Chapter 19

Mountain Bike Specifics

In This Chapter

➤ Tougher than the average frame

➤ To suspend or not to suspend

➤ Geometry lessons

➤ Off-road fun

Starting in the 1960s, bike manufacturers went all out to create lightweight, 10-speed road bikes for all riders. The United States market was a cornucopia of imported Raleighs, Peugeots, Gitanes, and higher-end Colgnagos, Paramounts, Singers, and dozens of other bike brands. The trend was away from the heavy three-speeds and old one-speed clunkers to sleek touring and racing frames with drop-style handlebars and narrow wheels.

Starting in the early 1970s, according to mountain bike historians, the old balloon-tire bikes were rediscovered for their roadworthiness in places where there weren't any roads. The birthplace of this resurgence was Marin County, California, where one-speed Schwinns and similar bikes were used to explore the back roads and trails of Mt. Tamalpais. Downhill riding, as it ended up, really tested the ability of a rider to handle a bike under tough riding conditions.

The word spread by the late 1970s and the rest is history. These comfortable bikes, which allow for more upright riding, have lightened and increased in gears and the quality of components. Mountain bike sales have exceeded road bike sales for years, and generally have renewed interest in cycling both here and in Europe.

Mountain bikes basically operate the same as other types of bikes, but quality models come with the latest and greatest components such as disc brakes, threadless headsets, and crack suspension systems. There are entire books and magazines devoted to mountain bikes and this chapter by no means attempts to exhaust the subject; it simply covers some of the basics.

Derailed

Buying a mountain bike doesn't make you qualified to ride it over any trail or course. This is a different style of riding and can cause injuries to a novice who jumps in without any training. Start on easy trails, take your time, and consider taking a class if one is offered in your area. All those riders who make it look easy have practiced and ridden extensively—and have had their share of spills.

Mountain Bike Features

As a bicycle category, mountain bikes have shown tremendous growth and innovation since their first wide-scale commercial introduction in the 1980s. As riders pushed the boundaries further ("Hey, look—a 15-foot drop! Let's do it!"), manufacturers responded with more advanced bikes, and riding enthusiasts became bicycle designers.

Freewheelin' Facts

In cooperation with the U.S. Consumer Product Safety Commission, Dynacraft Industries, Inc., of San Rafael, California, is voluntarily recalling about 24,800 mountain bikes. Because some were not welded properly, the front suspension forks on these bicycles can break apart during use, resulting in serious injury to the rider. Dynacraft is aware of 23 reports of injury to riders when the forks on these bikes broke apart. Injuries included concussions, fractures, cuts, bruises, back strain, and chipped and lost teeth. The recall involves 26-inch Vertical XL2, as well as 24- and 26-inch Magna Electroshock mountain bikes. Both model bikes sold for between $100 and $140.

Mountain bikes are available in a range of prices, from the low $300s to as high as you want to go. You can pay less, but I wouldn't define those as real mountain bikes. The higher you go in price, the lower the bike goes in weight. As you spend more, you can expect to see the following features:

➤ 27 speeds

➤ Professional-quality alloy parts

➤ Usually Shimano components that might be mixed with similar quality components from other manufacturers

➤ Hydraulic disc brakes

➤ Clipless pedals

➤ Reinforced, butted aluminum frame

➤ Superior suspension

Remember, it's most important that your frame fit you and fit your intended type of riding. You can always change out or replace individual components. Replacing a frame that doesn't fit or suit you is another matter altogether.

These Aren't Road Frames

Aluminum is regularly used for many mountain bike frames. It's appropriate because it is lightweight, strong, rust proof, and readily available. In fact, most of the components on modern bikes are made from aluminum alloys. Aluminum frame tubing is pretty stiff and doesn't have quite as much bending or ability to "give" as steel.

One difference between mountain bike frames and road bike frames is their "beefiness." Larger aluminum tubes means larger welding areas at the joints. Forks are in a class all by themselves, and the rear dropouts are especially strong. Better-designed frames offer mounts or tabs integrated into the rear dropouts to accommodate disc brakes. This is important because a disc brake increases the force applied to a chainstay.

Your mountain bike will not be the same size as your road bike, or at least it shouldn't be. Think of the kind of riding you'll be doing: jumping over logs, riding up and down washed-out trails, and probably falling off from time to time. Slipping off the saddle and onto a frame that's suitable for the road—that is, one to two inches between your groin and the top tube—can be a little tough off road, where conditions aren't too genteel. For this reason, a mountain bike frame can have as much as six inches of clearance between you and the top tube depending on the frame design and type of riding you'll be doing. Mountain bikes come with long seatposts to accommodate this smaller frame size.

Freewheelin' Facts

Weight savings are especially important on mountain bikes, which are already heavy from added suspension systems and oversized tubing. These fatter aluminum tubes do come with thinner walls, which help keep the weight down.

Derailed

Never raise a seatpost any higher than the manufacturer's maximum height, which is marked on the outside of the post itself: The seatpost can snap, endangering the rider.

Crashproof Components ... Sort Of

You could build a bicycle frame out of half-inch thick iron pipe, and someone would find a way to hammer it enough until it fails (my tech editor and his friends come to mind). Mountain bike manufacturers understand this challenge, and quality bikes are built to withstand off-road pounding—up to a point. No frame or component is indestructible, but some will last longer than others. Price isn't strictly a determinant of durability, although it usually denotes smoother operating components.

Bike Bites

If you do a lot of hardcore off-road riding, you'll probably end up trashing your wheels on a regular basis. It pays to get a good pair of wheels up front, as well as hubs with thick flanges that can be used again when you rebuild your wheels.

Some components found on road bikes, such as caliper brakes and down tube shifters, are impractical for a mountain bike. Sealed bearings are standard on mountain bikes because of the expected increased exposure to water and mud. Road bikes get this exposure, too, but their riders typically don't go looking for it the way off-road riders do. Crankarms on mountain bikes look like they're on steroids. These bikes aren't bulletproof, but it's not for lack of trying.

Wheels

Riding the back roads and roadless backwoods requires strong wheels. Mountain bikes come with 26-inch wheels (with various widths, such as 22 mm) rather than the narrower road bike wheels (27" × 1⅛" or 700C, for instance). These wider wheels are better able to stand up to the pounding from off-road riding. Extra-stiff rims and hubs with thicker flanges add to riding stability and fewer breakdowns.

Off-Road Stopping Power

Braking was an issue with the earliest conversions from one-speed clunkers to multi-speed bikes. These were heavy bikes before and after the conversions, and braking power was critical for off-road riding. Hub disc and drum brakes helped satisfy this need, but added more weight. The brakes of choice on modern mountain bikes are either disc brakes that mount outside each wheel hub or V-brakes, which are a deceptively simple, yet very affective rim brake. Both do a good job, but the disc brakes are superb because they are not affected by weather, the condition of brake pads, or a wheel rim. On the other hand, V-brakes are less expensive and simpler to repair.

Bike Bites

Some older-model mountain bikes routed the derailleur cables under the bottom bracket shell, which isn't the brightest idea in the world. Off-road biking means dirt and mud and gunk tossed up by the front tire. A better design—standard on better-quality, new bikes—is to run the cables along the top tube.

Suspension Systems

Early bikes of the nineteenth century—those built prior to the introduction of pneumatic tires—were tough on the riders. There's a reason some were called boneshakers. Air-filled tires were among the first shock-absorbing components on a bike. Full-suspension bikes offer the most forgiving rides of all, and it's a good thing, too, considering the kinds of off-road riding they're typically engaged in.

Mountain bikes offer fabulous suspension systems, ranging from simple shock absorbers built in to the front fork to full suspension with pivoting features for the rear. The same suspension systems have evolved over the years as manufacturers discovered what worked well and what didn't. A bike can have a front suspension system (suspension fork) that can feature *elastomer* (a springy kind of plastic) *bumpers* and springs, fluid *damping*, and various types of coil and air springs.

The simpler the design, the fewer the repairs. Front suspensions were added to mountain bikes to provide a more forgiving ride. It's easier to add suspension to the fork than to add a suspension to the rear triangle of a bicycle frame. The latter is a complicated and expensive matter, but is now available on more expensive models of mountain bikes. A suspension fork also can be retrofitted onto some existing frames—always a plus if you're upgrading and want to add some comfort at the same time.

Any suspension system adds weight to a bike and affects the handling. Your first experience with either a front or rear suspension can be disconcerting. Once you're used to it, you'll notice a huge difference in your comfort during off-road rides.

Bringing Up the Rear

Rear-suspension systems are quite complicated when compared with a suspension fork. Designs vary, and no one has a monopoly on ideas here. Different manufacturers pivot the rear at varying points on the frame. The design and performance issues include rigidity, added weight, and dealing with the chain.

The more suspension you add, the more expensive the bike. As much as riding a bike with front suspension takes getting used to, imagine riding a full-suspension bike. Some riders actually recommend riding a rigid bike without suspension for your first mountain bike to build your riding skills. This makes some sense, especially if you have a limited budget—but you'll be sore if you try any extreme riding.

The amount of travel varies with different rear-suspension systems. Some systems move as much as four inches. Some experienced riders feel this offers too much movement and bobbing up and down and makes for less efficient pedaling. Others think a full-suspension bike offers the most awesome, comfortable ride they've ever had and wonder what those other guys are whining about.

Look, Ma, No Suspension

You might deem them some kind of weird Puritan cyclists, but those who advocate riding a mountain bike without any suspension until your riding skills are developed might have a point. The advantages offered by a bike without suspension are lighter weight,

The Spoken Word

Damping is an adjustment to the suspension's shock absorbers to control how fast the suspension responds to a bump.

Derailed

A suspension fork is longer than a standard fork and won't be suitable for all bike frames. The longer length will raise many frames and affect the handling and feel of the bike. Check with your local shop before installing one of these forks on an older bike.

Bike Bites

Some front suspension systems allow you to control the degree of stiffness. This can be advantageous when you want to lock the system out during a climb and keep the frame stiff for peak pedaling efficiency.

fewer repair problems, and smoother handling. After riding without suspension for a while, you'll really appreciate it when you have it on your next bike. For that matter, you can upgrade a bike that doesn't have any suspension by adding a suspension seatpost, and possibly a suspension fork.

Read the Instructions!

Every suspension system, whether it's the front fork or full suspension, comes with an instruction and maintenance manual. Read it and follow the recommendations. It will explain how to adjust, clean, and lubricate your suspension and when to take it to a shop mechanic.

Some systems require special tools such as a bushing seater and a seal extractor, and special mineral oils that you are unlikely to invest in. As much fun as suspension systems are, you'll have to pay to keep them in top form. Additionally, as they advance, newer systems come out that eventually will render yours obsolete. After a few years, you might just want to replace the entire bike if you really want to keep up with the latest and greatest.

Derailed

Your choice of full-suspension bikes might be terrific off road, but not so on smooth pavement where you need a stiffer frame. These are two entirely different riding surfaces, and each of them calls for a specific frame type.

Bike Bites

If you replace your crankset, consider getting one that can be installed and removed with an Allen bolt (usually referred to as "self-extracting"). This allows you to easily tighten your crankarms with a 5mm Allen wrench, a tool you'll probably have in your bike pack anyway.

Hard Riding, Unavoidable Maintenance

You should follow a regular maintenance and safety check schedule for your mountain bike just as you would for any other type of bike. I'd say it's a little more critical with an off-road bike, given that the terrain and riding are tougher than that for a standard road bike. There are also the suspension systems, which are added components not found on most road bikes.

The following is a good general outline of mountain bike maintenance and pre-ride checks:

➤ Check your headset for free movement before each ride.

➤ Check shocks for travel and for leakage at the seals.

➤ Make sure that the brakes make a solid contact and that the levers don't travel too far before the brakes make contact.

➤ Give the wheels a spin and check for trueness and cuts in the tires. Be sure that each quick release is tight.

➤ Wash the bike after every muddy ride, making sure to avoid spraying water into the hubs, headset, or crankset; follow up by lubricating the chain, derailleurs, and brake pivots.

➤ Check the frame for cracks after every rough ride.

➤ Spot true wheels every month or so (or as needed).

➤ Inspect chain rings, sprockets, and crankarms for bends once a month or so.

➤ Check chain-ring bolts and crankarm bolts for tightness at least once a month or after every hard ride.

➤ Inspect pedals for play in the axles once a month or so.

➤ Depending on the amount of riding you do, repack the headset, wheel hubs, and bottom bracket every 6 to 12 months.

➤ Follow your owner's manual regarding suspension maintenance.

Retro Retro

The original mountain bikes—the old one-speed Schwinns that were cast aside by the growing use of lightweight 10-speeds—were cast aside as mountain bikes were designed and built as multi-speed machines with the full core of components found on road bikes. Now there are riders who are returning to the simplicity of the early one-speeds. Some are stripping away the gearing; others are ordering new bikes built as one-speeds. The latter aren't simply multi-speed frames with a single sprocket and single chainwheel. Frame builders are designing with the unique demands of a one-speed in mind (for instance, the tougher torque demands).

Advocates of one-speeds tout the lighter weight as they shed derailleurs, cassettes, and extra chain rings. They also claim their riding skills improve as they concentrate more on the riding itself and not on gear shifting. Then there's the dependence on one's own power to get around on a trail rather than downshifting. To some, these riders are bicycle Luddites, but I can appreciate their desire to strip away the toys and enjoy the purity of the ride. They even have their own races. The first Single Speed World Championships were held in Southern California in 1999—tattoos went to the winners.

Bike Bites

All new bikes come with warranties, one on the frame and one for the components. A lifetime warranty on the frame sounds great, but read the paperwork. Warranties exclude abusive riding (always a point of definition) and accidents caused by your enthusiastic riding practices.

The Least You Need to Know

➤ A quality mountain bike is built to withstand uneven off-road riding, but it can't survive abusive riding.

➤ Take your time getting used to off-road riding and develop your skills before trying the tougher trails.

➤ Suspension systems offer a more comfortable riding experience, but add weight and expense to the bike.

➤ Regular maintenance probably is more critical with a mountain bike given the more strenuous riding requirements to which it's exposed.

➤ A mountain-bike frame will be smaller than any road frame to which you're accustomed.

Chapter 20

On-the-Road Emergencies

In This Chapter

➤ Prevention is best

➤ Tired tires

➤ Road kill

➤ Metallurgy

➤ Cable connections

Being prepared for emergencies and foreseeable problems seems to be a matter of training. In California, you'll find plenty of people who have stored away bottled water, first-aid kits, batteries, flashlights, and other sundry items in case of an earthquake. Automobiles come with spare tires and tire jacks, but how many of us carry flares, emergency blankets, and water in case we get stuck on a road less traveled?

Bicyclists are more vulnerable than motorists when it comes to breakdowns on the road. For lack of a chain tool or because of a bent rim, you could be stuck out in the elements. A motorist, on the other hand, can be stuck inside a cushy SUV with all the comforts of home (or even more comforts). Roadside repairs sometimes go beyond the tools and patches you're carrying inside your handlebar or seat bag. Of course, sometimes the best thing to do is just stick out your thumb and hope one of those SUVs will come by and take pity on you. However, with a little imagination and some techniques you wouldn't practice in your garage workshop, you can get yourself home or at least to some shelter.

Before You Ride ...

Insurance companies, auto mechanics, and fire departments all say the same thing: Prevention always beats reaction. This is a good time to review preventive maintenance and your basic carry-along tool kit. Even a trip around town can take you a longer distance than you might want to walk—far from the nearest bike shop.

By now you know about maintenance schedules and how to perform that maintenance. It's pretty simple to figure out that replacing a frayed brake cable before it breaks on you is a better idea than having it snap while you're out riding. A quick inspection before you ride can save you trouble later. Before each ride …

Derailed

A lot of problems result from a lack of regular lubrication, especially with chains. If you keep your moving parts lubed, you'll have fewer unscheduled roadside stops.

➤ Give the brake levers a tight squeeze to check the cables and pads.

➤ Check the air pressure in each tire.

➤ Give each wheel a spin and look for wobbles.

➤ Make sure each wheel is secured to the bike frame.

➤ Make sure the headset and bottom bracket are adjusted properly and don't have any play in them.

➤ Make sure you have some basic tools and parts in your handlebar bag.

➤ Give your chain a quick lube if it needs it.

For a few minutes of your time, you can be ready to roll with confidence. Can you still have a problem on the road? Of course, but your brief inspection reduces the chances of this happening.

Carry-Along Tools and Stuff

Remember your list of "should haves" when you ride. These tools and parts will see you through most common road repairs, as well as emergencies. They don't take up much room and can be carried with you when you park the bike:

Derailed

Be sure that any universal cables you carry have the unneeded head cut off unless you plan to carry a cable cutter. The cable is useless with a head on each end.

➤ Tire pump

➤ Patch kit, spare tube, tire patch, and tire levers

➤ Chain tool

➤ Spare cables

➤ Multi-tool or its equivalent

➤ Small adjustable wrench

➤ Small piece of bailing wire

➤ A few wire twist ties

➤ An empty film container with extra nuts and bolts

If you don't want to carry everything with you, at least grab the multi-tool, because the whole tool kit is expensive to replace if someone decides to go through your handlebar bag and remove any of the tools.

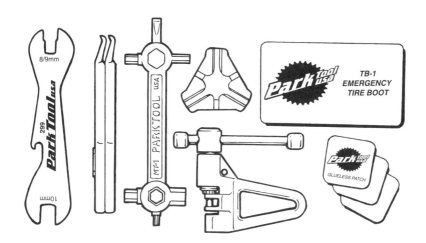

Don't let its size fool you: This tool kit can make the difference between getting stuck on the road and getting home.

(Courtesy of Park Tool)

Neutral Switzerland Makes Great Knives

A Swiss Army knife is a multi-tool unto itself and is good to carry around even when you're not biking. Most have one or two screwdriver blades—both slotted and Phillips. The knife blades can be used for cutting tire patches. Some models even have a corkscrew, which might come in handy if you happen to break down near a wine store.

Wallet Tools

Carry an ID in your handlebar bag and tape another ID inside your helmet so you can be identified in case of an accident. Include any pertinent health information that an EMT might need (allergies to certain medicines, blood type, the name of your physician). Also carry spare change for a pay phone, unless you're carrying a cellular phone with you. It's not a bad idea to tape some change and a dollar or two inside a plastic sandwich bag to the bottom of your saddle for a little added insurance.

Roadside Mechanics

With so many moving parts, it's not unheard of for something on your bike to break, loosen, or snap during a hard or long bike ride—especially if it's been a while since your bike had any scheduled maintenance. Demanding riders and demanding riding conditions can take their toll. Off-road cyclists have been known to break forks, bend crankarms, and trash wheels during rides. Your experiences might be tamer, but you can find yourself in similar situations during even the most benign ride.

Bike Bites

You can't be a purist when you're on the road or biking through the woods and have a bike problem to fix. You just want to get home or back to your car. This might mean riding with a single working brake or only one usable gear. Most of the time it beats walking.

Bike Bites

Depending on how steep the remainder of your ride is and what kind of shifters you have, you might be able to remove the rear brake cable and use it to replace a rear derailleur cable. This works best with old-style friction shifters.

Unchained

Chains come in two common sizes: ⅛" and ³⁄₃₂".

Chains are under a lot of stress, especially during a long climb. They don't snap all that often, but they do snap. If your chain breaks during a ride, do the following:

1. Stop pedaling.

2. Remove the broken link and the one next to it.

3. Install extra two links or, if you don't have spares, simply reconnect the chain, keeping in mind that it's shorter than its optimal length and you might have some trouble going into some gears. When you get home, replace the entire chain.

Bike Bites

If you don't have a chain tool, you can patch your chain together with a small piece of wire. It isn't a terrific repair, but it can keep you riding. Stay in a low gear range so the chain isn't stressed excessively and replace the chain when you get home.

Derailed

A misadjusted rear derailleur can cause big problems on the road if it travels into the spokes. Not only will you be stuck somewhere during your ride, but you'll have to replace your rear wheel and most likely the derailleur. Practice some preventive maintenance and check its adjustment periodically.

Slipping Away

If a derailleur is out of adjustment, the chain can slip between the chain rings or between the small front chain ring and the frame. It can be a real nuisance to pull it free, especially if there isn't much clearance between the chain ring and the frame. If this happens, do the following:

1. Stop pedaling and stop the bike.

2. Grab the rear derailleur cage, push it forward to get some slack in the chain, and pull the chain out and over the appropriate chain ring.

3. Check the derailleur cage travel and adjust with a screwdriver.

Some bikes have only a small amount of room between the small chain ring and the bike frame. If your chain slips in this space, you'll have to carefully pull it out. Spray the chain and the frame with lubricant if you have any with your tools. You want to be careful so you don't scratch the paint when freeing the chain.

A Crimped Rim

Wheel problems on the road can range from a broken spoke to the famous taco. Either way, you have to do what you can to get it spinning straight (this is a relative term here). Bent rims result from crashes, running into or over something, or a broken spoke.

If the wheel is usable as it is, but out of true, the simplest thing to do is release your brake arms. Unless you're at the peak of Mt. McKinley, you can finish many rides safely with one brake, although you'll have to apply it frequently when descending.

A broken spoke will allow the rim to pull to the opposite side from the break. If you don't have a spare spoke, simply loosen the spoke opposite the broken one to get the wheel a bit more in true. Wrap the broken spoke around an intact spoke with tape or a wire twist to keep it from dangling. Replace the spoke and true the wheel later.

Sometimes a badly bent (taco'd) wheel can be straightened out by pushing it against a tree or rock. Another approach is to grab the wheel and smash it against the road, tree, or rock with the wobble or bend facing down. After each attempt, give it a spin and see if it's becoming truer. You need only to get it to the point where it's usable, so don't get ridiculous here.

Chain Ring Crisis

Bent chain rings aren't a common occurrence, but anything can happen during off-road riding. A bad enough bend means the chain won't stay on the chain ring's teeth, and you'll have to do without that chain ring for the remainder of the ride. If you want to straighten it out, here's what you need to do:

1. Place your adjustable wrench on the bent ring.

2. Be sure that the wrench clears the teeth; otherwise you can snap some of them off.

3. Pull or push against the ring until it's as parallel to the other rings as you can get it.

4. If you cannot straighten out the ring, use another chain ring until the bent one can be replaced.

Derailed

Before you start messing with a bent chain ring or front derailleur, make sure your bottom bracket isn't loose. If it's sliding around or the spindle is somehow bent, you'll have to address these repairs. You don't want to misdiagnose and make things any worse.

When Cables Collapse

Cables that are regularly replaced during major overhauls are unlikely to break, but older or misadjusted cables can snap during a ride. A broken derailleur cable is more unusual than a broken brake cable; but if a brake cable does snap and you haven't got a spare, you can still finish your ride safely. You'll have to depend on the remaining brake until the cable can be replaced.

A broken derailleur cable can be more of a nuisance because you can lose gearing range. You have a couple of choices of repairs if you don't have a replacement cable:

➤ If the front derailleur cable snaps, move the derailleur over a chain ring (that will allow you to finish the ride comfortably) and turn the adjustment screws until they lock the derailleur cage in place over that chain ring.

➤ When a rear derailleur cable snaps, position the derailleur over the desired sprocket and turn the adjustment screws until the derailleur stays in this position (the derailleur will maintain chain tension on its own).

What if the rear derailleur itself gets mangled? You won't like the answer if you like using 20-plus speeds, but you can convert your bike into a 1-speed by doing the following:

1. Remove the chain.

2. Remove the derailleur with an Allen wrench or adjustable wrench depending on how it's attached to the frame.

3. Place the chain in the middle rear sprocket and the middle or low chain ring (depending on how level the remaining ride is).

213

4. Remove enough links so your chain is snug enough to stay on the gear teeth.

5. Ride carefully.

Think of this as an opportunity to relive the early days of bicycling when everyone had fixed-gear machines. After your bout of nostalgia, slap on a new derailleur as fast as you can and be thankful that bicycle technology is so advanced.

Bottoming Out

My first 10-speed was an Italian Corso that I purchased when I was in college. The cottered bottom bracket went out of adjustment constantly as the adjustable cup and lockring came loose. I eventually fixed it so it would stay put, but it's doubtful that anyone is going to carry bottom bracket tools when out riding. If you have a cottered or cotterless bottom bracket (not the sealed cartridge types) and the cup comes loose, you can use a screwdriver or any other pointed tool to stick it into the pin hole on the cup and pound it with whatever is handy, including a rock. Follow up by tightening the lockring as well. Be careful not to get so enthusiastic that you overtighten.

Bike Bites

If worse comes to worse, you can always try to join two broken ends of a cable with some intermediary material such as bailing wire. You might even use a key chain if you can somehow wrap the cable around both ends of it (remove your keys first). Basically, you can use anything that gets the job done.

Loose Headset

Unless you have a wrench or channel locks, you'll have to tighten a threaded headset with your hands. To improve your grip, you might loosely wrap a section of inner tube around the locknut and/or adjustable cup. If you have a threadless headset, simply tighten the stem bolt with an Allen wrench.

Tire Troubles

A blown inner tube can always be replaced (well, if you brought a spare tube), but a blown tire is another matter. A tire has three functions: to cushion your ride, improve the rolling resistance of the wheel, and contain the inner tube. The point is, a hole in the tire will not contain the tube at that point and a new or patched tube will expand through the hole and burst. As long as you can seal the hole, you can use the tire until it can be replaced.

Bike Bites

Sometimes, if you're out of patches or spare tubes, you actually can tie a tight knot in a blown inner tube, underinflate it, and still ride your bike. This works better with bigger 26-inch tubes because you have plenty of room between the rim and the wheel. Just cut the tube on one side of the hole and tie the two ends together. Remember to make the knot really tight.

To seal a blown tire, you can use the following:

➤ A section of old tire

➤ Any piece of paper or cardboard including a dollar bill or even a candy bar wrapper

➤ A large patch from an inner tube patch kit

➤ Duct tape

Simply insert the patching material or boot on the inside of the tire so it will stay in place when the tube is installed. Inflate the tube carefully, making sure the patch is staying in place. If it appears to be bulging, lower the air pressure in the tube.

Frame Fractures

Occasionally, a cheap frame actually can come apart at one of the joints. No amount of bailing wire will put one of these bikes back together safely. More common frame problems result from crashes during which the fork or rear stays get bent. A bike shop will straighten out a repairable frame with a number of tools that will properly align the different tubes. The only tools you'll have on the road are your hands, feet, and eyes.

In the event of a crash that requires straightening out of a bike frame, do the following:

1. Remove the respective front or rear wheel.

2. Determine which section of the fork or stays must be pulled out.

3. Place your foot on the opposing fork tip or stay and pull up on the bent one until it's in approximately the correct position.

4. Hold the frame upright on its other wheel and look carefully at your work. If you need to bend the frame further, do so and reinstall the wheel.

A fork on a road bike is tougher to straighten out than the stays. All bets are off with full suspension mountain bikes, but they are built tougher and are less likely to bend in the first place. Take your bike to a shop that does frame repairs after you get home and see if it's salvageable. Seat stays can often be realigned, and forks can be replaced.

Bike Bites

As the last desperate measure—and I mean really desperate—a trashed tube can be replaced with leaves, scrap paper, or anything else that can fill up the tire. This repair can allow you to ride okay on a smooth road, but off-road riding is more dicey.

Bike Bites

One of the best emergency repair tools is a flashing light. This will warn off motorists if you're stuck by the side of the road or end up riding home after dark because you stopped for a repair.

The Least You Need to Know

➤ Preventive maintenance will save you unnecessary roadside repairs.

➤ Unexpected and emergency repairs don't need to look pretty; they just need to get you home safely.

➤ Some repairs will reduce your bike to a single speed, but this usually is better than walking.

➤ Being creative with tools, spare parts, and items you find on the side of the road or trail will get you through even the toughest repair situations.

Glossary

adjustable cup   The left-side cup of a bottom bracket that is secured in place by a lockring. This cup is easily removable so the bottom bracket can be serviced.

adjusting barrel   A hollow bolt, located at the end of a brake cable or gear cable, that facilitates tension adjustment of the cable by hand and without the use of tools.

Aero bars   Handlebar attachments or special handlebars that support a rider by the forearms, thus allowing the upper body to be bent over into a lower, aerodynamic position and allowing faster speeds.

Allen wrench   An L-shaped stool with six sides used to adjust Allen bolts.

alloy   In the bicycle world, alloy usually refers to aluminum rather than a blended metal. Aluminum parts found on bikes often include the cranksets, wheel rims, handlebars, stems, and derailleurs.

anchor bolt   A bolt that secures the end of a cable at its termination point.

Ashtabula crank   One-piece cranksets once made in Ashtabula, Ohio (a city where, coincidentally, many of the author's distant cousins live).

axle   A shaft located between two sets of bearings. Also referred to as a *spindle*.

cable   A group of twisted wire used to control hand brakes and derailleurs. Some section of each cable is enclosed in cable housing.

cable guide   An attached fitting or braze-on used to guide a cable along the bike frame to its destination.

cable stop   A fitting or braze-on through which the end of a cable passes out of its housing and onto a component.

cadence   Revolutions per minute (or RPMs) of the pedals.

caliper   An arm of a caliper-style brake that moves a brake shoe against a wheel rim.

Campagnolo   The big cheese of Italian-made bicycle parts.

cantilever brake   A brake with two separate arms (the cantilevers) that pivot independently against the wheel rim.

carbon fiber A material that is mixed with resin to make composite frames.

cassette A modern set of sprockets, spacers, and freehubs used on multi-speed derailleur bikes.

center-pull brake A caliper-style brake in which the brake cable attaches to a yoke that in turn attaches to a transverse cable to activate the calipers; this brake style is rarely used on modern bikes.

chain Component that connects the front chain rings to the rear sprockets.

chain ring A front sprocket, sometimes called a chainwheel.

chain stays The frame tubes that run from the bottom bracket to the rear fork ends.

chain tool A tool for removing chains that do not have a master link.

chain whip A tool for removing cassette sprockets.

cleat An attachment to the bottom of a cycling shoe that fits on the specially designed bike pedals.

clincher tire A tire that has an inner tube.

cluster A group of rear sprockets.

coaster brake A foot brake located in the rear hub.

cog Rear sprocket.

composite Bicycle frame made from carbon or boron fiber and bonded with epoxy resin.

cone A special nut on a wheel axle against which the bearings sit.

cone wrench A wrench used to adjust cones.

cottered cranks Steel cranks that use cotter pins to secure the cranks to the bottom bracket axle.

cotterless cranks Three-piece crank system in which the alloy cranks are secured to the bottom bracket axles with bolts.

crank An arm that attached to the bottom bracket axle and secures a pedal

crank extractor A tool that removes cotterless cranks.

crown The upper section of a front fork.

cruiser An old, heavy, balloon-tire, one-speed bike; some modern, lighter-weight cruisers are manufactured today.

cyclocross A specific type of off-road bike racing.

derailleur A component that moves a chain from one rear sprocket to another and from one chain ring to another.

diamond frame The most common bicycle frame.

disc brake A type of hub brake.

dish The tightening done to the right side of a rear wheel to pull it over enough so that it's centered within the bike frame.

dish stick A tool that checks a wheel's dish.

double butted   A thickening of a tube or spoke at both ends.

down tube   The frame tube that runs from the bottom of the head tube to the bottom bracket.

drop   On the bike frame, the difference in height between the fork ends and the bottom bracket.

dropout   The section of the frame that secures the rear wheel.

drum brake   Another type of hub brake.

dual suspension   A bike with suspension at both wheels.

Dura Ace   A top line of Japanese bicycle components.

ferrule   An eyelet in a wheel rim or metal or plastic cap at the end of cable housing.

fixed cup   The right-side bottom bracket cup that can be removed, but is not adjustable.

fixed gear   A one-speed bike without a freewheel mechanism (typically, a track bike).

flange   The section of a wheel hub to which spokes are attached.

fork   The section of a frame that secures the front wheel (a rear fork secures the back wheel).

frame   A bike's skeleton.

freehub   A trademark name for a rear hub that uses cassettes.

freewheel   The ratchet mechanism that allow the bike to coast. Also, the entire cluster of rear sprockets that have been replaced with cassettes.

gear   Motion transmitted by the movement of the chain rings, rear sprockets, and wheels working together.

generator   Mechanism for running bicycle lights; a rubber wheel or roller on the generator rubs against a moving tire, producing a current; some generators are built in to the wheel hubs using an armature and rotating magnet to produce a current.

hardtail   A bike without rear suspension.

head tube   The front frame tube through which the threaded end of the fork passes through.

headset   Consists of two sets of bearings and their races, allowing the front fork to turn.

high wheeler   A nineteenth-century bike with a large front wheel (up to 60 inches across).

housing   The protective tube-like material through which cables pass.

hub   The center part of a wheel.

hub brake   Opposite of a rim brake.

hybrid   A bicycle that combines features of a mountain bike and a touring bike.

indexed shifting   Assisted shifting in which the shift control has pre-set stops that correspond to different gears.

internal cable routing   Gear and brake cables that run inside a bike frame.

internal gearing   Hub gears (such as a three-speed).

219

left-hand threads   Threads on a fastener that tighten in a counterclockwise direction rather than turning clockwise.

limit stop screws   Screws that limit how far a derailleur can travel, or move to the left and right.

locknut   A nut that secures another nut by screwing against it and locking it in place. On a bicycle, locknuts are used to maintain components that contain bearings.

lockring   A type of locknut typically found on a bottom bracket assembly.

lug   A section of a bike frame to which frame tubes connect.

master link   A removable chain link found on $^1/_8$" chains and occasionally $^3/_{32}$" chains.

mixte   A type of women's bike frame or step-through frame.

mountain bike   An off-road bike that generally has a minimum of 15 speeds and cantilever brakes.

nipple   The nut that secures the threaded end of a spoke to a wheel rim.

pannier   A storage bag that hangs off of a bike rack.

pedal   The component on which you put your foot to start the bike moving.

penny farthing   A high-wheeler bicycle; the term originated in England where the penny was a large coin and the farthing was smaller.

pitting   A type of damage done to metal surfaces, especially cones and bottom bracket cups, in which small pits appear due to grit or worn bearings.

pneumatic tire   A tire with an inflatable inner tube.

presta   A narrow valve used on inner tubes and normally found on high-end bikes.

puller   Refers to a crank puller or freewheel puller, which are tools for working on these two separate components. Also called *extractors*.

quick-release wheels   Wheels that release through the use of a cam mechanism instead of nuts; quick releases also are used in seat bolts.

radial spoking   Wheel construction in which the spokes do not cross each other, but run straight from the hub to the rim.

reaction arm   Connects a hub brake to the frame.

recumbent bicycle   A type of bike on which the rider essentially is in a horizontal position.

retainer   A clip that holds ball bearings.

rim   The metal hoop part of a bike wheel.

saddle   The bike seat.

Schrader   A type of air valve found on automobile tires and many bike tubes.

sealed bearing   A bearing that is encased or otherwise protected from dirt by plastic or rubber gaskets.

seatpost   The metal tube to which the saddle is attached.

seatpost bolt   A binder bolt that tightens to secure the seatpost.

seat stays   Frame tubes between the seat cluster and the rear fork ends.

seat tube   The frame tube between the seat cluster and the bottom bracket.

sew-up   A tubular bicycle tire.

shifter   A control used to shift gears (either for derailleurs or multi-speed hubs) that is frame-mounted or located on the handlebars.

Shimano   A well-known Japanese manufacturer of bicycle parts.

side-pull brake   A caliper-type brake whose cable runs down the side.

skewer   The locking mechanism in a quick-release hub.

solid axle   The opposite of a quick-release axle; this axle secures the wheel to the frame with standard nuts.

spider   The "arm" to which chain rings attach.

spindle   An axle.

spoke   A thick wire that connects a wheel rub to the rim.

spoke patterns   The different ways of lacing or installing spokes.

spoke protector   A protective metal or plastic disk that's installed between the rear sprockets and the right-side spokes to prevent the derailleur from moving into the spokes and causing damage.

sprocket   A front or rear toothed gear.

standover height   The distance between the top tube and the ground; it should be low enough for a rider to comfortably mount and dismount the bicycle.

stay   A thin frame tube including the seat stay, fender stay, and chain stay.

steerer   The upper part of the front fork to which the handlebar stem attaches.

stem   The connecting piece between the handlebars and the steerer.

stoker   Usually the rear rider on a tandem who pedals and does not control the steering or the shifting.

straight gauge   Frame tubing that is not butted and has uniform wall thickness throughout.

Sturmey-Archer   Well-known manufacturer of internal-gear hubs.

tandem   A bicycle built for two.

third-hand tool   A tool that clamps brake shoes against a rim to facilitate cable adjustment.

tire lever   Also called a *tire iron;* a prying tool for removing clincher tires.

toe in   To adjust a brake shoe so the front of the brake shoe hits the wheel rim before the rest of the pad does.

top pull   A front derailleur whose cable is installed from above the component rather than below.

top tube   The frame tube that runs between the head tube and the seat cluster.

transverse cable   A horizontal cable that connects the arms of a center-pull or cantilever brake.

triple butted   A double-butted tube with a different thickness at each end of the tube.

true wheel   A perfectly concentric wheel. *Truing* is the process that results in a true wheel. A "true" wheel is one in which the rim is perfectly concentric and runs along a plane perpendicular to the axle. A wheel that is "out of true" vertically will be out of round, and will give a bumpy ride even on a smooth road.

tubing   The metal tubes that make up a bicycle frame.

tubular   A sew-up tire. A racing tire with an inner tube sewn inside the tire casing that fits on the special sew-up rims and uses presta valves.

U-brake   A form of cantilever brake.

V-brake   A direct-pull cantilever brake and a Shimano trademark.

yoke   The component that connects with a cantilever or center-pull brake's transverse cable.

Buying a Bike

A few days ago, I went down to a local St. Vincent de Paul store and looked at the used bikes, which were selling for a whopping $6 each unless otherwise marked. From what I could see, none of them were marked so the $6 price applied to all of them. Snooping through America's two-wheel discards, I came across the following:

➤ A used, mid-level 10-speed French Peugeot with a taco'd rear wheel, all-alloy parts, and chipped paint

➤ A roughly 20-year-old Raleigh Gran Prix (an introductory-level 10-speed) in clean condition

➤ A Schwinn Le Tour with terrific alloy wheels, bar end shifters, and a handlebar bag

➤ A nondescript but clean Japanese 10-speed with alloy parts, a rear rack, and a fairly new Avocet saddle

All of these bikes featured old technology: freewheels instead of cassettes, 10 speeds instead of 24 or 27, and caliper brakes that are no longer manufactured. Keep in mind that a wheel hub that takes a freewheel cannot take cassettes; some people want more than 10 speeds; and although older caliper brakes work well, they can't compare to new disc brakes or even V-brakes.

The nondescript bike and the Raleigh were the most ready to ride, but all of the St. Vincent bikes were quite repairable using the existing parts (after cleanup and lubrication, of course). And at $6 a piece, how could you lose? I considered buying all four of them and piecing together the best parts into a single bike, but decided I didn't want to deal with the leftovers.

There are plenty of used bikes around at secondhand stores, garage sales, and police auctions. With the knowledge you've gained in this book, you could pick up a decent bike, overhaul it, and save a ton of money. You probably will have to compromise on features and the latest technology, but if you're looking for only basic transportation at a bargain price, you won't be disappointed.

Not every used bike is available for pocket change. If you increase your budget, you increase your choices. Some marvelous old 10-speeds built on custom European frames are often available at good prices. For example, our local shop currently has a top-of-the-line, eight-year-old, barely ridden Schwinn Paramount in as-new condition for about a third of its new bike price.

Used Bike Tips

The biggest component of any bike is the frame. Whenever you buy a used bike, scrutinize the frame for rust, dents, cracks, and alignment problems, especially on mountain bikes. Look for hairline cracks on the welding or brazing on all the joints. Check for serial numbers (if they're filed off or otherwise obscured, the bike might be stolen). Give the wheels a spin and check for trueness.

Used mountain bikes offer some interesting deals as riders upgrade to newer equipment. Of course, because they're mountain bikes and often used for off-road use, you can expect that individual bikes have seen what can politely be called challenging rides. Keep this in mind when you scrutinize these bikes for possible purchase.

Suspension bikes have their own issues including leaking seals and rebound performance. If it doesn't bounce back the way it should, your body will pay for it every time you take it off road. Disc brakes are terrific performers, but check them for leaks as well. Every part that you have to replace, from cables to bearings to tires, has to be figured into the selling price.

By all means, give your prospective purchase a good, hard ride and really put it through the paces. This will tell you if all the gears are working and how effective the brakes are, and give you an opportunity to hear all the creaks and groans that are present. Stand up on the pedals, slam on the brakes, and check for loose headsets and bent crankarms. Make sure the cables are taut and the shifters move freely.

Buying New

A new bike can be a significant expenditure, going as high as thousands of dollars (more than some used cars). Before you buy any bike, consider the following:

➤ A realistic budget

➤ The type of riding you plan to do

➤ The frequency of your riding

➤ Equipment preferences

You only have so many dollars to spend, and your budget obviously will limit your purchase choice. Keep in mind that you don't have to max your budget out if you can find a less expensive bike that will suit your riding purposes. You don't want to buy less than you need, but you don't need to spend more for features you won't fully use or appreciate, either.

If you've nailed down the type of riding you will be doing (commuting, off-road, touring), but you're not sure which style of bike will suit your purposes, test-ride everything. Ask a lot of questions. Comparison shop. Don't settle for a no-name, heavy clunker from a store for whom bicycles are simply a sideline or one of many sporting goods departments. Go to a good bike shop and become an informed consumer.

The Advantages of Bike Shops

Not all independent bicycle shops are created equal, but they have one thing in common: They sell and service only bikes and bike accessories. Larger shops carry a complete range of bike types and prices and have a knowledgeable sales staff. This isn't to say that a shop isn't without its biases. After all, they choose to represent and sell certain manufacturers' lines of products. They might do so because they truly believe in the individual product or because one manufacturer is more dealer-friendly than another. In any event, visit at least two or three shops if you want a full range of opinions and available brands.

An independent bike shop offers other advantages, such as ...

➤ Test rides.

➤ Assistance in finding the correct frame size.

➤ Full assembly and warranty tune-ups.

➤ Better-quality bicycles than discount and department stores.

➤ Parts availability.

➤ Year-end closeout sales on brand-name bikes.

Bike shops are like every other retailer in that they have to move out stock by the end of the calendar year to make room for the newest and coolest. Every bike from the previous year that sits on the shop floor simply ties up money that could be spent on a newer model. You can get some pretty good discounts if you shop around in December.

Size Matters

A bike that doesn't fit you isn't a bargain, no matter how low its price. You can't make up for an oversize frame by somehow stretching yourself out. An over- or undersize bike will be both uncomfortable and unsafe.

You have two major measurement concerns when you purchase a bicycle:

➤ The clearance between you and the bike

➤ Your reach as you hold on to the handlebars

Frame size is measured from the top of the seat tube to the bottom bracket spindle. Stand over and straddle the top tube and look for a comfortable clearance between your groin and the top tube, typically 1 to $1^1/_2$ inches of space for a road bike. A mountain bike rider wants more space; as much as 4 inches for safety reasons (off-road riding presents more opportunities to slide off the saddle and on to the top tube). The reach should be comfortable and appropriate for the type of riding you will be doing.

There are other considerations, including the following:

➤ The position of the saddle

➤ The length of the crankarms

➤ Riding style

➤ The measurements of the rider

The saddle should be high enough for you to comfortably reach the pedals without rocking side to side. With the ball of your foot on one pedal and the other pedal at its lowest point, your leg should be almost fully extended and still maintain a slight bend in the knee. This gives you more power and protects your knee joint.

Some riders place the saddle higher than the handlebar; others set it so the two are approximately level with each other. A sprinter who regularly stands on the pedals pulls up on the handlebar rather than rest on it in the manner of a long-distance touring rider. A lower bar allows the sprinter to both pull up and lean over some, thus decreasing wind resistance. The best height for the handlebars will be one that's comfortable for both riding positions. Most people seem comfortable with handlebars that allow them to put their hands at approximately shoulder width.

To some extent, you can adjust the position of the handlebars with different-size stems. You're better off with an appropriate size frame rather than trying to make up for its size deficiencies with long or short stems or by moving the saddle forward or back so much that you cannot cycle efficiently.

An undersized bike can be uncomfortable, inefficient to ride, and difficult to handle. An oversized bike can be uncomfortable and dangerous if you ever fall on the top tube. Typically, the larger the frame, the longer the top tube; thus the reach will be uncomfortable to a rider for whom the bike it too big.

Some shops employ sizing systems, such as the New England Cycling Academy FitKit, that come up with the proper frame size after computing various body measurements from the rider. These systems are fine as far as they go, but only you can determine if the bike is comfortable or not. Trial and error will be your best determinants.

Riding Your Bike

A professional bike rider—kind of an odd profession, when you think about it—learns all kinds of riding techniques for hill climbing, sprints, and long distance. These also can be useful to a more casual rider, but in toned-down versions. You should be more concerned with safe, legal riding that will keep you from getting injured and allow you to get the most out of your bicycle.

The basics of riding include the following:

➤ Be sure the bike fits you properly and that you can comfortably reach and maneuver the brake levers, gear shifters, and pedals.

➤ Give your bike a quick once-over (checking cables, brakes, and tires) every day that you ride.

➤ Follow all traffic rules.

➤ Wear a helmet!

Local laws vary, but a bicycle is basically treated like any other moving vehicle. This means you must do the following:

➤ Stop at stop signs and stoplights.

➤ Equip your bike with lights for night riding.

➤ Stick to the speed limit.

➤ Observe one-way street signs.

➤ Change lanes properly.

➤ Ride in marked bike lanes when available.

➤ Walk your bike on sidewalks unless you are allowed to ride on them.

➤ Stay to the right of the road.

➤ Do not block a sidewalk or pedestrian right-of-way when parking your bike.

Too many adult riders have the annoying habit of barely stopping at stop signs or stoplights before barreling on through. This is not only dangerous, but it gives all riders a bad name with motorists. The latter, driving increasingly bigger and faster vehicles, are not exactly known for being tolerant of cyclists. Children, in particular, need to know safe riding rules—especially the idea of stopping before riding out into a street.

As in driving a motor vehicle, your best riding technique is to look ahead and anticipate. It's one thing to run into another car when driving at 10 miles an hour. Do this on a bike, and you're going to have some big problems. This doesn't mean your riding should be shrouded in a fog of paranoia; but you should stay sharp and assume that car drivers are not going to be paying as much attention to you as they will be to other automobiles.

Riding alone is different from riding in a group. Riding side by side is the usual format, but needs to give way to single file when traffic conditions demand it. You can whine all you want about cyclists having their rights to use the road as much as any automobile, but the fact is that you can endanger yourself and others by unnecessarily blocking the road. On the other hand, if the road is too narrow for traffic to safely pass you, the group is safer riding double until road conditions improve—and should do so to protect themselves.

Off-road riding brings other concerns for the rider. Observe the rules of the trail. If it's marked for walking and hiking only, respect this rule and don't see it as a challenge to your riding ability. If you're riding a shared trail, walkers normally will have the right-of-way, so slow down and announce your presence, especially if coming up from behind. Inquire with park officials about riding off the trails.

Finally, remember to brake gradually and to slow down in advance, especially on wet surfaces. You'll be depending more on your front brake than the rear, gradually squeezing it on and off instead of a last-minute hard pull.

Resources

In the Internet Age, we have virtually unlimited information on any topic we choose; this certainly is true of bicycling. I'm not going to try and list all Web sites related to bicycling, but here are a few that you might find helpful.

Web Sites

www.massbike.org/bikelaw   Lists bicycling laws by state.

http://sheldonbrown.com/harris/index.html   Sheldon writes prolifically on bicycle topics from the vantage point of a mechanic. He presents articles on all kinds of topics, from three-speed hubs to tandems.

http://sheldonbrown.com/bicycling-links.html   This is Sheldon's personal site with about a zillion links to everything bicycle-related, including manufacturers.

www.danenet.wicip.org/bcp/makers.html   Another site that links to manufacturers.

The following three sites link to many bicycling sites as well:

www.bikelane.com/   A zillion sites

www.geocities.com/Colosseum/6213/   Another zillion sites.

www.bikecrawler.com   A cycling search engine.

Books

Anybody's Bike Book, by Tom Cuthbertson and Rick Morall (Illustrator), Ten Speed Press, 1998.

The first edition of *Anybody's Bike Book* was published more than 20 years ago and was one of the first accessible bike repair books. The author really wants you to enjoy your bike without getting caught up in the latest and the greatest. A reliable source of information for more than one generation of cyclists.

Bicycle Repair Step by Step: The Full-Color Manual of Bicycle Maintenance and Repair, by Rob Van Der Plas, Van der Plas Publications, 1994.

The author is an engineer—and an opinionated one at that. He has written quite a few books on all facets of bicycling and doesn't hesitate to throw in a physics lesson now and again.

Complete Guide to Bicycle Maintenance and Repair, by Jim Langley (*Bicycling Magazine*), Rodale Press, 1999.

Published by the same people who produce *Bicycling Magazine,* this book offers plenty of photos and clear explanations, including a section on suspension systems.

Index